THE RIGHT TO REPRODUCTIVE CHOICE:
A STUDY IN INTERNATIONAL LAW

THE RIGHT TO REPRODUCTIVE CHOICE

A STUDY IN INTERNATIONAL LAW

by

Corinne A. A. Packer

Åbo Akademi University, Institute for Human Rights
Turku/Åbo, 1996

Cataloguing-in-Publication Data

The right to reproductive choice : a study in international law / Corinne A. A. Packer – Turku / Åbo : Åbo Akademi University. Institute for Human Rights, 1996.

ISBN 951–650–546–5 (PB)

UDC 396.2; 347.63; 613.888; 613.99

Index words: reproductive rights / women / children / family rights / population policies / health

Cover: Elina Hildén

Published and sold by:
Institute for Human Rights
Åbo Akademi University
Gezeliusgatan 2
FIN–20500 Turku/Åbo
Finland

fax: 358–21–2654699

http://www.abo.fi/instut/imr/

Åbo Akademis tryckeri
Åbo 1996

To my parents,

who chose not to stop at seven

Acknowledgements

I would like to thank Professor Allan Rosas of the Institute for Human Rights at Åbo Akademi University for having demonstrated initial interest in this study, offering direction for the broadening of its scope and encouraging me to bring it to press. This last taxing task was performed by Raija Hanski with admirable patience and skill. I also wish to thank my husband, John, for providing endless constructive comments, ceaseless assistance at the computer, bottomless cups of coffee and interminable amounts of love and support throughout the endeavour.

TABLE OF CONTENTS

FOREWORD	v
LIST OF TABLES	viii
GLOSSARY OF ACRONYMS AND ABBREVIATIONS	ix

I. UNDERSTANDING THE RIGHT TO REPRODUCTIVE CHOICE ... 1

    1. Locating the Rationale for the Right to
Reproductive Choice: What is the Issue? ... 1
    2. The Links Between the Right to Reproductive
Choice and Contemporary Problems ... 5
    3. The Formation of the Right to Reproductive
Choice at the International Level ... 9

II. ARTICULATIONS OF THE RIGHT TO REPRODUCTIVE
CHOICE IN INTERNATIONAL LAW ... 14

    1. Defining the Right to Reproductive Choice ... 14
    2. Sources of the Right to Reproductive Choice:
In General ... 18
    3. Sources of the Right to Reproductive Choice
in International Law ... 23
        3.1 Introduction ... 23
        3.2 Sources of the Right to Found a Family ... 24
        3.3 Sources of the Right to Decide the Number
and Spacing of Children ... 27
        3.4 Sources of the Right to Family Planning
Information and Education ... 29
        3.5 Sources of the Right to Access to Family
Planning Services ... 32

III.	ESTABLISHING THE PARAMETERS OF PROTECTION OF THE RIGHT TO REPRODUCTIVE CHOICE IN INTERNATIONAL HUMAN RIGHTS LAW	42

1. Introduction — 42
2. The Scope of the Right to Reproductive Choice — 43
   2.1 The Scope of the Right to Found a Family — 43
   2.2 The Scope of the Right to Decide the Number and Spacing of Children — 55
   2.3 The Scope of the Right to Family Planning Information and Education — 65
   2.4 The Scope of the Right to Access to Family Planning Services — 69
3. Beneficiaries of the Right to Reproductive Choice — 76
   3.1 Introduction — 76
   3.2 Gender, Marital Status and Couples — 76
   3.3 Adolescents — 82
   3.4 Mentally Disabled Persons — 88
   3.5 Individuals with Hereditary Illnesses — 90
4. Obligations of the State — 91
   4.1 Establishing State Responsibility — 91
   4.2 Negative and Positive Obligations — 93
   4.3 Reproductive Choice as a Private Matter Publicly Protected — 94

IV.	OBSTACLES AND CHALLENGES TO THE FULL REALIZATION OF THE RIGHT TO REPRODUCTIVE CHOICE	98

1. Population Policies — 98
   1.1 State Interpretations of 'Responsible' Reproductive Choice — 98
   1.2 The Use of Incentives for 'Responsible' Decision-Making — 102
2. Cultural and Religious Norms — 104
3. The Cost of Reproductive Choice — 110
   3.1 State Obligations: The Principle of Relativity — 110
   3.2 Examining the Real Costs — 111

V.	SECURING RESPECT FOR THE RIGHT TO REPRODUCTIVE CHOICE THROUGH THE WOMEN'S CONVENTION	115

1. Implementation in General ... 115
2. The System of Supervision ... 116
   2.1 Weaknesses in the Reporting System and Efforts Towards Improvement ... 116
   2.2 CEDAW's Monitoring of the Right to Reproductive Choice ... 119
3. The Problem of Reservations Affecting Reproductive Choice ... 120
   3.1 Introduction ... 120
   3.2 Admissibility of Reservations in General ... 127
   3.3 Reservations on the Grounds of Religion ... 132
   3.4 Reservations Concerning Discrimination Rooted in Culture ... 136
   3.5 Reservations Concerning Settlement ... 137
   3.6 Strengthening the Women's Convention ... 138

VI.	SECURING RESPECT THROUGH OTHER MEANS	140

1. Other Legal Means ... 140
2. Non-Legal Means ... 143
   2.1 Extra-Conventional Mechanisms ... 143
   2.2 The Role of International Assistance ... 145

VII.	EXPANDING THE REACH OF THE RIGHT TO REPRODUCTIVE CHOICE	149

1. Expanding the Recognition of Serious Violations of the Right to Reproductive Choice ... 149
   1.1 The Recognition of Forced Pregnancy as a Serious Violation ... 149
   1.2 The Right to Asylum as a Result of Serious Violations of the Right to Reproductive Choice ... 153
2. Expanding Implementation through the Work of International Organizations ... 156
3. The Way Forward ... 158

APPENDIX A. EXCERPTS FROM THE PROGRAMME OF ACTION
OF THE 1994 INTERNATIONAL CONFERENCE ON POPULATION
AND DEVELOPMENT 162

APPENDIX B. EXCERPTS FROM THE PLATFORM FOR ACTION OF
THE 1995 FOURTH WORLD CONFERENCE ON WOMEN 169

APPENDIX C. STATES PARTIES TO INTERNATIONAL HUMAN
RIGHTS TREATIES WITH RELEVANCE TO THE RIGHT TO
REPRODUCTIVE CHOICE 173

APPENDIX D. GENERAL COMMENT NO. 19 ADOPTED BY THE
HUMAN RIGHTS COMMITTEE, REGARDING ARTICLE 23
(ON THE RIGHT TO MARRY AND FOUND A FAMILY) 178

APPENDIX E. GENERAL RECOMMENDATION NO. 21 ADOPTED
BY THE COMMITTEE ON THE ELIMINATION OF DISCRIMINATION
AGAINST WOMEN REGARDING EQUALITY IN MARRIAGE AND
FAMILY RELATIONS 181

APPENDIX F. EXCERPTS FROM GENERAL COMMENT NO. 24
ADOPTED BY THE HUMAN RIGHTS COMMITTEE, REGARDING
ARTICLE 52 (RELATING TO RESERVATIONS) 184

BIBLIOGRAPHY 187

TABLE OF TREATIES 204

TABLE OF CASES 206

INDEX OF TERMS 208

Foreword

At the international level, the human right to reproductive choice, that is, the right of individuals to obtain the knowledge and means to determine freely and responsibly the number and spacing of their children, was first enunciated in the 1968 Proclamation of Teheran. Since then, much headway has been made in terms of providing legal support for the right to reproductive choice as a universal human right, the strongest instrument being the 1979 Convention on the Elimination of All Forms of Discrimination against Women. In spite of this progress, access to family planning information and services and the practical exercise of freedom of choice in reproductive decision-making is still elusive for many people. Laws and governmental policies, or the lack thereof, continue to frustrate efforts to ensure the right to reproductive choice.

If the commitment to reproductive choice is to mean anything in practice, that is, if it is to be ruled by law which informs, if not instructs, States in their law- and policy-making, we must first closely examine what is really meant by an individual human right to reproductive choice in a world which is culturally complex and faces significant demographic challenges. This book, therefore, takes a legal approach in examining the status of the right to reproductive choice as articulated in international human rights law, both at the universal and regional levels.

The basic structure of this book begins with a discussion on the significance of reproductive choice in the present day. The enjoyment of the right to reproductive choice meaningful impacts on a full constellation of other rights; effectively, without the right to reproductive choice, the enjoyment of other rights may be thwarted. Chapter I discusses the underlying rationale for the right to reproductive choice and reviews the links between this right and contemporary problems.

The right to reproductive choice is protected by international treaty law as a composite right. Chapter II defines the right to reproductive choice in international law and establishes the sources of the elements which compose this right, including interpretations which can be derived from the treaty provisions in which the elements appear. This study endeavours to use the existing international treaties on human rights to identify the full breadth of the right to reproductive choice. Rather than relying on the non-binding and non-enforceable human rights provisions of the documents adopted at the successive United Nations conferences on population, specific obligations are drawn from relevant provisions of human rights treaties that are legally binding—the breach of which constitutes an international wrong incurring State responsibility. In examining the content of the right to reproductive choice in Chapter III, this book also endeavours to demonstrate that issues of reproductive choice are relevant to both developing and developed States. However, available figures clearly demonstrate that protection of the right to reproductive choice is particularly needed in developing countries. While such protection is the focus of this study, issues which give rise to frequent debate in more developed countries, such as access to safe abortion or to medically-assisted reproduction, are also addressed.

The relationship between the community and the freedom of individuals to choose the number of children they raise is at issue in every population policy. However, a number of policies have come under particular scrutiny in recent years because of the coercive measures with which they enforce 'responsible' childbearing. General trends in national population programmes are thus studied to assess the extent to which policies aimed at curbing population growth are compatible with obligations to respect the right to reproductive choice. The age-old influences of social and religious norms on spousal relationships, how we choose to control our fertility, and the value we attribute to childbearing are also considered in Chapter IV. An examination of the practical challenge posed by the real cost of family planning information, education and services concludes this chapter.

As the most significant mechanism for supervision of implementation of the right to reproductive choice, the functioning of the United Nations Committee on the Elimination of Discrimination against Women (CEDAW) is discussed in Chapter V. The strengths and weaknesses of CEDAW are examined, after which recommendations are put forth with a view to improving the functioning of the body. The penultimate chapter of this book deals with other legal mechanisms for supervision of implementation (i.e. bodies established to oversee compliance by States Parties to the other relevant conventions). Politically important (but non-legal) means of securing respect for the right to reproductive choice are also examined. For example, insofar as international donor agencies are also influential in contributing to the realization of the right to reproductive choice, their work is considered.

As a general matter, new areas of progress in the protection of the right to reproductive choice are appearing. These and other measures must be taken to protect the right to reproductive choice while realistically tackling the problem of population growth. This entails a responsible reconciliation of sometimes conflicting individual and collective desires and interests. It is to this end that this book concludes with recommendations responding to the global population and resources crises through provision of better family planning information, advice and freedom in decision-making for the many millions who require it.

The ultimate purpose of this study was to produce a resource which would help human rights advocates, lawyers, policy-makers, health and social workers, indeed professionals from all related fields of work, understand the meaning of the right to reproductive choice and how to obtain its better protection.

LIST OF TABLES

Table 1	Unmet Need for Family Planning	4
Table 2	The Composition and Sources of the Right to Reproductive Choice in International Law	36
Table 3	Exercising the Right to Reproductive Choice / Implications for the State	97
Table 4	Reservations to Provisions in the Women's Convention Affecting Reproductive Choice	123
Table 5	Interpretive Declarations on, and Reservations to, Provisions Affecting Reproductive Choice in Other Universal Human Rights Treaties	126

GLOSSARY OF ACRONYMS AND ABBREVIATIONS

ACHR	American Convention on Human Rights
CCPR	International Covenant on Civil and Political Rights
CEDAW	Committee on the Elimination of Discrimination against Women
CESCR	International Covenant on Economic, Social, and Cultural Rights
CIOMC	Council of International Organizations of Medical Sciences
CRC	Committee on the Rights of the Child
ECHR	Convention for the Protection of Human Rights and Fundamental Freedoms (European Convention on Human Rights)
ECJ	Court of Justice of the European Communities (European Court of Justice)
ECOSOC	Economic and Social Council
ETS	European Treaty Series
EU	European Union
FGM	Female genital mutilation
HRC	Human Rights Committee
IBRD	International Bank for Reconstruction and Development
ICJ	International Court of Justice
ICPD	International Conference on Population and Development (Cairo, 1994)
I.L.M.	International Legal Materials
ILO	International Labour Organisation
INA	U.S. Immigration and Nationality Act
IPPF	International Planned Parenthood Federation
IUD	Intra-uterine devices
IWRAW	International Women's Rights Action Watch
OAS	Organization of American States
OAU	Organization for African Unity
ODA	Official development assistance
NGO	Non-governmental organization
UDHR	Universal Declaration of Human Rights
UNFPA	United Nations Fund for Population Activities (UN Population Fund)

UNHCR	United Nations High Commissioner for Refugees
UNICEF	United Nations Children's Fund
UNIFEM	United Nations Fund for Women
UNTS	United Nations Treaty Series
WHO	World Health Organization
WPPA	World Population Plan of Action

Chapter I

Understanding the Right to Reproductive Choice

1. LOCATING THE RATIONALE FOR THE RIGHT TO REPRODUCTIVE CHOICE: WHAT IS THE ISSUE?

Procreation is among the most basic features of the human experience. Reproduction, implies creating a family, community and connecting with the future, raising the most profound questions of existence. At the same time, humans desire to live life with dignity, in which life can be enjoyed to the fullest, in good health, and with the freedom to develop according to one's desires. Control over one's fertility is closely related to life with dignity, giving humans the unparalleled power of choice in the creation of human life itself.

Only the individual or couple can decide what children mean to them, whether they wish to have a family, how many children they desire and when they wish to have them. States must respect these decisions. To interfere with human reproduction would represent the most intimate attack on dignity, striking at the nature and spirituality of human existence. Yet the procreation of individuals is a matter which also affects the welfare of the community in which they live. This community may be faced with limited resources and geographical space and there may be legitimate concerns over guaranteeing minimum standards of life for everyone in the community, including new children brought into the world. Consequently, the desires of individuals to procreate must be balanced with community interests. In seeking to achieve this balance, the dictates of human dignity place limits on the interests of the community vis-à-vis the desires and needs of the individual.

International human rights law proclaims the inalienable rights and freedoms of every human being, which effectively limit the power of the community (in the sense of the State) over the individual. Moreover, to foster life with dignity, the community (the State) is obliged to assist the individual with the fulfilment of minimum needs. In matters of procreation, limitations on what the State may do and obligations concerning what the State must do are equally important. These limitations and obligations are stipulated in terms of precise proscriptions and prescriptions in international human rights instruments.

Yet, while the human right to reproductive choice has been affirmed in a number of international instruments (as discussed below), millions of men and women are denied this right in practice every day. Of the dozen or so significant issues considered at the third United Nations International Conference on Population and Development (ICPD) held in Cairo from 5 to 13 September 1994, the subject of human reproduction and the human rights relating to this intimate facet of life posed the greatest difficulty in achieving consensus. The same subject was hardly less controversial at the fourth World Conference on Women held one year later in Beijing from 4 to 15 September 1995. Nonetheless, the resultant Programme of Action adopted in Cairo (hereafter the Cairo Programme of Action), which is intended to guide population activities and social advancement into the twenty-first century, devotes an entire chapter to the issue of reproductive rights and family planning,[1] while the Platform for Action adopted in Beijing (hereafter the Beijing Platform for Action) re-emphasized the principles agreed to in Cairo.[2] These events reflect the importance which the subject of reproductive choice has gained worldwide. The Cairo Programme of Action builds upon the considerable international consensus which has developed since the 1968 Proclamation of Teheran with regard to the right to reproductive choice.[3] Considering the diversity of the participants in Cairo, including representatives of more than 150 governments and 700 non-governmental organizations (NGOs),[4] consensus was understandably difficult to achieve. After all, the issue inherently involves deeply held views on family, gender and

---

[1] UN, Report of the International Conference on Population and Development, Cairo, 5–13 September 1994, Programme of Action of the International Conference on Population and Development (hereafter Cairo Programme of Action), UN doc. A/CONF.171/13, paragraphs 7.1 to 7.40.

[2] UN, Report of the Fourth World Conference on Women, Beijing, 4–15 September 1995, Beijing Declaration and Platform for Action (hereafter Beijing Platform for Action), UN doc. A/CONF.177/20.

[3] Proclaimed by the International Conference on Human Rights at Teheran on 13 May 1968; see: UN, Final Act of the International Conference on Human Rights, Teheran, 22 April to 13 May 1968, UN doc. A/CONF.32/41; and as reproduced in: UN, *Human Rights: A Compilation of International Instruments, Volume I (First Part)* (1994), pp. 51–54.

[4] See 'Wirth Urges ICPD to Adopt Universal Family Planning', *Daily Bulletin* of the Mission of the United States of America to the United Nations Office at Geneva, 6 April 1994, p. 4.

religion.[5] Moreover, many indicators demonstrate that, even with consensus achieved on paper, it may not be followed by determined action.

Despite the international consensus and various public declarations of intent, a large number of men and women throughout the world remain unable to exercise their right to reproductive choice because of restrictive laws and policies or because of the practical inability to gain access to family planning information and services necessary for its exercise. One indicator of this is the large unfulfilled demand for family planning in the developing world, as evidenced in Table 1 below.

While access to family planning is almost universal in Europe, North America and much of East Asia, in most of Sub-Saharan Africa, modern (i.e. effective) methods of family planning are either not available or not accessible such that contraceptive use is on average below 15 per cent of the fertile population and most women will bear six or more children.[6] The tremendous desire of individuals to control their fertility is further evidenced by high rates of illegal abortion and infanticide.[7]

---

[5] Leading into the Conference in Cairo, and following several preparatory committee meetings open to all participants, the final draft's chapter on reproductive rights featured heavily bracketed language (i.e. language still not agreed upon) including significant terms such as 'fertility regulation', 'reproductive rights' and 'family planning'; see UN, Third Session of the Preparatory Committee for the International Conference on Population and Development, 4–22 April 1994, UN doc. A/CONF.171/PC/1 and in UN Press Release POP/94/3 of 25 April 1994.

[6] See the UNFPA's *Population Issues (Briefing Kit 1992)*, p. 12. See also the UNFPA's *Index of Demographic, Social and Economic Indicators* (1995), p. 67.

[7] See Petchesky and Weiner, *Global Feminist Perspectives on Reproductive Rights and Reproductive Health* (1990), p. 20. See also UNFPA, *Population Issues, supra* note 6, p. 8.

TABLE 1. UNMET NEED FOR FAMILY PLANNING

as the per cent of currently married women 15 to 49 years of age who desire to postpone their next pregnancy or to bear no more children, but who do not use any form of modern contraception.

Sub-Saharan Africa

Botswana	27	Liberia	35	Rwanda	36
Burkina Faso	29	Madagascar	31	Senegal	27
Burundi	26	Malawi	34	Tanzania	27
Cameroon	21	Mali	30	Togo	42
Ghana	37	Namibia	12	Uganda	27
Guinea	25	Niger	18	Zambia	27
Kenya	32	Nigeria	20	Zimbabwe	23

Asia, Middle East, Northern Africa

Bangladesh	24	Nepal	28	Thailand	12
Egypt	20	Pakistan	27	Tunisia	20
Indonesia	14	Philippines	26	Turkey	12
Jordan	23	Sri Lanka	13	Vietnam	11
Morocco	20	Sudan	27		

Latin America, Caribbean

Bolivia	24	Ecuador	25	Paraguay	20
Brazil	14	El Salvador	22	Peru	16
Colombia	16	Guatemala	30	Trinidad and Tobago	27
Dominican Rep.	17	Mexico	27		

Source: DHS Program, *Women's Lives and Experiences: A Decade of Research Findings from the Demographic and Health Survey Program* (1994).

2. THE LINKS BETWEEN THE RIGHT TO REPRODUCTIVE CHOICE AND CONTEMPORARY PROBLEMS

The documents for action adopted in 1994 and 1995 at the World Summit on Social Development, the International Conference on Population and Development and the World Conference on Women have emphasized the strong link between reproduction and the health, social, economic and demographic dimensions of population growth.[8] The most recent International Conference on Population and Development was explicitly given a broader mandate than the previous UN conferences on population in order to reflect 'the growing recognition of global population, development and environmental interdependence'.[9] Certainly, achieving balance in all of these areas is no small feat. As will be examined at a later point, advances in some areas have more often than not been gained at the expense of reproductive choice (e.g. forced sterilization and coercion in planning family size) or have been stymied by failure to secure reproductive choice (e.g. forbidding the use of contraceptives by a certain part of the population).

2.1 Health

Reproductive choice plays a significant role in the general health and well-being primarily of women, but also that of children and the family as a whole. Just as the world cannot sustain an unlimited number of people, so women's bodies cannot sustain unlimited pregnancies. The denial of family planning services condemns many women to a life beset with the irreversible difficulties resulting from pregnancies too early or too late in life, too frequent, or too close together. In the extreme, women die from complications caused by pregnancy or childbirth. Unfortunately, the 'extreme' is all too common in many parts of the world: one-fifth of all deaths among women in the developing world are ascribed to maternal causes.[10] Even more startling, it is estimated that one in three women in the developing world suffer from some reproductive illness related to pregnancy, childbirth, abortion, HIV or a sexually transmitted disease. In addition, children born to

---

[8] For greater detail, see generally the Cairo Programme of Action, Chapters III, IV, VII and VIII, and the Beijing Platform of Action in its entirety.

[9] Cairo Programme of Action, paragraph 1.1.

[10] See: WHO, *The World Health Report 1995* (1995), pp. 35–36; and Black, *Better Health for Women and Children Through Family Planning* (1988), p. 12.

women suffering from reproductive ill-health may suffer from malnutrition and retarded growth and have a greater risk of death. Studies have shown, for example, that if all babies were born after at least a two-year birth interval, infant mortality in many developing countries would be reduced by 20 per cent.[11] Clearly, the individual's ability to make a choice regarding the number and spacing of pregnancies would make a positive contribution to the health of both mothers and children. Furthermore, improved maternal and infant health helps create the conditions for more effective family planning programmes.[12]

2.2 Population Growth

The right to reproductive choice goes beyond a focus on access to family planning methods or freedom in reproductive decision-making. Any discussion on this subject has broader implications involving the consideration of major issues which confront the world today. Primary among these is population growth. Indeed, it is this conceptual and moral nexus which largely explains the discussion of reproductive health and choice at the United Nations conferences on *population* and *development*.

As of mid-1995, the world population stood at about 5.75 billion.[13] The rate of population growth is increasing faster than ever before with three people being born every second.[14] Whereas it took 123 years for the world's population to move from the one billion to two billion mark, it will take only 11 years to increase from five billion to six billion, the population figure anticipated for 1998.[15] UN population projections for the year 2015 range from a low of 7.10 billion to a high of 7.83 billion.[16] In other terms, the world's population will grow by nearly the equivalent of the current population of the African continent over a period of just one decade.[17] If we aim to keep within the low projections, it is absolutely critical that we move towards universal

---

[11] Black, *ibid.*

[12] UNFPA, *Population Issues, supra* note 6, p. 8.

[13] Sadik, *The State of the World Population 1995*, p. 16.

[14] Sadik, *The State of the World Population 1993*, p. 1.

[15] Sadik, *supra* note 13, p. 16.

[16] *Ibid.*

[17] At mid-1995, Africa's total population was just over 728 million; *ibid.*, p. 67.

effective family planning before the end of this decade. Irrespective of which population projections are met, the problem of our increasing population relates directly to some of the other central concerns of our time: the state of the environment, the eradication of poverty, and the elimination of gender inequalities.

2.3 Sustainable Development and the Environment

The obstacles to sustainable development and a clean and inhabitable environment are closely linked with the failure to disseminate family planning information and offer fertility regulating services. Owing to population expansion, growing pressures for access to water, energy and food transcend all cultural and national boundaries. However, approximately 95 per cent of the world's population growth is occurring in the developing countries[18] since, despite falling mortality rates in most of these countries, many have not undergone the transition to lower fertility as experienced in the developed States. The real effects of population growth, therefore, will be especially felt in the developing world where the availability of resources is already failing to respond sufficiently to all the demands placed upon them. For example, by the end of the twentieth century, over half of the developing countries will be unable to feed their people without importing food.[19] If any effort towards sustainable development is to be successful, universal access to family planning and reproductive choice must first be addressed.[20] To this end, the call for universal access to family planning services by the year 2015 must be headed.[21]

---

[18] UNFPA, *Population Issues*, supra note 6, p. 2.

[19] See Johns Hopkins University, 'The Environment and Population Growth: Decade for Action', in: *Population Reports* (1992), Series M, No. 10, at p. 12.

[20] This reasoning underlies the provisions stipulated in the 1989 Amsterdam Declaration adopted at the International Forum on Population in the Twenty-first Century which was organized under the auspices of the United Nations Population Fund. At the Forum, the participating States reiterated the need to respect the human right to reproductive choice with emphasis placed on the crucial importance of population trends for the well-being and quality of life of future generations. Overall, the Declaration sets a firm course of action towards sustainable development and the protection of the environment. See: UN, Amsterdam Declaration on A Better Life for Future Generations, adopted by the International Forum on Population in the Twenty-first Century, Amsterdam, 6–9 November 1989, UN doc. A/C.2/44/6; and as reproduced in: UNFPA, *Meeting the Population Challenge* (1992), pp. 44–47.

[21] See the Cairo Programme for Action, paragraphs 7.6 and 7.16, as reproduced in Appendix A.

2.4 Social Disadvantages and Gender Inequalities

In the developing world where social security is absent or lacking, poverty breeds high rates of fertility since parents who lack adequate income from employment require children as a source of income and labour as well as security in one's old age.[22] While it may not appear evident at first glance, schooling is closely linked to quality of health and level of fertility (especially age at first pregnancy).[23] Women and girls with a poor level of education are at greater risk of poverty and high fertility. By improving the education of adolescents in general and girls in particular, age at marriage is delayed, the desired number of children is reduced and the risks of child and maternal mortality are considerably diminished.[24] According to the conclusions of the World Commission on Environment and Development (also known as 'the Brundtland Commission'), improved health, social security and labour laws would reduce the need for 'extra' children and more couples would opt for limiting their fertility.[25]

Without the ability to control their fertility, women are unable to shape their lives. Consequently, women are subjugated by their reproductive role which is determined by society at large and by their husbands in particular. Effectively, the status of women is greatly reduced in the absence of reproductive choice. Women cannot complete their education, maintain gainful employment nor make independent decisions.[26] Conversely, gender inequalities in the form of unequal access to education and the inferior status of women pose a significant barrier to women's exercise of reproductive choice. In most countries, the better educated a woman, the more likely she is to use family

---

[22] See report of the World Commission on Environment and Development, *Our Common Future* (1987), p. 106.

[23] For example, in Uganda (with a GNP of US$181 per inhabitant), women are likely to be illiterate (45 per cent), bear an average of 7.1 children, and can expect to live only until age 44. By comparison, the GNP of Denmark stands at US$27,551 per person, the rate of literacy is over 99 per cent, the average couple has 1.88 children and a woman lives until the age of 79. See generally Sadik, *supra* note 13, pp. 63–71.

[24] For example, one recent sample survey shows that countries with high literacy tend to have low infant mortality which, in turn, is followed by low fertility. See charts, WHO, *supra* note 10, p. 14. See also the Beijing Platform for Action at paragraph 268.

[25] *Supra* note 22.

[26] See Black, *supra* note 10, p. 11.

planning.²⁷ One study has demonstrated that women in the developing world who receive seven or more years of education marry, on average, more than five years later than women without any education; they also have two to three fewer children.²⁸ Equal access to education for young girls is thus a critical component in any policy aiming at the reduction of fertility.²⁹ Raising the status of women by improving their standards of education, health, employment and overall living is essential to promote healthy reproductive lives and reduce high fertility.³⁰ Evidently, if women are always pregnant, they have little chance of improving their status or their health. Following this reasoning, it is understandable why reproductive choice is addressed in a United Nations convention concerning the elimination of discrimination based on gender.³¹ Clearly, freedom in fertility decision-making plays a central role in making overall equality achievable.³²

3. THE FORMATION OF THE RIGHT TO REPRODUCTIVE CHOICE AT THE INTERNATIONAL LEVEL

The human right to reproductive choice has coalesced over the years as the result of a gradual evolution which, in its early developmental stages, was principally hortatory in nature.³³ The legal formulation of the right reflects this evolution in its full content insofar as it responds to the same fundamental concerns and embodies the international consensus for protection. Consequently, some review and examination of the concepts which contributed to the formulation of a human right to reproductive choice in international law is useful for a full under-

---

²⁷ See Johns Hopkins University, 'Fertility and Family Planning: An Update', in: *Population Reports* (1985), Series M, No. 8, at p. M–298.

²⁸ See Harrison, *The Third Revolution: Environment, Population and a Sustainable World* (1992), p. 287.

²⁹ This issue is also addressed in the Cairo Programme for Action at paragraph 6.7.

³⁰ See UNFPA, *Population Issues, supra* note 6, p. 5.

³¹ For discussion, see generally: Cook, 'Women's International Human Rights Law: The Way Forward', and Byrnes, 'Toward More Effective Enforcement of Women's Human Rights Through the Use of International Human Rights Law and Procedures', both in: Cook (ed.), *Human Rights of Women: National and International Perspectives* (1994).

³² See Paxman, *Law and Planned Parenthood* (1980), p. 92.

³³ Johnson provides a historical review of provisions concerning population issues in hortatory international instruments and the procedure by which they were adopted, up to 1986. See generally Johnson, *World Population and the United Nations* (1987).

standing of the articulated right.

3.1 The Principle of Free Choice

In December 1966, the UN General Assembly unanimously adopted Resolution 21/2211 on Population Growth and Economic Development, which addressed the issue of national population programmes. Thereby, States recognized:

> ... the sovereignty of nations in formulating and promoting their own population policies, with due regard to the principle that the size of the family should be the free choice of each individual family.[34]

The resolution essentially reformulates the right of individuals to found a family, but stresses that it may be of whatever size they desire, thus providing an additional element which forms an important part of the right to reproductive choice. Although this provision implies the right of individuals to found a family of their choice, it also emphasizes the State's power to encourage or discourage certain choices in its attempt to control population growth. In a statement issued in 1967, then Secretary-General U Thant highlighted the important relationship between these two concerns, combining them as follows:

> There are important links between population growth and the implementation of the rights and freedoms proclaimed in the Universal Declaration of Human Rights ... population planning is seen not only as an integral part of national efforts for economic and social development, but also as a way to human progress in modern society ... [However] any choice and decision with regard to the size of the family must inevitably rest with the family itself, and cannot be made by anyone else.[35]

In making the above statement, Thant acknowledged that there exist two concepts which could be in conflict. At the time, the *second* concept was the right of prospective parents to make their own choices as to family size; this concept would henceforth receive the fullest recognition in all United Nations documents on population issues. However, the *first* concept arising in the discussion was the sovereign right of States to decide on population policy. In the light of this emphasis on an apparently primordial State prerogative to set population policy, one

---

[34] UN General Assembly resolution 21/2211 of 17 December 1966.

[35] See United Nations, *Population Newsletter*, Population Division of the Department of Economic and Social Affairs, UN, New York (No. 4), 10 December 1967.

may wonder what becomes of coercive national population programmes which may deny individuals the right freely to found a family of their choice, such as the case of China's 'One Child – One Couple' campaign. How is the principle of free choice to be reconciled with the sovereignty of States over population policy? The manner in which this conflict is to be resolved according to contemporary international law is an issue which will be addressed in Chapters III and IV.

One year later, the International Conference on Human Rights was convened in Teheran under the auspices of the United Nations and a new step forward was made with the recognition of reproductive choice as a *human right*. The Conference concluded with the unanimous adoption of the Proclamation of Teheran on 13 May 1968 which proclaims, *inter alia*, that:

> The protection of the family and of the child remains the concern of the international community. Parents have a basic human right to determine freely and responsibly the number and spacing of their children.[36]

This contributed significantly to the clarification of the relationship between individual choice and the State's power over population policy: the priority apparently shifted, with individual choice gaining primordial status through its character as a 'basic' (and presumably inalienable) human right.

3.2 The Requirement of Responsibility

The right of parents to decide on matters of procreation was further elaborated in the Declaration of Social Progress and Development adopted by the General Assembly in 1969.[37] In Article 4 of the Declaration, the fundamental message of the Proclamation of Teheran is repeated:

> Parents have the exclusive right to determine freely and responsibly the number and spacing of their children.

In examining both the Proclamation and the Declaration, there appears to be a growing consideration of the role of parents with regard to *responsible* reproductive decision-making. Whereas prior emphasis had

---

[36] UN, Final Act of the International Conference on Human Rights, *supra* note 3, Article 16.

[37] UN General Assembly resolution 24/2542 of 11 December 1969.

been placed on the right of individuals to found a family of their choice,[38] there had entered into the equation a proviso: a responsibility of the couple not to have more children than they are able to support. These were the earliest articulations of a duty of parents to guarantee their children a life of dignity (a duty which was later included among the rights of the child). It also provided a legitimate basis for the State to intervene to limit 'irresponsible' behaviour.

3.3 Access to Family Planning for Meaningful Choice

In August 1974, the first World Population Conference was held in Bucharest. This Conference represented a major step forward in the growing movement to stem population growth not only because it was the first official inter-governmental conference on the subject but also because it approved a ten-year World Population Plan of Action (WPPA). Many had hoped that the Bucharest Conference would provide the global consensus needed to tackle population problems, but instead the Conference was characterized by controversy and discord.[39] Provisions for family planning fared poorly. While the original draft Plan of Action called for immediate action so that reproductive choice could be guaranteed to everyone by 1985, the text was rejected and an alternative, less ambitious, text adopted in its place.[40]

Gradually, building on the statements, resolutions and declarations issuing from international gatherings, an international norm to decide the number and spacing of one's children and an increasing commitment on the part of governments and international agencies to carry out population and family planning programmes was being formed. The second International Conference on Population, which took place in Mexico City in 1984, followed the incremental pattern established in previous conferences and proved a net advance on Bucharest. Clearly, it was determined, the most effective means by which a couple can responsibly found a family is through modern family planning. The weak support for family planning agreed to in Bucharest contrasted sharply with 1984 data from the World Fertility Survey for developing countries which indicated that one in every four births had not been

---

[38] Article 16(1) of the 1948 Universal Declaration of Human Rights (UDHR) provides that all 'men and women of full age . . . have the right . . . to found a family' without discrimination.

[39] See Johnson, *supra* note 33, pp. 81–90.

[40] *Ibid.*, p. 118.

desired.[41] This time, 'Recommendation 25', in clear no-nonsense language, was adopted, stating that:

> Governments should, as a matter of urgency, make universally available information, education and the means to assist couples and individuals to achieve their desired number of children . . . [These] should include all medically approved and appropriate methods of family planning, including natural family planning, to ensure a voluntary and free choice in accordance with changing individual and cultural values.[42]

The next year, four paragraphs solely devoted to empowering women with the ability to control freely their fertility through family planning information and services were adopted in the Nairobi Forward-looking Strategies for the Advancement of Women.[43] These paragraphs represented the culmination of the work in this area during the United Nations Decade for Women, which was intended to promote the status of women and equal enjoyment of their human rights worldwide.

---

[41] *Ibid.*, pp. 277–278.

[42] UN, Report of the International Conference on Population, Mexico City, 6–14 August 1984, UN doc. E/CONF.76/19.

[43] UN, Report of the World Conference to Review and Appraise the Achievements of the United Nations Decade for Women: Equality, Development and Peace, Nairobi, Kenya, 15–26 July 1985, UN doc. A/CONF.116/28/Rev.1, paragraphs 156–159.

CHAPTER II

ARTICULATIONS OF THE RIGHT TO REPRODUCTIVE CHOICE IN INTERNATIONAL LAW

1. DEFINING THE RIGHT TO REPRODUCTIVE CHOICE

The right to 'reproductive choice' does not exist *expressis verbis*. Rather, the term is used for reasons of ease and represents a shorthand way of referring to the 'rights to decide freely and responsibly on the number and spacing of [one's] children and to have access to the information, education and means to enable [one] to exercise these rights'—rights which are provided *expressis verbis* in an international human rights treaty, specifically in Article 16(1)(e) of the 1979 Convention on the Elimination of All Forms of Discrimination against Women[44] (the Women's Convention). Any discussion on the definition of the right to reproductive choice, and consequently the scope inferred in the definition, necessarily begins with the recognition that it is protected as a composite right (comprised of a number of core elements) and through a compound effect. Along with the above stipulation expressed in the Women's Convention, the individual elements are recognized separately as basic human rights in various conventions (see the discussion on 'sources' below). Each of the core elements, which can also be referred to as core rights, stand their own ground and yet are not insulated; they interact dynamically with each other (as, indeed, do all human rights) and thus lend strength to the right to reproductive choice. To understand fully the content of the right to reproductive choice, it is therefore equally important to understand the scope of application of these core elements (as discussed below in Chapter III). However, before addressing the sources and content of the right to reproductive choice, the core elements must be clearly identified and the concept generally defined.

---

[44] Adopted 18 December 1979; for the full text of the Convention, see 1249 UNTS 13. Also reproduced in: UN, *Human Rights: A Compilation of International Instruments, Volume I (First Part)* (1994), pp. 150–163.

the free exercise of one's intellect to decide on matters relating to one's development (in particular one's own reproduction) seems the essence of human dignity. It is because the essence of the subject matter is *choice* in relation to *reproduction* that this author prefers the abbreviated term 'reproductive choice'.

To better define reproductive choice, further examination of Article 16(1)(e) of the Women's Convention reveals that it contains a *principal* clause which ensures individuals the right 'to decide freely and responsibly on the number and spacing of their children'. Only in relation to this principal clause did the drafters choose to specify in a secondary *enabling* clause two further rights of individuals: 1) to have access to (relevant) information and education; and 2) to have access to the means to enable exercise of 'these rights' (referring to the right to decide on the number and spacing of children). While the latter 'enabling rights' are also expressly stipulated in other human rights instruments, as will be discussed below, their expressed stipulation in Article 16(1)(e) of the Women's Convention underscores the vital nature of their relationship to the principal right to decide the number and spacing of one's children; the principal right cannot be disconnected from the enabling rights (which explains why these rights are expressed in a single provision).

One element which is not stipulated in Article 16(1)(e) of the Women's Convention is the right to found a family. However, it is evident that the very concept of a right to decide the number and spacing of one's children naturally presupposes a right to found a family. Indeed, the *choice* of founding a family would involve, at a minimum, an initial decision to have or not to have children. How many more children (if any) and at which intervals are issues which arise only thereafter. Information and services necessary to exercise these rights would vary according to the basic desires of the persons concerned, i.e. bringing into play elements which enable meaningful choices on founding a family and deciding the number and spacing of children.

With the above in mind, it is the inseparable nature[50] of the composite elements which give form and content to a right which may be referred to on its own, i.e. 'the right to reproductive choice'. Thus, following the logic of the inseparability of the principal and enabling

---

[50] For a practical example, one author correctly points out that 'limiting access to contraceptive methods cannot be reconciled with the right [to reproductive choice]'; Lieberson, 'The Population Explosion and Contraceptive Ethos', in: Spicker et al. (eds.), *The Contraceptive Ethos* (1987), p. 75.

rights, the core elements of the composite right to reproductive choice are:

(a) the right to found a family;
(b) the right to decide (freely and responsibly) the number and spacing of one's children;
(c) the right to access to family planning information and education;
(d) the right to access to family planning methods and services (facilities).

2. SOURCES OF THE RIGHT TO REPRODUCTIVE CHOICE: IN GENERAL

A great many of the international texts referred to in Chapter I (including the documents adopted at the Cairo and Beijing Conferences) which advance the existence of general 'reproductive rights' or specific rights regarding reproductive choice and health are hortatory (or, at best, of uncertain legal value). This is of fundamental and critical importance because hortatory instruments and provisions articulate aims or goals, but they do not establish legal obligations. In the absence of a legal obligation, there is no duty of performance and, consequently, no possibility of breach. Since there can be no breach, there can be no international wrong for which a State may be found responsible and, in turn, since there arises no issue of State responsibility there is no basis for claims to restitution or compensation and no basis for lawful sanctions. Perhaps from a more practical perspective, the absence of a legal obligation obviates the need for *supervision of compliance* and essentially prevents the establishment of *procedures* relating to implementation. This means that hortatory declarations are usually less effective instruments than legal ones. For advocates of reproductive health and choice, this is a serious concern which demands adequate consideration.

Despite the hortatory nature of various instruments, particularly the texts adopted at the successive international conferences on population and women, many commentators who have written extensively on the right to reproductive choice claim the texts to be 'binding' in a legal sense.[51] However, in asserting the binding nature of the texts, most of

---

[51] For example, see generally: Freedman and Isaacs, 'Human Rights and Reproductive Choice', 24 *Studies in Family Planning* (1993), pp. 18–30; Dixon-Mueller, *supra* note 47; and IPPF, *The Human Right to Family Planning* (1984).

these commentators fail to identify and establish the precise source of law.

There is no secret about the sources of international law.[52] The legal nature of a specific text may be determined by reference to the known and limited sources. Article 38(1) of the Statute of the International Court of Justice (ICJ) lists the sources of international law as follows:

> (a) international conventions, whether general or particular, establishing rules expressly recognized by the contracting States;
> (b) international custom, as evidence of a general practice accepted as law;
> (c) the general principles of law recognized by civilized nations;
> (d) . . . judicial decisions and the teachings of the most highly qualified publicists of the various nations, as subsidiary means for determination of rules of law.

While these sources were stipulated in the Statute in order to instruct the ICJ as to what to apply in order to decide cases before it, 'Article 38 is generally regarded as a complete statement of the sources of international law'.[53] The critical and foundational nature of the three sources listed in sub-paragraphs (a) to (c) is that they derive from the principle of *consent*; sub-paragraph (d) only refers to a '*subsidiary* means for determination of rules of law' (emphasis added). The principle of consent is itself founded upon the sovereign equality of States which constitutes the first principle of contemporary international law and relations; since no State has more legitimacy than any other State, no State can be required to follow prescriptions or proscriptions against its will. Even 'the general principles of law' referred to in sub-paragraph (c) turn (dubiously) upon a *recognition* by 'civilized' nations. As for 'judicial decisions and the teachings of the most highly qualified publicists', the wording of sub-paragraph (d) makes it clear that, while these are useful subsidiaries, they require identification of sources prior to their invocation relative to the possible specific content or extent of

---

[52] On the sources of international law, see: Brownlie, *Principles of Public International Law* (1990), pp. 1–31; Detter, *The International Legal Order* (1994), pp. 146–251; Harris, *Cases and Materials on International Law* (1991), pp. 23–68; Higgins, *Problems and Process; International Law and How We Use It* (1994), pp. 17–38; Reuter, *Droit international public* (1983), pp. 89–174; Rousseau, *Droit international public* (1987), pp. 17–92; Schachter, *International Law in Theory and Practice* (1991), pp. 34–65; and Shaw, *International Law* (1991), pp. 58–100.

[53] Brownlie, *ibid.*, p. 3. With the same conclusion, see: Detter, *ibid.*, p. 148; Harris, *ibid.*, p. 24; Reuter, *ibid.*, pp. 92–93; and Shaw, *ibid.*, p. 59. Cf. Higgins (*ibid.*, pp. 17–18) who essentially agrees, but qualifies her accord with an interesting analysis of some 'problems'.

an obligation.[54]

To return to the legal nature of the hortatory texts referred to above, it is difficult to place them within any of the three sources (and one subsidiary means) of international law listed above. First, the language used in many of the texts clearly demonstrates that they were intended only to be hortatory. For example, the document adopted at the 1984 International Conference on Population issued mere 'Recommendations'. Similarly, the 1989 Amsterdam Declaration on A Better Life for Future Generations only *called* for a course of action for the future.[55] The 1994 Cairo Programme of Action clearly states in its preamble that it 'recommends to the international community a set of important population and development objectives' (paragraph 1.12) and, moreover, that it 'does not create any new international human rights' (paragraph 1.15).[56] The 1995 Beijing Platform for Action sets an 'agenda for women's empowerment' (paragraph 1).[57] Nevertheless, some commentators employ these instruments as legally binding texts on the basis that they were subsequently adopted by resolutions of the United Nations General Assembly,[58] e.g. the 1985 Nairobi Forward-

---

[54] In making it clear that there are only '*three* law-creating processes: treaties, international customary law or the general principles of law recognized by civilized nations', Schwarzenberger (as quoted in Harris, *supra* note 52, p. 23, emphasis added) adds that '[t]he significance of this enumeration lies in its exclusiveness. It rules out other potential law-creating processes such as natural law, moral postulates or the doctrine of international law'. In his interesting and critical assessment of the overall character of the value of scholarly works in relation to the sources of international law, Schachter (*supra* note 52, pp. 38–39) concludes: 'whether one or many, the jurists still engage in generalizing and abstraction that adds to the distance between their pronouncements of *lex lata* and the raw data of the sources'. Likewise, Schachter (pp. 39–43) cautions against over-reliance on judicial decisions (even—or especially—those of the ICJ).

[55] See the Amsterdam Declaration, *supra* note 20.

[56] Cairo Programme of Action, *supra* note 1, at Chapter I, Preamble. Indeed, the introductory paragraph of Chapter II, entitled 'Principles', reads: 'The implementation of the recommendations contained in the Programme of Action is the sovereign right of each country, consistent with national laws and development priorities, with full respect for the various religious and ethical values and cultural backgrounds of its people, and in conformity with universally recognized international human rights'. This implies a very flexible understanding of the 'recommendations' of the document and largely explains the absence of an independent monitoring system.

[57] Beijing Platform for Action, *supra* note 2.

[58] Article 10 of the Charter of the United Nations provides that the General Assembly 'may make *recommendations*' (emphasis added). For a commentary on the 'Form and Legal Nature of Recommendations' within the meaning of Article 10 of the Charter, see Simma (ed.), *The Charter of the United Nations: A Commentary* (1994), pp. 237–240. For an excellent analysis of the legal value and implications of UN General Assembly resolutions (and

looking Strategies—another document with language which is inconsistent with a binding instrument. Quick reference to the sources of law listed in Article 38(1) of the ICJ Statute would indicate that such resolutions are not sources of law. But, this is too quick and shallow an analysis. In fact, the principle of consent[59] functions such that everything turns on the nature of the specific resolution and its adoption since there is the possibility that a resolution adopted by the UN General Assembly may reflect customary law or may be 'law-making' as an interpretation or specific and subsequent application of obligations under the Charter of the United Nations (i.e. that it may be rooted in treaty law). The intention of the States as evidenced by the specific wording of the resolution, the explanations of votes before and after voting, and the voting itself are all relevant to determining the legal nature of a resolution.[60] Thus, as Shaw observes, while certain (rare) resolutions of the UN General Assembly are binding upon UN Member States, others 'are not legally binding and are merely recommendatory, putting forward opinions on various issues with varying degrees of majority support'.[61] He goes on to explain that one must be aware of the 'dangers in ascribing legal value to everything that emanates from the Assembly', particularly resolutions which may never have been intended to constitute binding norms.[62] Sloan further clarifies that unless the resolution 'purports to declare existing law' thus confirming 'the absence of contrary practice (or confirming practice within the organization)' it is more likely to be *de lege ferenda* (law in the making).[63] In most cases where a resolution is asserted to be binding, its real

---

similar texts), see Schachter (*supra* note 52), Chapter VI entitled 'Resolutions and Political Texts', pp. 84–105. See also Harris (*supra* note 52) at pp. 59–64. For another interesting discussion of the legal value of 'resolutions of international organizations', see Higgins (*supra* note 52, pp. 22–28).

[59] On the principle of consent, see Detter (*supra* note 52), pp. 157–165, who describes as 'very few indeed' the 'general international rules which *"break through"* the sovereign walls of a State' (her emphasis); Detter lists only 'genocide, slavery, torture and apartheid', pp. 163–164.

[60] For a thorough recount and critique of arguments concerning voting, see *ibid.*, pp. 234–243.

[61] Shaw, *supra* note 52, at p. 93.

[62] *Ibid.*, p. 95.

[63] Sloan, quoted in Harris (*supra* note 52) at p. 61. This reference to what is also known as 'soft law' raises the possibility of something of an *inferior*, if of any, legal value. Interestingly, Detter treats the issue of 'recommendations' within her chapter on 'Soft Law'; Detter (*supra* note 52), pp. 212–251, at pp. 224 ff. After lengthy consideration, Detter concludes that recommendations 'usually denote a facultative measure that can be adopted

source of law is usually said or implied to be found in custom insofar as the vote is seen to constitute both *opinio juris* (the belief that there is a legal obligation) and the general practice of States. However, in the case of the right to reproductive choice, one cannot easily assert a customary norm of reproductive choice because, irrespective of any voting, there is certainly no consistent practice in this area. Therefore, it stretches the idea of law-making resolutions by the UN General Assembly well past the point of tenability simply to assert a right to reproductive choice on the basis of the adoption of a resolution. This, of course, is to say nothing of the specific wording of the resolutions in question, none of which indicate an intention to create binding law.[64]

In light of the above, it is submitted that the great majority of the existing literature on the right to reproductive choice focuses erroneously (and in large measure *unnecessarily*) on the large number of hortatory international instruments (such as those referred to above) as a basis to claim a binding obligation on the part of States to protect the right to reproductive choice. While these 'instruments' may represent important contributions to the genesis of treaty law, may raise public awareness and consciousness, may be rallying points for advocacy movements, and may stimulate positive changes within States, they are not sources of law and cannot be invoked to secure legal protection. At best, their texts support a notion of reproductive choice which is socially and politically persuasive: they reflect a common endeavour by the international community to address issues under the rubric of 'reproductive rights'. Unfortunately, the rather broad misconception that such texts are legally binding renders much of the discussion over the right to reproductive choice misleading. If the right is to be protected by international law, it is essential that we correctly establish the sources of the right in international law. Indeed, reference to existing 'hard' law reveals that a high degree of protection has already been secured for the right to reproductive choice. It is in this sense that an over-emphasis on hortatory texts is 'unnecessary'; there exist solid legal bases to

---

or dismissed at will' (pp. 249–250). While acknowledging that they may contribute *'support'* and *'a cadre de référence'* for action, they remain *'proteiforme'* which 'may be useful as *material'* (her emphasis, p. 250). Higgins (*supra* note 52, p. 28) considers the resolutions of international organizations in a similar fashion, determining that 'they undoubtedly play a significant role in creating norms'. Still, Detter concludes, '[t]he important principle of security of law in international society is endangered if there is uncertainty of existing legal commitments. Therefore, the meaning of recommendations must not be distorted and construed to entail obligations *per se*' (pp. 250–251).

[64] On the 'legal impact of standards and recommendations in international society', see Detter (*supra* note 52), pp. 249–251.

protect the right to reproductive choice and more attention should be paid to these sources with, accordingly, more energy devoted to achieving their effective implementation.

Since there is far from any 'general practice' of States regarding reproductive choice, there is no customary law basis for 'the right to reproductive choice'. Similarly, the right to reproductive choice (nor any of its component elements) can be said to constitute a 'general principle of law' recognized by States. However, provisions protecting the elements forming the right to reproductive choice, as well as the right itself, have been established in various international human rights treaties. As such, the right to reproductive choice is protected *solely* by conventional law which is, as such, binding only between States Parties. The relevant provisions may thus be examined.

3. SOURCES OF THE RIGHT TO REPRODUCTIVE CHOICE IN INTERNATIONAL LAW

3.1 Introduction

Since this is a study of the right to reproductive choice in international law, it is necessary to identify sources at the universal (i.e. globally applicable) and regional (i.e. applicable within a defined geo-political part of the world) levels. Universal standards have been developed under the auspices of the United Nations Organization. Regional standards have been developed under the auspices of the Council of Europe, the Organization of American States (OAS), and the Organization for African Unity (OAU).[65]

The sources of the right to reproductive choice, and the composite of rights which lend it strength in the universal and regional human rights treaties elaborated under the auspices of the various inter-

---

[65] While no regional standards yet exist in Asia (nor does an Asia-wide organization exist within to elaborate such standards), it is perhaps worth noting that an important step in international human rights law was taken in September 1994 by the League of Arab States with the adoption of the Arab Charter on Human Rights (adopted on 15 September 1994 by the Council of the League of Arab States, meeting at its 102nd session, by resolution 5437). However, disappointingly, the Arab Charter on Human Rights is of no apparent value in securing the right to reproductive choice; it does not provide for either the right to found a family or the right to decide the number and spacing of children, nor does it secure the right to information or the right to health. Moreover, the Arab Charter has yet to be ratified by any State and has yet to enter into force; see Marie, 'International Instruments relating to Human Rights', 17 *Human Rights Law Journal* (1996), No. 1–2.

governmental organizations, are considered below. While the universal texts are often the better known, it is important for human rights advocates to be aware of and understand the existing provisions in regional instruments[66] since these are accompanied by implementation procedures and supervisory organs which may be easier to access and are more effective, particularly in the developed regional systems of Europe and the Americas. The precise provisions in the various universal and regional instruments are listed in abbreviated fashion in Table 2 below.

3.2 Sources of the Right to Found a Family

3.2.1 Universal. The 'right of men and women of marriageable age to marry and to found a family' is recognized under Article 23(2) of the 1966 International Covenant on Civil and Political Rights[67] (CCPR). Article 2(1) of the same instrument equally ensures the right 'without distinction of any kind'. This right is understood to be derived from Article 16(1) of the 1948 Universal Declaration of Human Rights[68] (UDHR) which, while expressing values which may enjoy universal recognition, is of uncertain legal value.

The right to found a family is also protected under the special case of genocide in the 1948 Convention on the Prevention and Punishment

---

[66] It is perhaps necessary to sound a cautionary note at this point concerning the contents of the 1981 African Charter on Human and Peoples' Rights which appears to provide for virtually everything in its Article 18(3) which stipulates as follows: 'The State shall ensure the elimination of every discrimination against women and also ensure the protection of the rights of the woman and the child as stipulated in international declarations and conventions'. However, commentaries on this provision within the Charter convincingly demonstrate the extreme weakness of protection owing largely to its absence of specificity; see: Adjetey, 'Reclaiming the African Woman's Individuality', 44 *American University Law Review* (1995), No. 4; Welch, 'Human Rights and African Women: A Comparison of Protection under Two Major Treaties', 15 *Human Rights Quarterly* (1993), No. 3. For the full text of the African Charter, as adopted in Nairobi on 26 June 1981, see 21 I.L.M. 59. Also reproduced in: Council of Europe, *Human Rights in International Law: Basic Texts* (1992), pp. 342–362.

[67] Adopted and opened for signature, ratification and accession by UN General Assembly resolution 2200 A (XXI) of 16 December 1966; for the full text of the Covenant, see 999 UNTS 171. Also reproduced in: UN, *Human Rights: A Compilation of International Instruments, Volume I (First Part)* (1994), pp. 20–40.

[68] Adopted and proclaimed by the United Nations General Assembly by resolution 217 A (III) of 10 December 1948; for the full text of the Declaration, see UN, *Human Rights: A Compilation of International Instruments, Volume I (First Part)* (1994), pp. 1–7. On the relationship of Article 16(1) of the UDHR to Article 23(2) of the CCPR, see Nowak, *U.N. Covenant on Civil and Political Rights: CCPR Commentary* (1993), p. 412.

of the Crime of Genocide.[69] Article 2(d) of the Genocide Convention condemns measures imposed with the intention of preventing births (such as involuntary sterilization) with the object of limiting the numbers of racial, ethnic or religious groups.[70]

3.2.2 Regional

Europe. The right to found a family is stipulated in the principal human rights instrument adopted by the Council of Europe. Article 12 of the 1950 Convention for the Protection of Human Rights and Fundamental Freedoms[71] (the European Convention on Human Rights; ECHR) is the same as the provision in the CCPR regarding the right to found a family, with the exception that it expressly foresees variations in domestic law as follows: 'Men and women of marriageable age have the right to marry and to found a family, according to the national laws governing the exercise of this right'.

Americas. In the Americas, provisions for the formation and protection of families take a considerably different approach. According to Article 17(2) of the 1969 American Convention on Human Rights[72] (hereafter the ACHR or the American Convention), States Parties are required to respect:

> The right of men and women of marriageable age to marry and to raise a family . . . if they met the conditions required by domestic laws, insofar as such conditions do not affect the principle of non-discrimination established in this Convention.

---

[69] Approved and proposed for signature and ratification or accession by United Nations General Assembly resolution 260 A (III) of 9 December 1948; for the full text of the Convention, see 78 UNTS 277. Also reproduced in: UN, *Human Rights: A Compilation of International Instruments, Volume I (Second Part)* (1994), pp. 673–677.

[70] While this may seem an extreme and implausible occurrence, there have been a number of such cases reported where persons belonging to, e.g., a minority group are forcibly sterilized. For example, see: Whitfield (ed.), *June Fourth Briefing Papers on China* (1993), pp. 46–47 as well as 'Family, Population, AIDS and Abortion', 24 *Impact International* (1994), No. 5, p. 16, with regard to allegations of forced sterilization of members of the Tibetan minority in China.

[71] Adopted in Rome on 4 November 1950; for the full text of the Convention, see ETS No. 5. Also reproduced in: Council of Europe, *Human Rights in International Law: Basic Texts* (1992), pp. 159–181.

[72] Also known as the Pact of San José, Costa Rica, adopted in San José on 22 November 1969; for the full text of the Convention, see 1144 UNTS 331. Also reproduced in: Council of Europe, *Human Rights in International Law: Basic Texts* (1992), pp. 293–326.

This focus on *raising* (rather than founding) a family is further elaborated in the 1988 Additional Protocol to the American Convention on Human Rights in the area of Economic, Social and Cultural Rights[73] (hereafter the Additional Protocol). According to Article 15 of the Additional Protocol:

> 1. The family is the natural and fundamental element of society and ought to be protected by the State . . .
> 2. Everyone has the right to form a family, which shall be exercised in accordance with the provisions of the pertinent domestic legislation.

One is immediately struck by the slight change in the wording of this provision as compared to the relatively well-established provision in universal and European usages: the right to 'raise' or 'form' a family is apparently different from, and arguably *broader* than, the right to 'found' one.[74] Worded as such, the American Convention and its Additional Protocol would initially appear to provide insufficiently for this aspect of reproductive choice, securing protection of the family only as a private entity rather than securing the choice of individuals regarding its initial foundation. However, it would have to be assumed that the drafters had intended a similar meaning to that established in the UDHR (to which reference is explicitly made in the Preambles of the ACHR and its Additional Protocol) and to the CCPR and the 1966 Covenant on Economic, Social and Cultural Rights[75] (CESCR) (to which reference is implied, respectively, in the Preambles of each of the conventions), as there is no outward indication (nor plausible reason) that the intention was to distinguish the *foundation* of a family from the *raising* of a family especially since logic would infer that one would not normally be in a position to raise a family without somehow having founded one. This interpretation is further supported by the juxtaposition in Article 17(2) of the ACHR of the right 'to raise a family' with the

---

[73] Also known as the Protocol of San Salvador, adopted in San Salvador on 17 November 1988; for the full text of the Additional Protocol, see OAS Treaty Series No. 69. Also reproduced in: Council of Europe, *Human Rights in International Law: Basic Texts* (1992), pp. 327–339.

[74] To 'raise' a family implies parental prerogatives concerning child-rearing—which responds to concerns over private family life and social and cultural formation in the family unit, rather than any concern about reproduction.

[75] Adopted and opened for signature, ratification and accession by United Nations General Assembly resolution 2200 A (XXI) of 16 December 1966; for the full text of the Covenant, see 999 UNTS 3. Also reproduced in: UN, *Human Rights: A Compilation of International Instruments, Volume I (First Part)* (1994), pp. 8–19.

'right of men and women of marriageable age to marry' thereby clearly connecting the ideas of marriage and family in a traditional manner with the implication that family (i.e. child-bearing) follows marriage.

Doubt over the status of the right to found a family in the Inter-American system is largely resolved by reference to the 1948 American Declaration of the Rights and Duties of Man (hereafter American Declaration).[76] Article VI of the American Declaration provides that '[e]very person has the right to establish a family'; to 'establish' a family is virtually synonymous with founding a family.[77] Consequently, for all Member States of the OAS there exists a legal obligation (derived from the OAS Charter, which is a treaty) to respect the right of everyone to establish (found) a family.

3.3 Sources of the Right to Decide the Number and Spacing of Children

3.3.1 Universal. At the universal level, only one convention provides expressly for the right to decide the number and spacing of one's children. According to Article 16(1)(e) of the Women's Convention, States Parties must take all appropriate measures to ensure individuals have the right 'to decide freely and responsibly on the number and spacing of their children'. While it may be said that the right to decide the number and spacing of one's children logically implies an inherent right to found a family (which explains why the Women's Convention does not provide expressly for the right to found a family), choice over the number and spacing of children clearly goes beyond founding a family.

The right to decide the number and spacing of one's children may also be considered a matter of 'privacy'. Article 17(1) of the CCPR provides that '[n]o one shall be subjected to arbitrary or unlawful interference with his privacy'. While the exact meaning of the term

---

[76] Adopted in Bogotá on 2 May 1948; for the full text of the Declaration, see OAS doc. OEA/Ser.L/V/II.65, doc. 6, p. 19. Also reproduced in: Council of Europe, *Human Rights in International Law: Basic Texts* (1992), pp. 284–292.

[77] It is important to note in this connection that the Inter-American Court of Human Rights has pronounced that the American Declaration 'contains and defines the fundamental human rights referred to in the Charter [of the OAS]' . . . 'with the result that . . . the American Declaration is for these [Member] States a source of international obligation related to the Charter of the Organization'; Inter-American Court of Human Rights, *Interpretation of the American Declaration of the Rights and Duties of Man within the Framework of Article 64 of the American Convention* (pursuant to the request of the Government of the Republic of Colombia), Advisory Opinion OC–10/89, of 14 July 1989, at paragraphs 43–45.

'privacy' has not been defined with regard to this provision,[78] Nowak observes that it concerns, *inter alia*, the individual's 'identity' and 'autonomy' insofar as 'human beings strive to achieve self-realization by way of actions that do not interfere with the liberty of others'.[79] However, the Human Rights Committee (the expert body established pursuant to Article 28 of the CCPR) has stated that, '[a]s all persons live in society, the protection of privacy is necessarily relative'.[80] Consequently, decisions regarding the number and spacing of one's children are protected by the right to privacy to the extent that such decisions 'do not interfere with the liberty of others'.

Insofar as too many pregnancies, or pregnancies spaced too closely together, may adversely impact on maternal health, the right to decide the number and spacing of one's children may be protected under the right to health as stipulated in Article 12 of the 1966 CESCR. On the same basis, adolescents may be protected under Article 24 of the 1989 Convention on the Rights of the Child[81] (hereafter the Children's Convention). The relationship between the right to health and the right to reproductive choice is further developed below with regard to sources of the right to access to family planning services, both at the universal and regional level.

3.3.2 Regional. At the regional level, there is no expressed right to decide the number and spacing of children. However, the right to privacy is protected by Article 8(1) of the ECHR and Article 11(2) of the ACHR. Unfortunately, no mention of a right to privacy exists under the 1981 African Charter on Human and Peoples' Rights (hereafter the African Charter).

All regions have at least one instrument which ensures the right to health and arguably, therefore, the right to decide the number and spacing of one's children in certain circumstances. The right to health is protected under the regional systems as follows: paragraph 11 of Part

---

[78] See Nowak, *supra* note 68, p. 294.

[79] *Ibid.*, p. 297.

[80] Paragraph 7 of General Comment No. 16(32) of 23 March 1988; for the full text of the General Comment, see UN, Report of the Human Rights Committee, General Assembly, Official Records, Forty-third Session, Supplement No. 40 (A/43/40), Annex VI, pp. 181–183. Also reproduced in Nowak, *supra* note 68, pp. 864–865.

[81] Adopted and open for signature, ratification and accession by United Nations General Assembly resolution 44/25 of 20 November 1989; for the full text of the Convention, see 28 I.L.M. 1456. Also reproduced in: UN, *Human Rights: A Compilation of International Instruments, Volume I (First Part)* (1994), pp. 174–195.

I and Article 11 of Part II of the 1961 European Social Charter[82] (elaborated under the auspices of the Council of Europe); Article 10(3) of the 1990 European Code of Social Security (Revised)[83] (also elaborated under the Council of Europe); Article 10(1) of the Additional Protocol to the ACHR; and Article 16 of the African Charter.

3.4 Sources of the Right to Family Planning Information and Education

3.4.1 Universal. The right to obtain information specifically[84] on the subject of family planning is expressly provided in international treaty law. As mentioned earlier, the right to information and education on family planning is provided in the grouping of rights in Article 16(1)(e) of the Women's Convention as a means to ensure the right to decide the number and spacing of one's children.

The right to access to information in general (including in relation to family planning) is protected under Article 19(2) of the CCPR which ensures the individual the:

> . . . freedom to seek, receive and impart information and ideas of all kinds, regardless of frontiers, either orally, in writing or in print, in the form of art, or through any other media of his choice.

Freedom for children, in particular, to obtain information in general is similarly provided in Article 13 of the Children's Convention.[85] With respect to the right to education, or at least to *educational* information, it could also be argued that the CESCR provides for access to family planning education or information pursuant to Article 13(1) insofar as 'education shall be directed to the full development of the human personality and the sense of its dignity'.

Finally, information for men and women on family planning is key

---

[82] Adopted in Turin on 18 October 1961; for the full text of the Charter, see ETS No. 35. Also reproduced in: Council of Europe, *Human Rights in International Law: Basic Texts* (1992), pp. 211–235.

[83] Adopted in Rome on 6 November 1990; for the full text of the Code, see ETS No. 139.

[84] Coliver suggests an alternative 'right to reproductive information and choice' which consists of the grounding and constitutive rights to: equality and non-discrimination; life; health; dignity, liberty and security; private and family life; and to decide freely and responsibly on the number and spacing of one's children. See generally Coliver, 'The Right to Information Necessary for Reproductive Health and Choice Under International Law', in: Coliver (ed.), *The Right to Know* (1995).

[85] The possibility of limitations on the right of a child to information, particularly with reference to family planning information, is examined in detail in Chapter III below.

to good health. It enables a woman to space births at intervals which do not damage her health, to delay child-bearing until her body is physically mature, and to reduce the likelihood of ill-health resulting from too many pregnancies. As such, the right to health may also be invoked to obtain family planning information. It is precisely for this reason that Article 10(h) of the Women's Convention provides that men and women, on a basis of equality, are to have:

> access to specific educational information to help to ensure the health and well-being of families, including information and advice on family planning.

It is important to note that the obligation to ensure access to 'information' is coupled with an obligation to provide 'advice', thus entailing active engagement by the State.

3.4.2 Regional

In each of the three specific regions with applicable human rights texts, the right to information in general is protected in some shape or fashion. While the text of each of these provisions regarding the right to information does not expressly specify information on family planning (as articulated in the Women's Convention), the regional provisions are broad enough to be interpreted so as to include access to information on family planning, especially where supported by jurisprudence in this direction.

Europe. Article 10(1) of the ECHR provides that '[e]veryone has the right . . . to receive and impart information and ideas without interference by public authority and regardless of frontiers'. Article 10(2) of the ECHR allows some restrictions on this freedom including, *inter alia*, 'for the protection of health or morals'. However, States which restrict individuals from seeking and receiving information on family planning on the grounds of the protection of 'public morals' would first have to establish that family planning information represents a breach of public morals. In the case of *Open Door and Dublin Well Woman v. Ireland*, the European Court of Human Rights found that an injunction preventing these two Irish counselling agencies from providing women with information concerning abortion facilities abroad violated Article 10 of the ECHR.[86] The implications of the ruling are examined in Chapter III below.

Broad support for freedom of information, with very few restrictions, has been strongly reiterated in the European region over the decades. For example, the Council of Europe's 1982 Declaration on the Freedom of Expression and Information[87] states that Member States consider that 'the freedom of expression and information is necessary for the . . . development of every human being' (Article 4), so States must 'guard against infringements of the freedom of expression and information' (Article 6). Texts adopted by the participating States of the Organization for Security and Cooperation in Europe (which, with a membership of 53 States stretching from Vancouver to Vladivostok, encompasses all Member States of the Council of Europe) provide broad recommendations to facilitate 'the freer and wider dissemination of information *of all kinds*' (emphasis added), as provided in universal and other European human rights instruments.[88] While such instruments are not legally binding, they reflect the consistent and firm commitment within Europe to a broad interpretation of freedom of information which suggests that the decision of the European Court of Human Rights in the case of *Open Door and Dublin Well Woman v. Ireland* would be confirmed in similar cases (which, in fact, has been the case as explained in Chapter III below); no limitation on access to information regarding family planning technology and methods would appear to be justified by the expressed restrictions of Article 10(2) of the ECHR nor by the intended meaning of the entire provision.

As observed above in relation to universal instruments, the right to health may be invoked to obtain family planning information. In the European context, the European Social Charter ensures that every

---

[86] See *Open Door and Dublin Well Woman v. Ireland*, judgment of 29 October 1992, Publications of the European Court of Human Rights, Series A. No. 246. Also reproduced in: 13 *Human Rights Law Journal* (1992), No. 9–10, pp. 378–395.

[87] Adopted by the Committee of Ministers on 29 April 1982; for the full text of the Declaration, see Council of Europe, *Human Rights in International Law: Basic Texts* (1992), pp. 269–271.

[88] See, in particular, paragraph 34 under 'Co-operation in Humanitarian and Other Fields' of the Concluding Document of the Vienna Meeting on the Follow-Up to the [then] Conference, adopted on 15 January 1989; for the full text of the Document, see Bloed (ed.), *The Conference on Security and Co-operation in Europe: Analysis and Basic Documents, 1972–1993* (1993), pp. 327–423, especially at pages 355–369. Relevant extracts of the Vienna Document, including the chapter on 'Co-operation in Humanitarian and Other Fields', have also been reproduced in: Council of Europe, *Human Rights in International Law: Basic Texts* (1992), pp. 403–423.

person 'has the right to benefit from any measures enabling him to enjoy the highest possible standard of health attainable' (paragraph 11 of Part I). Article 11 of the Charter further states that advice and education is needed for the individual to take active responsibility for his health, a statement which can very easily be interpreted to provide a right to family planning information. As for the European Code of Social Security (Revised) which provides in Article 10 for medical care, it is a matter of interpretation whether 'care' necessarily includes information; neither information nor education in relation to care are expressly stipulated in the Code and they do not appear to be implied.

Americas. Article 13(1) of the American Convention on Human Rights provides for the right to information and is identical in text to the provision in the CCPR. Restrictions are permitted under sub-paragraph 2 for, *inter alia,* the protection of public order and morals. In the absence of relevant jurisprudence of either the Inter-American Commission or Court of Human Rights, it is not clear whether 'public morals' could be invoked to restrict access to information concerning family planning. The right to health is also provided under Article 10(1) of the Additional Protocol to the ACHR.

Africa. The African Charter stipulates in very simple terms that 'Every individual shall have the right to receive information' (Article 9). The right is unconditional. In equally unfettered language, it is provided that everyone is entitled 'to enjoy the best attainable state of physical and mental health (Article 16).

3.5 Sources of the Right to Access to Family Planning Services

The specific right to access to family planning services is provided in the Women's Convention and the Children's Convention. In addition, the right to family planning services is also inferred in provisions for the right to health. At the ICPD in Cairo, international consensus was clearly achieved that *reproductive health* is one aspect of health in general: in order to ensure reproductive health, men and women must 'have access to safe, effective, affordable and acceptable methods of family planning of their choice, as well as other methods of their choice for regulation of fertility which are not against the law'.[89] The explana-

---

[89] Cairo Programme of Action, paragraph 7.2, as reproduced in Appendix A.

tion for this linkage is well-established in medical science[90] and was recognized to be so by the ICPD at Cairo.[91] Thus, the right to obtain the means of family planning would be an essential component of the right to health.[92] However, this interpretation would have to be confirmed by States Parties or, at least, authoritative bodies such as the relevant expert bodies or competent organs established under the conventions in relation to the precise provisions within the conventions. With this in mind, it is important to identify provisions for the right to health in human rights instruments as possible sources of the right to access to family planning services.

3.5.1 Universal. Three articles of the Women's Convention stipulate the freedom to obtain the means for family planning so that individuals may regulate their fertility as they desire. The provision of Article 16(1)(e) has already been cited as a whole. In addition, Article 12(1) provides that:

> States Parties shall take all appropriate measures to . . . ensure, on a basis of equality of men and women, access to health care services, including those related to family planning.

Recognizing the frequent inaccessibility of family planning services in rural areas, the drafters of the Women's Convention in Article 14(2)(b) essentially repeated the provision of Article 12(1) for the specific circumstance of persons in rural areas, guaranteeing 'access to adequate health care facilities, including information, counselling and services in family planning'.

Article 24(2)(f) of the Children's Convention is also clear in its protection of access to fertility regulating methods as a means of preventive health care. In light of the close relationship between maternal and child health, States Parties undertake '[t]o develop preventive health care, guidance for parents and family planning education and services'.

---

[90] For more ample descriptions of the relationship between ill-health and the absence of family planning, see WHO, *supra* note 10, pp. 14–15 and 35–37; and the Beijing Platform for Action, paragraphs 92 and 97, as reproduced in Appendix B.

[91] See Cairo Programme of Action, Chapter VIII, sub-chapter C entitled 'Women's health and safe motherhood', paragraphs 8.19 and 8.27.

[92] For a lengthier description of the relationship between the right to reproductive health and the right to family planning, see Chapter I, Section 2, above as well as the excerpts from the Cairo Programme of Action in Appendix A.

The Covenant on Economic, Social and Cultural Rights provides in Article 12 for the 'right of everyone to the enjoyment of the highest attainable standard of physical and mental health'. Article 12(2)(a) specifically seeks to improve the chances for child survival by requiring that States Parties take steps 'for the reduction of the stillbirth-rate and infant mortality and for the healthy development of the child'. Stillbirths and infant mortality are often the result of poor maternal health arising from improper child-spacing.[93] Therefore, Article 12(2)(a) would imply that facilitation of access to family planning methods is an essential 'step' to prevent such deaths or ill-health.

3.5.2 Regional

None of the regional instruments make provision for the specific right to access to family planning services. However, as noted above, regional human rights texts do provide for the right to health.

Europe. The European Social Charter recognizes as a basic principle in Part I, paragraph 11, that '[e]veryone has the right to benefit from any measures enabling him to enjoy the highest possible standard of health attainable'. Under Article 11 of the Social Charter, the Contracting Parties agree to ensure the effective exercise of the right to protection of health and undertake:

> ... either directly or in co-operation with public or private organisations, to take appropriate measures designed *inter alia*:
> 1. to remove as far as possible the causes of ill-health;
> 2. to provide advisory and educational facilities for the promotion of health and the encouragement of individual responsibility in matters of health ...

This provision can be interpreted to include access both to family planning information and *services* as a means to encourage responsible preventive health care by the individual. For those persons who cannot afford to pay for medical assistance, Contracting Parties must undertake to ensure these individuals will receive adequate assistance, in particular by benefits under a social security scheme according to

---

[93] See, for example, Sadik, *The State of the World Population 1992*, pp. 11–12. See also the Cairo Programme of Action which calls for States to 'recognize the interrelationships between fertility and mortality levels' and asks that they 'aim to reduce high levels of infant, child and maternal mortality so as to lessen the need for high fertility and reduce the occurrence of high-risk births' (paragraph 6.5).

Article 13(1) of the Social Charter. This last provision can also be interpreted to imply that persons unable to pay for family planning methods and services must be assisted by the State.

In addition to respecting the provisions of the European Social Charter, Council of Europe Member States which have ratified the Revised European Code of Social Security are bound to firmer measures. Part II of the Code deals exclusively with medical care. According to Articles 9 and 10, 'all employees . . .' or 'economically active persons together with their dependent spouses and their children' or 'all residents' shall benefit from medical care aimed 'at preserving, restoring or improving the health of the person protected and his ability to work and to meet his personal needs'. Article 10(1) of the Code states that medical care shall comprise, *inter alia*, 'general practitioner care and specialist care' along with 'the provision of the necessary pharmaceutical supplies'. This may well include access to family planning services.

Americas. Parties to the Additional Protocol to the American Convention on Human Rights recognize that '[e]veryone shall have the right to health, understood to mean the enjoyment of the highest level of physical, mental and social well-being' (Article 10(1)). Although family planning is not explicitly mentioned, a number of measures are listed as a means to ensure the enjoyment of the right to health.

To a possibly lesser degree, the American Declaration of the Rights and Duties of Man provides in Article XI that '[e]very person has the right to the preservation of his health through sanitary and social measures relating to food, clothing, housing and medical care'. Again, to the extent that access to family planning contributes to preservation of one's health, this provision can be interpreted to infer a right to family planning services.

Africa. The African Charter similarly provides in Article 16 for the 'right to enjoy the best attainable state of physical and mental health' and urges States Parties to 'take the necessary measures to protect the health of their people'.

For a list of States Parties to the universal and regional human rights treaties referred to above, see Appendix C.

TABLE 2. THE COMPOSITION AND SOURCES OF THE RIGHT TO REPRODUCTIVE CHOICE IN INTERNATIONAL LAW

	Right to Found a Family	Right to Decide the Number and Spacing of Children	Right to Family Planning Information (and Education)	Right to Family Planning Services
Women's Convention	Article 16(1)(e) (implied)	Article 16(1)(e) to decide freely and responsibly on the number and spacing of their children	Article 16(1)(e) to information, education . . . to enable [the exercise of reproductive choice] Article 10(h) access to specific educational information to help to ensure the health and well-being of families, including information and advice on family planning	Article 16(1)(e) means to enable [the exercise of reproductive choice] Article 12(1) access to health care services, including those related to family planning Article 14(2)(b) in rural areas . . . access to adequate health care facilities, including information, counselling and services in family planning

	Right to Found a Family	Right to Decide the Number and Spacing of Children	Right to Family Planning Information (and Education)	Right to Family Planning Services
Children's Convention		Article 24(2)(f) [as] preventive health care, guidance for parents and family planning education and services	Article 13(1) freedom to seek, receive and impart information and ideas of all kinds, regardless of frontiers, either orally, in writing or in print, in the form of art, or through any other media of [his] choice Article 24(2)(f) [as] preventive health care, guidance for parents and family planning education and services	Article 24(2)(f) [as] preventive health care, guidance for parents and family planning education and services
CCPR	Article 23(2) to marry and to found a family	Article 17(1) no one shall be subjected to arbitrary or unlawful interference with his privacy	Article 19(2) freedom to seek, receive and impart information and ideas of all kinds, regardless of frontiers, either orally, in writing or in print, in the form of art, or through any other media of his choice	

	Right to Found a Family	Right to Decide the Number and Spacing of Children	Right to Family Planning Information (and Education)	Right to Family Planning Services
CESCR		Article 12(1) to the highest attainable standard of physical and mental health	Article 13(1) to education . . . directed to the full development of the human personality and the sense of its dignity Article 12(1) to the highest attainable standard of physical and mental health	Article 12(1) to the highest attainable standard of physical and mental health
European Convention (ECHR)	Article 12 to marry and to found a family	Article 8(1) to respect for his private and family life	Article 10(1) to receive and impart information and ideas without interference by public authority and regardless of frontiers	

	Right to Found a Family	Right to Decide the Number and Spacing of Children	Right to Family Planning Information (and Education)	Right to Family Planning Services
European Social Charter		Part I, para. 11 to benefit from any measure enabling him to enjoy the highest possible standard of health attainable	Part I, para. 11 to benefit from any measure enabling him to enjoy the highest possible standard of health attainable Article 11 to ... advisory and educational facilities for the promotion of health and the encouragement of individual responsibility in matters of health	Part I, para. 11 to benefit from any measure enabling him to enjoy the highest possible standard of health attainable
European Code of Social Security (Revised)		Article 10(3) medical care should aim at preserving, restoring or improving ... health ... and to meet his personal needs		Article 10(3) medical care should aim at preserving, restoring or improving ... health .... and to meet his personal needs

	Right to Found a Family	Right to Decide the Number and Spacing of Children	Right to Family Planning Information (and Education)	Right to Family Planning Services
American Convention (ACHR)	Article 17(2) to marry and to raise a family	Article 11(2) no one may be the object of arbitrary or abusive interference with his private life	Article 13(1) freedom to seek, receive and impart information and ideas of all kinds, regardless of frontiers, either orally, in writing, in print, in the form of art, or through any other medium of one's choice	
Additional Protocol to the ACHR	Article 15(2) to form a family	Article 10(1) to health, understood to mean the enjoyment of the highest level of physical, mental and social well-being	Article 10(1) to health, understood to mean the enjoyment of the highest level of physical, mental and social well-being	Article 10(1) to health, understood to mean the enjoyment of the highest level of physical, mental and social well-being
American Declaration	Article VI to establish a family	Article XI to the preservation of his health through sanitary and social measures relating to . . . medical care	Article XI to the preservation of his health through sanitary and social measures relating to . . . medical care	Article XI to the preservation of his health through sanitary and social measures relating to . . . medical care

	Right to Found a Family	Right to Decide the Number and Spacing of Children	Right to Family Planning Information (and Education)	Right to Family Planning Services
African Charter		Article 16 to enjoy the best attainable state of physical and mental health	Article 9 to receive information Article 16 to enjoy the best attainable state of physical and mental health	Article 16 to enjoy the best attainable state of physical and mental health

CHAPTER III

ESTABLISHING THE PARAMETERS OF PROTECTION OF THE RIGHT TO REPRODUCTIVE CHOICE IN INTERNATIONAL HUMAN RIGHTS LAW

1. INTRODUCTION

In order to assess the extent to which the right to reproductive choice is protected, we must first establish the nature of the obligations involved: their breadth and depth, whether they are absolute, positive or negative, etc. This is a matter of interpretation. The 1969 Vienna Convention on the Law of Treaties[94] (hereafter the Vienna Convention), which essentially codified the customary international law of treaties,[95] clearly articulates the manner in which treaty provisions are to be interpreted, thus enabling one to ascertain the extent of specific obligations on States Parties.

According to Article 31 of the Vienna Convention, a treaty or provision thereof 'shall be interpreted . . . in accordance with the ordinary meaning to be given to the terms of the treaty in their context and in light of its object and purpose'. Together with textual and contextual considerations, any agreement between the parties as to the interpretation or application of the treaty, and any subsequent practice by them which establishes the agreement of the parties as to its interpretation, shall be taken into account. Should the meaning of the treaty provision still be 'ambiguous or obscure', or should the result of interpretation lead to a conclusion which is 'manifestly absurd or unreasonable', then, according to Article 32 of the Vienna Convention, supplementary means of interpretation, such as the *travaux préparatoires* and the circumstances in which the treaty was concluded, may be employed. The latter sources may also be employed in order to confirm a meaning already established. If doubt should persist, the nature of

---

[94] Adopted on 23 May 1969; for the full text of the Convention, see 8 I.L.M. 679.

[95] See Reuter, *La convention de Vienne sur le Droit international des traités* (1970), pp. 7ff.

human rights treaties is such that the benefit of doubt belongs to the beneficiary; as Nowak has put it, 'generally recognized rules of interpretation for human rights texts call for a liberal interpretation of rights ("*in dubio pro libertate*") and a narrow interpretation of restrictions'.[96] This conclusion is sustained by Article 31 of the Vienna Convention insofar as such a benefit of doubt is in keeping with the object and purpose of human rights treaties which purport to protect 'inalienable' rights.

With regard to supervision of implementation of the conventional provisions which constitute the sources of the right to reproductive choice, independent bodies have been established either in the form of quasi-judicial expert committees or in the form of judicial organs. The interpretations made by these committees or organs in relation to specific provisions of the conventions are authoritative. Also important are official statements or declarations of States, made either unilaterally or in conjunction with other States. In addition, contributions to the development of legally significant 'doctrine', relevant for interpretation, are also to be found in the writings of the most highly qualified publicists of the world. Consequently, reference will be made to the above means of interpretation in determining the parameters of the right to reproductive choice in international law.

2. THE SCOPE OF THE RIGHT TO REPRODUCTIVE CHOICE

2.1 The Scope of the Right to Found a Family

The right to found a family did not appear to be much of a concern at the time of the drafting of the CCPR. In fact, the provision was adopted unanimously without much in-depth consideration.[97] Since this time, however, a number of contested interpretations have been put forward.

To begin with the least contested interpretation of one element, the right to found a family does not imply an *obligation* to establish a family. Nor does it imply an obligation on the part of the State to ensure use of a particular course or method of family planning leading to more or fewer children. Rather, the matter is left essentially to the will of the persons involved: it is a *freedom* in which the State should

---

[96] Nowak, *supra* note 68, p. XXIV.

[97] See Bossuyt, *Guide to the Travaux Préparatoires of the International Covenant on Civil and Political Rights* (1987), p. 444.

not interfere.

With regard to the scope of the right to found a family in Article 23(2) of the CCPR, the Human Rights Committee has explained in its General Comment on Article 23 as follows:

> The right to found a family implies, in principle, the possibility to procreate and live together. When State parties adopt family planning policies, they should be compatible with the provisions of the Covenant and should, in particular, not be discriminatory or compulsory.[98]

Thus, States may adopt laws and policies which encourage a certain family size or promote certain family planning methods, but they may essentially not interfere with the freedom of persons ultimately to disregard this encouragement or promotion and do as they wish. As Nowak further observes, '[b]ecause the right to found a family . . . is guaranteed without express proviso, the *permissibility of State restrictions* . . . *[are] to be interpreted narrowly*. In evaluating permissibility, it must particularly be taken into account whether a restriction is generally recognized in the States Parties and serves a legitimate purpose within the meaning of the Covenant'.[99]

2.1.1 Distinguishing between the Possibility *and the* Ability *to Procreate.* Today, a large part of the discussion on the scope of the right to found a family centres on technological advances and the issue of whether the right is divorced from the impact of these advances or expanded in scope by them.[100] Certainly, remarkable technological innovations over the last two decades in the areas of contraception, sterilization, safe abortion, *in vitro* fertilization, surrogate motherhood, fetal monitoring, etc. have greatly increased the possibilities of choice in relation to reproduction.[101] In an attempt to understand the impact of technologies to assist conception on the human personality, physical and intellectual integrity as well as the rights and freedoms of the individ-

---

[98] Paragraph 5 of General Comment No. 19(39) of 24 June 1990; for the full text of the General Comment, see: UN, Report of the Human Rights Committee, Volume I, General Assembly, Official Records, Forty-fifth Session, Supplement No. 40 (A/45/40), pp. 175–177. For ease of reference, the full text of General Comment No. 19(39) is reproduced in Appendix D.

[99] Nowak, *supra* note 68, p. 414, his emphasis.

[100] See Blank, *Fertility Control: New Technologies, New Policy Issues* (1991), p. 3.

[101] See Bok, 'Population and Ethics: Expanding the Moral Space', in: Sen et al. (eds.), *Population Policies Reconsidered: Health, Empowerment and Rights* (1994), pp. 16–17.

ual, independent studies on the ethical,[102] human rights,[103] and medical and legal[104] aspects of artificial reproductive technologies have been carried out, effectively serving as national monitoring or policy-making tools[105] and as guides for international standard-setting. In response both to the demands of persons seeking to limit or control their fertility and also to the demands of a significant minority of persons who are unable to have the children they desire owing, for example, to infertility, physical disability or sexual orientation,[106] advocates primarily from technologically advanced States have focused attention on the importance of making available medical technology to ensure the right to found a family.

The argument has been made by some human rights advocates that the right to reproductive choice protected by international human rights law supports the existence of an inherent right to procreate.[107] Indi-

---

[102] For example, see Bartels et al. (eds.), *Beyond Baby M: Ethical Issues in New Reproductive Technologies* (1989).

[103] For example, see: Baruch et al. (eds.), *Embryos, Ethics and Women's Rights* (1987); and Raymond, *Women as Wombs: Reproductive Technologies and the Battle over Women's Freedom* (1993).

[104] For example, see Mason, *Medico-Legal Aspects of Reproduction and Parenthood* (1990).

[105] See, for example: Blank's examination of reproductive technology policy issues in the United States (*supra* note 100, especially pp. 1–12); Norrie's review of regulation in the United Kingdom, 'United Kingdom: Legal Regulation of Human Reproduction', in: McLean (ed.), *Law Reform and Human Reproduction* (1992), pp. 201–219; and the compilation of various country studies on the specific issue of *in vitro* fertilization in Stephenson and Wagner (eds.), *Tough Choices: In Vitro Fertilization and the Reproductive Technologies* (1993).

[106] See Petchesky and Weiner, *supra* note 7, p. 2.

[107] Among others, see: Cook and Dickens, 'Ethics and Values in Family Planning: Legal and Legislative Aspects', in: Bankowski et al. (eds.), *Ethics and Human Values in Family Planning* (1989), pp. 117–140; and Cook, 'International Human Rights and Women's Reproductive Health', 24 *Studies in Family Planning* (1993), No. 2, pp. 73–86. According to Cook (*Women's Health and Human Rights* [1994], p. 30), 'the right to found a family is inadequately observed if it amounts to no more than the right to conceive, gestate and deliver a child'. Cook further states (*ibid.*) that the 'act of "foundation" goes beyond a passive submission to biology' and that Article 16(1)(e) of the Women's Convention provides us with a greater, and more appropriate, interpretation, namely that *foundation* involves 'the right of a woman positively to plan, time and space the births of children so as to maximize their health and her own'. However, it is the view of this author that, while Article 16(1)(e) certainly includes choice in planning, timing and spacing of births, the provision is not intended to define the 'right to found a family' *per se*. Reference to the Cairo Programme of Action is helpful in this regard: paragraph 7.6 states that reproductive health care (which is characterized as a right established under the *right to health*) includes, *inter alia*, 'prevention and appropriate treatment of infertility'. While the approach taken to advance a right to infertility treatment as provided through interpretation of the right to

viduals who so desire should, they argue, therefore have the right to have access to the medical technology which would enable procreation.[108] Proponents of the existence of such a right argue that the right to found a family 'may be invoked with regard to access to treatment for infertility, and to means of assistance to reproduce'.[109] One author expresses an even broader interpretation of some advocates' claims to a 'natural right to procreate' (seemingly superior to 'non-natural' human rights):

> The right to procreate has been conceived as a natural right and, by extension, technological reproduction has been recently promoted as the means to fulfil one's natural right to procreate. Thus the male-dominant tradition of property rights converges with a version of natural rights proclaiming a natural right to procreate, a natural right to a child, a natural right to use any means necessary to procreate, and thereby a natural right to use any person necessary to procreate.[110]

Cook advances the argument further in asserting that 'government inaction to prevent or remedy this source of infertility violates the right to found a family' whether it be classified as a positive right, in which case 'governments must serve through positive action', or a negative right where 'legal liability of the State for inaction might nevertheless arise not because of infertility itself but because of the differential impact that infertility has on the lives of women'.[111]

This understanding of existing provisions is far too broad and lacks

---

health is somewhat tenuous (since infertility does not involve ill-health or preventive care), it nevertheless would appear to confirm the general consensus that such a right has not been established under the *right to found a family*.

[108] For the contrary position, see the statement made by the Vatican in response to the enquiry of the UN Secretary-General which submitted (in decidedly religious terms) that *'in vitro* fertilization along with all other "artificial" forms of procreation [are] threats to the sanctity of the conjugal act, to the family, and to human dignity'; UN, Human Rights and Scientific and Technological Developments: Human Rights and Bioethics: Report of the Secretary-General, UN doc. E/CN.4/1995/74, paragraph 114.

[109] Cook and Dickens, *supra* note 107, p. 123.

[110] Raymond, *supra* note 103, p. 189.

[111] Cook, *Women's Health and Human Rights* (1994), p. 32. In an earlier article, the same author places a caveat on this assertion adding that it 'may not require public authorities to fund such services'; Cook, 'International Human Rights and Women's Reproductive Health', *supra* note 107, p. 80.

real foundation.[112] Specifically, the advanced interpretations of the relevant provisions imply greater protection than is to be derived either from their ordinary meaning or from the *travaux préparatoires* of the CCPR and the Women's Convention. Nor is support for infertility treatment to be derived from the general comments and recommendations of the expert committees established under the CCPR and the Women's Convention. In fact, most of the discussions in the course of drafting and interpreting existing provisions concern the definition of 'family' rather than of its 'founding'.[113] This may well be explained by the state of technological development at the time of the adoption of the various texts, i.e. at a time when procreation was essentially a matter of the birds and the bees. In other words, given that treatment for infertility and conception by medical intervention is relatively new (the first 'test-tube baby', Louise Brown, was born only in July 1978), it is implausible that the provisions of the 1948 UDHR, 1966 CCPR or 1979 Women's Convention inferred assisted procreation by medical intervention.

Reference to the *travaux préparatoires* of Article 23(2) of the CCPR supports the conclusion that there is as yet no right to the assistance of medical technology in order to procreate.[114] Subsequent authoritative interpretation by the Human Rights Committee also fully supports this conclusion insofar as paragraph 5 of its General Comment on Article 23 refers only to the implied 'possibility to procreate' and in no way refers to a State's duty to assist in creating such a possibility.[115]

---

[112] Similar misinterpretation seems to have arisen in relation to the right to health, with some advocates claiming the right to imply a certain degree of good health. This author shares the views expressed by Leary and Tomaševski. According to Leary ('The Right to Reproductive Health in International Human Rights Law', 1 *Health and Human Rights* [1994], No. 1, p. 28), '[s]uperficially, the *right to health* seems to presume that governments or international organizations or individuals must guarantee a person's good health. This interpretation is obviously absurd and the phrase is not given such an interpretation in the context of human rights law'. Similarly, Tomaševski ('Health Rights', in: Eide et al. [eds.], *Economic, Social and Cultural Rights: A Textbook* [1995], p. 125) has stated that the right to health 'does not mean that people have a right to be healthy' nor does it 'assure a specific state of health'; '[t]he substance of this right is thus necessarily relative'.

[113] For a review of the drafting of Article 16 of the UDHR, see Morsink, 'Women's Rights in the Universal Declaration', 13 *Human Rights Quarterly* (1991), No. 2, pp. 236–240.

[114] The *travaux préparatoires* reveal that Article 23(2) confers a 'negative' duty on States, i.e. to refrain from interfering in what is seen to be a most intimate and private social act: see: Nowak, *supra* note 68, pp. 412–414; and Bossuyt, *supra* note 97, pp. 441–444.

[115] See *supra* note 98. See also Nielsen, 'The Right to a Child Versus the Rights of a Child', in: Eekelaar and Sarcevic (eds.), *Parenthood in Modern Society: Legal and Social Issues for the Twenty-First Century* (1993), pp. 213–221.

Law, of course, is not static, and implementation of existing provisions should take into account technological and social advances to the extent they can be reconciled with the essence of each provision. However, to read into 'the right to found a family' a 'right to infertility treatment' would be to go well beyond a 'liberal' interpretation of the provisions since it would involve transforming an essentially passive obligation on the part of the State into a highly active and costly undertaking not likely to be borne by any but a very few States for a very long time. To conclude otherwise would be an extreme and untenable reading of the conventions which would lead to the further conclusion that, as a result of advancing technology, all States Parties are, therefore, in violation of their obligations. By analogy, the conclusion that the right to found a family obliges States to make available costly technology, e.g., *in vitro* fertilization, would be similar to concluding that the freedom of movement obliges States to make available supersonic jet planes to enable persons to move wherever they wish.

2.1.2 Invoking the Right to the Benefits of Science for the Ability *to Procreate.* It is equally interesting, and of some importance, to note that in a recent report of the UN Secretary-General regarding human rights and technological developments it was acknowledged that legally binding rules of international law bear in varying degrees on issues arising from rapid advances in technology-assisted procreation.[116] The Secretary-General expressed some concern over possible abuses and perversions, stating that '[t]he very idea of human rights arguably rests on a certain conception of what it means to be human, on a reverence for life and for autonomy, all of which could conceivably be undermined if the production, maintenance, manipulation and termination of embryos became commonplace, and particularly if this activity were carried on to a considerable extent for profit'.[117] However, the general conclusions of the report indicate an absence of clearly established principles.[118]

---

[116] As a result of the International Conference on Human Rights in Teheran, the UN Secretary-General was subsequently mandated to monitor human rights problems arising from scientific and technological developments and to issue periodic reports in this relation. The report issued at the end of 1994 considers artificial insemination and abortion; UN (*supra* note 108), paragraphs 101–118.

[117] *Ibid.*, paragraph 22.

[118] This is true both in international law and with regard to international and national policy. In fact, there has been a general lack of attention given to the overall problem. From an example cited in the report, the Commonwealth Medical Association, although having

From another point of view, it has been argued that Article 15(1)(b) of the CESCR, which ensures the individual's right '[t]o enjoy the benefits of scientific progress and its applications', infers a right to technology to found a family.[119] Although this may appear to present a strong argument in favour of a right to reproductive choice by medical intervention, such a conclusion would be misleading and erroneous. In the first place, the 'right to enjoy' indicates a duty on the State not to interfere with such a freedom; it does not confer an obligation on the State to furnish an individual with the means to enjoy according to the individual's desire. This is not only true in general, but it is fairly evident in the article in question insofar as Article 15(1)(a) of the CESCR also provides for the right 'to take part in cultural life'; clearly, the State is to respect such a freedom, but can hardly be obliged to provide culture (or its 'means')—something which would be highly problematic in relation to the implementation of human rights standards. Reading further in the same Article, paragraph 2 makes the duty of forbearance even clearer insofar as it specifies a slightly more active duty with regard to 'conservation', 'development' and 'diffusion of science'—but not a duty to provide the results of science to everyone. As already noted, an important factor in infertility treatment concerns the cost of some techniques which are far beyond the consideration of most countries.[120] From a legal perspective, the State's obligation vis-à-vis Article 15(1)(b) is, like most other obligations under the CESCR, a duty of conduct and not result. In interpreting duties generally, the Committee on Economic, Social and Cultural Rights (the expert body which supervises implementation of the CESCR) has concluded in its General Comment on Article 2 (regarding the 'nature of States parties obligations') that States are obliged to take steps which 'should be deliberate, concrete and targeted as clearly as possible towards meeting

---

established principles and commentaries on medical practice, inferred in its response to the enquiry of the UN Secretary-General that it has so far refrained from taking a decided view on technology-assisted reproduction and that its 'principles and commentaries' 'do not cover ethical and human rights aspects of medical practice that are not yet causing problems in developing countries, e.g. assisted conception, egg donation'; *ibid.*, paragraph 47.

[119] See Cook, *supra* note 111.

[120] It is interesting to note that the ethical discussions regarding reproductive technologies focus significantly on the cost factor. For further discussion, consult authors listed in Bartels et al. (eds.), *supra* note 102.

the obligations recognized in the Covenant'.[121] But, the specific obligation of a State Party pursuant to Article 2(1) of the CESCR is 'to take steps . . . to the maximum of its available resources' which, evidently, will vary by country and period. With this relativity clearly articulated in the CESCR, and in the light of the overall social and economic pressures on most States (including their many other obligations under international human rights law), this author is aware of virtually no State which can be expected to guarantee a right to the science of, e.g., *in vitro* fertilization because of its extreme cost.

2.1.3 The Implications of Disability. Although a State may not be obliged to assist with procreation, it is generally agreed that the individual has an inherent right to have children and that the non-consensual removal of this capacity amounts to a denial of that important right. Hence, the idea of sterilizing a person without consent is generally to be met with vociferous disapprobation on a number of grounds.[122] The issue of disability with respect both to the prospective parents and the prospective child raises some questions. Specifically, does a mentally disabled person have a right to found a family? Or, does one have the right to give birth to what will knowingly be a deformed or disabled child? These questions raise the spectre of further implied limitations on the right to found a family.

With regard to the ability or 'disability' of a prospective parent, it is clear from the unqualified relevant texts that essentially all persons have the right to found a family. Indeed, it is a general premise of human rights philosophy and law that a human being is no less human and is in no way diminished as a person by reason of physical or mental disability. However, the notion of founding a family surely implies some capacity to decide and to understand and control one's body and actions. The unfortunate reality is that a tiny number of human beings do not share this capacity and, as a result, they are usually placed under some form of guardianship. This particular concern regarding *mentally* disabled persons as beneficiaries of the right to reproductive choice (including the right to found a family) is addressed below in Section 3.4 of this Chapter. Suffice it to say here

---

[121] General Comment No. 3. UN, Committee on Economic, Social and Cultural Rights, Report on the Fifth Session, Economic and Social Council, Official Records, 1991, Supplement No. 3 (E/1991/23), pp. 83–87.

[122] For such a case, and the condemnation of competent judicial authorities, see *Aracelly Valencia Salazar v. Hospital General de Medellín*, No. 7795, Sala de lo Contencioso Administrativo, Santafé de Bogotá (1992).

that it is only in the case of an extreme limitation on the mental capacity to choose that the right to found a family may be limited, i.e. most mentally disabled persons retain the right to found a family.

By far the more problematic issue arises with respect to the disability of the prospective child. Again, modern technology has raised the spectre, indeed reality, of forced abortions and sterilizations in order to avoid the birth of disabled children—whether to able or disabled parents. For example, the widely reported 'Beijing Eugenics law' of 1 June 1995, which has been designed to 'avoid new births of inferior quality and heighten the standards of the whole population',[123] has come under international scrutiny.[124] The law reportedly requires persons with mental disabilities, illnesses (such as AIDS, gonorrhoea or leprosy) or serious hereditary illnesses (such as hepatitis) to undergo sterilization.[125] The law also reportedly stipulates obligatory pre-natal testing for all women; those found to carry abnormal foetuses are said to be 'advised' to abort. Critics of the law are legitimately 'worried that "advice" can turn into forceful persuasion, especially in poor rural areas'.[126]

Unfortunately, there is no clear answer to the question concerning foetal defects. Of course, it would have to be assumed that there would be a heavy burden of proof on the State to establish the factual and causal link in each case with presumptions in favour of the parental right to choose. Physical action by the State contrary to the wishes of the person concerned would also raise questions regarding respect for personal integrity rights. However, the larger society, i.e. the State, may have legitimate concerns about the viability of foetuses with demonstrably extreme defects. The statement made by the Government of Norway in response to the enquiry of the UN Secretary-General captures several of the necessary considerations:

---

[123] Words of the New China Agency, as cited in NGO Bulletin, Information Service (27 January 1995), p. 3.

[124] From its early consideration through to its adoption, see, e.g.: Walsh, 'Ordering up "Better" Babies', *Time Magazine*, 2 May 1994, pp. 48–49; 'China Moves to Ban Babies with Defects', *The Sunday Times*, 5 February 1995; and 'China Brings in Tough Law to Stamp out Birth Defects', *The Guardian*, 6 June 1995, p. 5.

[125] While this has caused moral outrage particularly in the Western world, it is to be noted that the People's Republic of China is not a party to the CCPR which protects the right to found a family.

[126] *The Guardian*, *supra* note 124, p. 5.

The knowledge gained from the potential in new diagnostic methods makes it necessary to define the line between foetal defects that would permit termination of a pregnancy once the 12-week limit had expired, and those that would not. This must be assessed in relation to the situation the woman finds herself in, or will find herself in. Consideration of legal protection for the foetus must be weighed against consideration of the consequences for the mother and the family if the pregnancy is allowed to go full-term. This assessment must also include consideration of the responsibility that society should be able to force expectant parents to accept the situation when the parents themselves do not feel able to bear it. The guidelines society must follow in these difficult evaluations must be based on a system of values that a great majority in society can follow and accept the consequences of.[127]

In sum, international human rights law at the universal level is relatively clear on the scope of the right to found a family. The right is not an absolute right. Yet, it is a right which implies a fairly unrestricted *possibility* to found a family with which the State virtually cannot interfere. Certainly, it does not impose any form of obligation on the State to provide the medical technology to assist procreation. This stems particularly from the fact that the right to found a family was never intended to imply an inherent right to procreate.

Essentially the same standards apply at the regional level. Article 12 of the ECHR provides for the right 'to marry and to found a family, according to the national laws governing the exercise of the right'. The clause 'according to the national laws' makes it clear that, under the convention, the right to found a family is not absolute. One obvious basis for permissible restriction would be in the case of lawful detention, i.e. in such a circumstance there would be no right to *become* pregnant (or to impregnate) as distinguished from the very different (and protected) right to bring a pregnancy to term and give birth while in detention. The right to found a family may also be restricted in the case of lawful deportation, extradition and refusal of admission to the territory of the State.[128] However, the essence of Article 12 is that it 'implies a prohibition for the authorities to interfere with the founding of a family, for instance by prescribing the compulsory use of contraceptives, ordering a non-voluntary sterilization or abortion, or tolerating

---

[127] As cited in UN, *supra* note 108, paragraph 102.

[128] See van Dijk and van Hoof, *Theory and Practice of the European Convention on Human Rights*, 2nd ed. (1990), pp. 449–450, citing relevant decisions of the European Commission of Human Rights.

the performance thereof';[129] 'family planning can therefore at most be stimulated on a voluntary basis'.[130]

With regard to a possible right to procreate, it is to be noted that, in the wider context of the Council of Europe (until recently, composed mainly of West European States), 'marriage' and 'the family' (and the link between the two) have undergone substantial changes in recent decades, including the gradual disappearance of the traditional family unit, the recognition of same-sex couples and increased reproductive rights.[131] The ready availability of technology for assisted reproduction coupled with the general wealth of Member States has given rise to demands for recognition of a right to have recourse to techniques of artificial procreation such as surrogate motherhood, embryo transfer, and treatment for infertility. As a result, the Council of Europe examined the issue and expressed its straightforward view on artificial reproduction via the Steering Committee on Human Rights.[132] The Committee declared that human rights cannot be interpreted to guarantee 'a right to procreate, if need be, in the absence of natural capacity, by means of artificial procreation'.[133] While some European Union States, such as Denmark and the United Kingdom, offer these services in the public domain, none have recognized the conferral of an *entitlement* to receive such services. It may be surmised that, if even the European Union States do not support the existence of a right to procreate (i.e. where the technologies and resources exist to make it possible), the likelihood of this right being acknowledged elsewhere is negligible.

In the Inter-American system, the above issues have not received the same attention or consideration whether within authoritative bodies (i.e. the Inter-American Commission on Human Rights or the Inter-American Court on Human Rights) or as a matter of international public debate. Nonetheless, it is to be recalled that each of the relevant

---

[129] *Ibid.*, p. 446.

[130] *Ibid.*, pp. 447–448.

[131] For a brief description of changing patterns within the European Communities, see Tomaševski, 'European Approaches to Enhancing Reproductive Freedom', 44 *The American University Law Review* (1995), No. 4, pp. 1037–1051, particularly pp. 1039–1041.

[132] See Council of Europe, Progress of Medicine, Biology and Respect for Private and Family Life, doc. DH–DEV (91) 1 (1 March 1991). While it is to be stressed that the Steering Committee on Human Rights is not empowered to make legal determinations, its views are important as a reflection of contemporary political standards to which the law must respond.

[133] *Ibid.*, at p. 45.

Inter-American instruments provides for the right to found a family under slightly varying, but essentially similar, formulations: the right 'to raise a family' pursuant to Article 17(2) of the ACHR, 'the right to form a family' pursuant to Article 15(2) of the Additional Protocol to the ACHR, and 'the right to establish a family' pursuant to Article VI of the American Declaration. Taking into consideration the socio-cultural make-up of Inter-American society, this repeated stipulation would appear to indicate a strong intention on the part of OAS Member States to accord a large measure of protection for the creation and maintenance of 'the family'. Consequently, permissible interferences with its *founding* (establishment, formation or raising) would have to be kept to an absolute minimum.

In conclusion, it is evident that the right to found a family is fairly well established in international law at both universal and regional levels. Only at the extremes of the right (which is a *freedom*) has its scope been challenged, particularly in the developed world. This is because, as Tomaševski has observed, technological developments have 'created demands that a right to parenthood be recognized: the availability of effective treatments of infertility, embryo transfer, and surrogate motherhood, have created a host of demands for entitlements concerning procreation'.[134] However, the law, for the most part, has not followed technology in its pace of advance.

As such, confusing the right to found a family (which is secured in international human rights law) or using it synonymously with the right to procreate (which is not established in international law), is misleading. Obviously, reproduction requires the capacity to procreate. Although some people by nature or circumstance do not have this capacity, and while modern technology may aid them to overcome their incapacity, the right to found a family cannot be interpreted to guarantee them the benefits of such technology. At the same time, for those persons who have such a capacity (notwithstanding all but a tiny number of persons with very particular mental disabilities), the real guarantee under international human rights law is that States cannot take away the right to found a family when persons are already capable of doing so (whether by nature or by their *own* initiatives).

---

[134] Tomaševski, 'Women', in: Eide et al. (eds.), *Economic, Social and Cultural Rights: A Textbook* (1995), p. 281.

2.2 The Scope of the Right to Decide the Number and Spacing of Children

The right to decide the number and spacing of one's children is essentially a private matter. The right to privacy is secured under Article 17(1) of the CCPR which provides in part that '[n]o one shall be subjected to arbitrary or unlawful interference with his privacy'. The concept of privacy is to be found near the roots of human rights philosophy inasmuch as individualism connotes a certain autonomy from others which is necessary to enable the full development of one's personality and identity. The related ideas of 'autonomy' and 'identity' are especially relevant for decisions regarding reproduction. Autonomy requires a certain degree of distance (both physical and mental) from the larger society in order to choose a course of action or behaviour. Development of one's identity is closely linked to notions of one's 'self', including ideas of 'family', 'ethnicity', 'spirituality' and a sense of relatedness with the future—possibly through biological descendents. All of these ideas have much to do with control over one's destiny.

As important as the right to privacy is, it is not unlimited. Indeed, Article 17(1) is specifically formulated in the negative to emphasize that only 'arbitrary or unlawful interference' would constitute a violation. This is because human beings do not live in isolation and their decisions concerning their own destinies generally affect others. This fact has been recognized by the Human Rights Committee in its General Comment regarding Article 17(1) of the CCPR: 'As all persons live in society, the protection of privacy is necessarily relative'.[135] For this same reason, Article 16(1)(e) of the Women's Convention expressly qualifies the right to decide the number and spacing of children by the term 'responsibly'. However, evident questions arise: what would be 'arbitrary', and 'responsibly' vis-à-vis whom?

Perhaps not surprisingly, the term 'arbitrary' gave rise to considerable discussion in the drafting process for Article 17(1) of the CCPR.[136] It is encouraging to note that it is not a unique term within the CCPR and so reference to its other locations leads toward a standard meaning. In summary, Nowak observes that 'arbitrary interference contains elements of injustice, unpredictability and unreasonableness'.[137] In relation to decisions on the number and spacing of children, it is evident that the number of children has an affect on society as a

---

[135] *Supra* note 80.
[136] See Nowak, *supra* note 68, p. 291.
[137] *Ibid.*, p. 292.

whole—which is the explanation for population policies. Whether too many or too few, the socio-economic effects of children are to be taken into account in government and have direct relations to such things as access to limited resources. Moreover, obligations on the State regarding the assurance of respect for the human rights of all persons within its jurisdiction, including social and economic rights, places the State in the position of having to be concerned with the number of children since the State must ensure their care. Whether a particular law, policy or act constitutes an 'arbitrary interference' will turn on the facts of the specific situation. However, it would seem that there would have to be an overwhelming public interest to legitimize interference with this fundamental freedom.

The *spacing* of one's children would appear to be a different matter. Whether one decides to have children in quick succession or spaced over many years seems hardly a matter of public interest or concern insofar as the effects of such decisions upon others would be extremely few if any. To interfere with this decision by specifying a specific interval would thus seem manifestly and always arbitrary. As such, the right to decide the spacing of one's children would seem to be an absolute freedom.

The question of responsibility is more difficult. While Article 16(1)(e) seems to be stated in clear language and to convey a plain meaning, there has been growing concern regarding the notion of *responsible* reproductive decision-making. Only a few decades ago, couples were left to procreate if and when they chose, and this was not thought to pose any threat to society or the State. Indeed, procreation was encouraged by population policies in Europe especially after the two World Wars. But human reproduction today is no longer necessarily the exclusive concern of the individuals most intimately involved. Consequently, in defining the right to reproductive choice, virtually every resolution or declaration made since the 1968 Proclamation of Teheran (including the Women's Convention) has used the same core language, i.e. the 'right to decide *freely and responsibly* on the number and spacing of their children' (emphasis added).[138]

Although reference is made to this duty in Article 16(1)(e) of the Women's Convention, a definition of the term 'responsibly' does not

---

[138] As noted in Chapter I, only the Forward-looking Strategies adopted by the Women's Conference in Nairobi in 1985 modified the terminology, declaring a 'right to decide *freely and informedly*', perhaps in the belief that an informed choice is a responsible choice; see UN, *supra* note 43, paragraph 156. Of course, what matters from a legal perspective is the fact that the term 'responsibly' remains in the *treaty* under discussion.

appear. Surprisingly, neither did any discussion of the term take place during the *travaux préparatoires* of the treaty.[139] Thus, the implications of the terms 'freely and responsibly' cannot be established definitively with regard to the *travaux préparatoires*. However, the term does seem to infer a limitation on the right by coupling a freedom with a qualifying and constraining individual duty regarding parental responsibility in the process of reproductive decision-making. As Boland et al. argue, '[o]ne is left to wonder just what "responsibly" means, in particular when yoked with the word "freely".'[140] This begs *both* the questions 'Responsible to whom?' and 'According to what criteria?'—questions which very few have ventured to address, let alone answer. Yet, these questions demand clear answers when individuals are faced with national population policies which may be coercive or family planning programmes which may function only on negative incentive schemes, both of which promote responsibility towards the community at large (and the State's right to set the policy).[141]

To date, the only effort of the international community to come to some terms with the meaning of the word 'responsibly' was achieved in the Declaration on Population and Development resulting from the 1984 Mexico City Conference. While not detailing what States should do to encourage 'responsible' choices, paragraph 26 describes its implications:

> Any recognition of rights also implies responsibilities: in this case, it implies that couples and individuals should exercise this right, taking into consideration their own situation, as well as the implications of their

---

[139] Belgium first suggested an additional paragraph on the equal rights of women to decide on the number and spacing of their children as well as a reference to their access to family planning education and information. India followed by proposing a new sub-paragraph, slightly altering the text to include the phrase 'freely and responsibly'. This proposal received overwhelming support and was adopted by consensus. For the drafting history of the provision, see Rehof, *Guide to the Travaux Préparatoires of the United Nations Convention on the Elimination of All Forms of Discrimination against Women* (1993), pp. 177–178.

[140] Boland et al., 'Honoring Human Rights in Population Policies: From Declaration to Action', in: Sen et al. (eds.), *Population Policies Reconsidered: Health, Empowerment and Rights* (1994), p. 93.

[141] While acknowledging that the word 'responsibly' and references to 'responsibilities towards the community' in the various programmes for action 'makes it possible for governments to argue that they are entitled to limit the right in the interest of achieving national goals', Coliver (*supra* note 84) asserts that Article 16(1)(e) of the Women's Convention 'does not include the notion of responsibility to the community'. However, no evidence is provided in support of this assertion, nor is any alternative explanation given for the meaning of the expressed term.

decisions for the balanced development of their children and of the community and society in which they live.[142]

The Cairo Programme of Action provides a similarly evasive response to the concern. According to paragraph 7.12, the success of numerous family planning programmes 'demonstrates that informed individuals everywhere can and will act responsibly in the light of their own needs and those of their families and communities'.[143] In other words, while affirming a right to reproductive choice, the right is coupled with the implication of a responsibility to care for the children which one bears and to consider their interests and the interests of the larger community. However, the Cairo Programme of Action did not address the prospect of *irresponsible* behaviour or the limits on State power to interfere in such cases.

In his study, Sass examines why an obligation of 'responsibility' is valid in the case of the right to reproductive choice. Under favourable conditions, he concludes:

> . . . societies enable me to choose, but also make it unavoidable for me to choose responsibly (i.e. to choose in response to what I understand to be the goals, values and norms which enrich and cultivate my life and my environment, and make it more enjoyable).[144]

As noted above, the reason why a private issue such as reproduction comes into the public domain is that 'while the metaphysical and cultural concepts of sex and love are not government issues . . . the reproductive outcome . . . is both a private and a public matter'.[145] Non-interference by government (i.e. a government not taking responsibility for influencing reproductive behaviour), Sass argues, is surely less morally acceptable than its interference.[146] Moreover, it is unrealistic to rationalize that no matter how many children are born, the State is responsible for their well-being: even the greatest desire and efforts of the State to fulfil its obligations will be checked by physical (i.e. resource) limitations. While many States refrain from making declarations attesting to this concern, there is no doubt that, as

---

[142] UN, *supra* note 42, paragraph 26.

[143] See Appendix A for full text of paragraph 7.12.

[144] Sass, 'Responsibilities in Human Reproduction and Population Policy', in: Spicker et al. (eds.), *The Contraceptive Ethos* (1987), pp. 137–138.

[145] *Ibid.*, p. 145.

[146] *Ibid.*, p. 149.

population grows and resources become more scarce, public concern over increasing population numbers will rise. The fact is that there are natural limits, and responsible law and policy must take this into account.

How each State interprets this notion of responsibility is another matter. In recent times, concern has arisen that 'responsible' child-bearing may justify government intervention, be it with regard to the choice of, and access to, means of fertility regulation or in enforcing the use of the means provided.[147] Conceptually, the right freely to choose one's family size protects individuals from two possible infringements: (a) interference with their decisions on child-bearing; and (b) interference with their use or non-use of contraceptive services. A State Party to the Women's Convention not only has a duty to enable individuals to make their choice, but also an obligation not to enforce its own will or the use of services it provides.[148] Yet, to repeat, freedom to choose is not absolute, as it may conflict with other responsibilities towards the community and, ultimately, with other people's rights. But at what threshold may persons be required to have fewer children than they desire?[149] Another question is to what extent can the responsibility be assumed freely and without coercion, particularly since the right which is at issue is most basic to the human experience? Put more directly, can the State forcibly sterilize an individual after a certain number of children? The answer to all these questions lies in their 'reasonableness', the determination of which may draw on the principle of proportionality. In some instances, it may be relatively easy to determine that a State's action imposing 'responsibility' is in violation of the individual's right to reproductive choice because the element of coercion is in disproportion to the stated need or object. These cases, however, are rare. Generally, it is difficult to establish at what point the steps taken by a State 'to encourage' responsible reproductive choice become coercive. This challenge is addressed in Chapter IV.

---

[147] See Fincancioglu, 'Contraception, Family Planning and Human Rights', in: UN, *Population and Human Rights: Prroceedings of the Expert Group Meeting on Population and Human Rights, Geneva, 3–6 April, 1989* (1990), p. 89.

[148] *Ibid.*, p. 90.

[149] Examples of the varying (and often extreme) interpretations which States have adopted in the past and at present regarding the individual's reproductive responsibility towards the community at large include: China's one-child policy whereby couples are strongly urged, if not effectively forced, not to bear more than one child for the common good of the community; and India's use of economic incentives to encourage sterilization (often targeted at the poor); see Freedman and Isaacs, *supra* note 51, pp. 20–21.

The absence of any consensus or clear and simple formula by which these questions may be answered is problematic as human rights and government action to influence population growth (with a population policy) cannot be entirely reconciled in the abstract. Another part of the problem lies in the schizophrenic background of reproductive rights in general which arose out of two somewhat conflicting international movements: the population movement and the women's rights movement.[150] The result is the 'articulation of a right that, so far, lacks the clarity to be an effective tool in influencing [population] policy'.[151] Without some declared principles by which we can determine the limits of *free and responsible* choice, 'that kind of judgment will continue to be based more on the whims of politics than on the principles of international law, thereby effectively destroying its credibility as a principled basis for challenging violations by local governments'.[152]

Despite the difficulties raised above, one point remains clear: the need for responsible reproductive behaviour on the part of the individual in no way releases a State from its obligation to ensure access to family planning information and services since an individual must have these *in order* to behave 'responsibly'.[153] This fact implies positive obligations on the State. In its General Recommendation No. 21 concerning 'Equality in marriage and family relations',[154] the Committee on the Elimination of Discrimination against Women (CEDAW, the expert body established pursuant to Article 17 of the Women's Convention) essentially reiterated the plain wording of Article 16(1)(e) in stating that 'women are entitled to decide the number and spacing of their children' and that, '[i]n order to make an informed decision about safe and reliable contraceptive measures, women must have information about contraceptive measures and their use, and guaranteed access to sex education and family planning services, as provided in article 10(h) of the Convention'.[155]

---

[150] See *ibid.*, p. 21.

[151] *Ibid.*

[152] *Ibid.*, p. 24.

[153] Fincancioglu, *supra* note 147, p. 90.

[154] Relevant excerpts of General Recommendation No. 21 are reproduced in Appendix E. For the full text of General Recommendation No. 21, see UN, Report of the Committee on the Elimination of Discrimination against Women, Thirteenth session, General Assembly, Official Records, Forty-ninth Session, Supplement No. 38 (A/49/38), pp. 1–10.

[155] *Ibid.* Interestingly, while CEDAW observes in its General Recommendation that '[s]ome [State] reports disclose coercive practices which have serious consequences for

As pointed out in Chapter II, the right to decide the number and spacing of one's children is also a matter of health for women.[156] Pregnancy, of course, is not to be confused with ill-health. Consequently, a healthy woman who is considering becoming, or has become, pregnant would only have concerns for preventive care (as opposed to curative care). Evidently, family planning is not a matter of preventive care for pregnant women; what pregnant women seek to prevent is ill-health in the course of the pregnancy and ill-health for the foetus, but they clearly do not seek to *prevent* their pregnancy.[157]

Family planning as preventive care is of relevance to women for whom the condition of pregnancy poses a threat to their physical or mental health. Physical health may be endangered by, for example, too many pregnancies or pregnancy at too early an age. Mental health may be endangered by unwanted pregnancy/ies irrespective of the cause; the cause of an unwanted pregnancy may be an aggravating issue and also raises other issues such as moral and criminal offenses which dehumanize women.[158]

At the universal level, Article 12 of the CESCR may be invoked to obtain family planning information and services insofar as such information and services contribute to achieving 'the highest attainable standard of physical and mental health'. While there has yet to be any authoritative interpretation of Article 12 by way of a General Comment issued by the Committee on Economic, Social and Cultural Rights, the Committee has made it clear in its General Comment on Article 2 that States Parties are obliged to take positive actions, including through legislation, to progressively realize the protected rights.[159] Moreover, since Article 2(1) of the CESCR requires States Parties 'to take steps, individually and through international assistance and cooperation, especially economical and technical, to the maximum of its available resources', States Parties are essentially obliged to accept international assistance and to cooperate with international organizations which seek

---

women, such as forced pregnancies, abortions or sterilizations', CEDAW fails to condemn such practices, to explain how exactly they constitute violations of the Convention or to call for modifications of policies in this regard.

[156] This observation has also been made by CEDAW in its General Recommendation No. 21.

[157] While many pregnant women may seek to prevent *birth* for a number of health and other reasons, termination of pregnancy as *curative care* is not discussed in this study.

[158] On the issue of forced pregnancy, see Chapter VII below.

[159] General Comment No. 3, *supra* note 121.

to increase the enjoyment of the rights enumerated in the Covenant. Moreover, with a view to preventing the ill-health of *children*, the Children's Convention provides in Article 24(2)(f) that 'guidance for parents and family planning education and services' are to be available so that parents will be able to decide the number and spacing of their children and optimize the quality of health to be enjoyed by the infant.

In Europe, the rights to privacy and health similarly may be invoked to secure the right to decide the number and spacing of one's children. Article 8(1) of the ECHR stipulates the right to respect for 'private and family life' the object of which has been interpreted by both the European Commission and Court of Human Rights to be 'essentially that of protecting the individual against arbitrary interference by the public authorities'.[160] In contradistinction to Article 17(1) of the CCPR, Article 8(1) of the ECHR is phrased in positive terms. However, it is followed by a lengthy limitations clause in Article 8(2) which entitles the State to interfere on a variety of grounds including 'the economic well-being of the country', 'for the protection of health or morals, or for the protection of the rights and freedoms of others'. While the specific issue of the right to decide the number and spacing of children has not been dealt with under the ECHR, it would appear that the reasoning offered above in relation to the private sphere at the universal level would apply under the ECHR. As for the right to health, paragraph 11 of Part I of the European Social Charter affords individuals the right 'to benefit from any measure enabling . . . the highest possible standard of health attainable'. According to Article 11 of the Charter, Contracting Parties are obliged:

> . . . either directly or in co-operation with public or private organizations, to take appropriate measures designed *inter alia*:
> 1. to remove as far as possible the causes of ill-health;
> 2. to provide advisory and educational facilities for the promotion of health and the encouragement of individual responsibility in matters of health;
> 3. to prevent as far as possible epidemic, endemic and other diseases.

Similar obligations arise in relation to Article 10(3) of the Revised European Code of Social Security as pertains to health for the beneficiaries of States Parties to this treaty. For the same reasons offered above in relation to Article 12 of the CESCR, these provisions may be invoked

---

[160] *Case relating to Certain Aspects on the Use of Languages in Education in Belgium* (Belgian Linguistic Case), judgment of 23 July 1968, Publications of the European Court of Human Rights, Series A, No. 6, pp. 24–25.

to secure the right to decide the spacing and number of children.

Turning to the Inter-American system, the same arguments hold as at the universal and European levels with regard both to the right to 'private life' (pursuant to Article 11(2) of the ACHR) and to the right to health (pursuant to Article 10(1) of the Additional Protocol to the ACHR and Article XI of the American Declaration). It is to be noted in this regard that the right to private life is stipulated in terms similar to those of the CCPR (i.e. in terms of non-arbitrary interference) and the obligations of implementation of the Additional Protocol are stipulated in Articles 1 and 2 in terms very similar to those of Article 2 of the CESCR.[161]

Since Article 1 of the African Charter requires States Parties 'to adopt legislative or other measures to give effect' to the right recognized therein, protection of the right 'to enjoy the best attainable state of physical and mental health' (pursuant to Article 16) may also be invoked within the jurisdiction of States Parties with regard to the right to decide the number and spacing of one's children as argued above.

2.2.1 The Implications of Sex Determination Technology. Another issue regarding medical intervention in reproduction which is insufficiently addressed by human rights law is the use of technology which makes it possible for couples to determine the sex of young foetuses. This has led to the exercise of reproductive choice by the practice of sex-selective abortions, particularly in countries where sons are prized over daughters. The use of amniocentesis tests, sonography (ultrasound) and increasingly developed technological methods for sex determination are reported to be contributing to sex-selective abortion of female foetuses—a concern which is heightened in places like Bombay where 99 per cent of pregnant women are reported to undergo amniocentesis.[162] Evidence of gender-based abortions can be seen in disproportionate sex ratios at birth: although the normal (i.e. official) sex ratio in the

---

[161] This is not surprising inasmuch as the Inter-American instruments were adopted after the two universal Covenants and were evidently influenced by them. With regard to the legal value of the Additional Protocol to the ACHR, it must here be added that, as at 1 January 1996, the Additional Protocol has yet to enter into force due to a lack of ratifications. However, the treaty remains binding for States signatories insofar as they may not conduct themselves in variance with the object and purpose of the treaty.

[162] See Patel, *In Search of Our Bodies: A Feminist Look at Women, Health and Reproduction in India* (1987).

developing world is approximately 97 females to 100 males,[163] in Pakistan the ratio is about 93 girls to 100 boys. More shocking, in China today there are 85 girls being born for every 100 boys, representing a ten per cent drop in a short period of time.[164] As a result, there are already tens of millions fewer women than men in China.[165] This phenomenon can only be attributed to gender-based abortions.[166] The gender bias is further aggravated by female infanticide after birth. However, insofar as Article 16(1)(e) of the Women's Convention provides for the right of individuals to decide 'the number and spacing of their children' and *not* 'the sex of their children' in founding a family, the provision probably could not be invoked to this end. Of course, such a practice could well be considered contrary to all provisions against discrimination by gender.[167] While it remains extremely unlikely that any universal human rights provisions apply to foetuses,[168] Article 2 of the ECHR on the right to life (read alone or in

---

[163] In Europe and North America, the normal sex ratio at birth is 106 females to 100 males. It would be safe to assume that this is closer to the 'natural' ratio and strongly suggests that fewer official and unofficial sex-selective abortions are performed in these regions as there would be no other scientific explanation for the difference in ratios (the argument that the difference is based on dubious 'ethnic' or 'racial' biological grounds is equally discarded given the higher ratios in many Asian countries, e.g. in Laos the ratio of female to male births is 103 to 100 and in Cambodia 108 females are born to every 100 males; see table created from United Nations and World Bank figures in 'Perish the Baby Girl', *Newsweek*, 28 August 1995, p. 23. Indeed, it has been estimated that only 600,000 of the six million abortions performed in India are legal (*ibid.*, p. 25), spawning the probability that a large number of the illegal abortions occur because of the undesired sex of the foetus.

[164] See table cited in footnote 163 above. See also Carrillo, 'Violence against Women: An Obstacle to Development', in: Bunch and Carrillo (eds.), *Gender Violence: A Development and Human Rights Issue* (1991), p. 24.

[165] Carillo, *Battered Dreams: Violence against Women as an Obstacle for Development* (1992).

[166] In is interesting to note that the UN Special Rapporteur on Violence against Women, includes abortions of female foetuses and female infanticide as forms of violence against women; UN, Preliminary report submitted by the Special Rapporteur on violence against women, its causes and consequences, Ms. Radhika Coomaraswamy, in accordance with Commission on Human Rights resolution 1994/45, UN doc. E/CN.4/1995/42, paragraphs 154–157.

[167] The Special Rapporteur on Violence against Women condemned the use of reproductive technology in this way; *ibid.*, paragraph 56.

[168] With regard to application of the right to life protected by Article 6 of the CCPR, it appears clear from the *travaux préparatoires* that it was specifically *not* the intention to extend protection to the unborn, at least not from the moment of conception; see Nowak, *supra* note 68, pp. 122–125. However, according to Nowak and others (*ibid.*, p. 124 with references), there may be some protection to the unborn foetus when it attains the ability to survive on its own.

conjunction with Article 14 on non-discrimination) may be invoked to protect a foetus from abortion on this basis.[169] In the Americas, Article 4(1) of the ACHR stipulates clearly that the right to life applies 'from the moment of conception'.

2.3 The Scope of the Right to Family Planning Information and Education

Article 16(1)(e) of the Women's Convention regarding the right to obtain family planning information is relatively straightforward. As a result, there has been very little discussion of this right. Yet, what is the standing of the general right to information in the relevant conventions with respect to fertility regulation? To date there has never been a case concerning this issue before the Human Rights Committee pursuant to Article 19(2) of the CCPR. However, it has been suggested that there is a potential problem of harmonization between the right to obtain information or education specifically relevant to family planning, as provided in at least one treaty, and provisions of the right to information (in general) in others.[170] Notwithstanding this concern, there is no apparent reason why information sought and received could not be family planning related, especially since Article 19(2) expressly applies to 'information and ideas of *all* kinds' (emphasis added). Indeed, the general provisions in other instruments should serve partly to explain and to reinforce the specific provision for family planning information in the Women's Convention. Of course, there are provisions in the Children's Convention (Article 13(2)) and the CCPR (Article 19(3)) which States may call upon to place limitations on the freedom to information, *inter alia* on the grounds of national security, public order, public health and public morals. However, the limitations may not serve to destroy the rights and freedoms provided therein, and it is difficult to see how information on family planning could negatively affect at least the first three bases for permissible limitations. By contrast, much concerning reproduction and family planning is about 'public morals' for which the Human Rights Committee has considered

---

[169] In its decision on a different, but related matter, the European Commission of Human Rights left open the possibility that Article 2 of the ECHR, concerning the right to life, applies to foetuses (at least after the first trimester); Application No. 8416/79, *X. v the United Kingdom*, Decisions and Reports 19 (1980), paragraph 23.

[170] See UN, United Nations Secretariat, 'Relationship Between Human Rights and Population Issues: Standard-Setting Activities of the United Nations, 1980–1988' in: UN, *Population and Human Rights: Proceedings of the Expert Group Meeting on Population and Human Rights, Geneva, 3–6 April, 1989* (1990), p. 58.

that 'a certain margin of discretion must be accorded to the responsible national authorities', i.e. States.[171] How much of a margin has yet to be established in relation to family planning information, but the Committee has also observed that 'public morals differ widely', raising the disturbing prospect of considerable relativity in the enjoyment of this right.[172]

The right secured in the CCPR and the Children's Convention includes imparting and receiving information. While this study is generally more centred on the right to receive family planning information, the ability of persons (including NGOs) to impart relevant and necessary information is evidently important. It is this *flow* of information which is at issue. The essence of the right is again one of freedom with which the State should *a priori* not interfere. Certainly, what this obligation implies is that no State Party to the relevant convention providing for the right to information can generally refuse private initiatives to obtain information nor restrict the assistance of non-governmental and donor organizations in providing information. Indeed, recent hortatory texts strongly recommend that access to family planning education/information (and services) should never be restricted; the fear is that, in the absence of such information, the success of State population programmes intended to curtail population growth could be immediately endangered.[173]

The most complete provision in relation to family planning information and education is Article 10(h) of the Women's Convention which ensures women '[a]ccess to specific educational information to help to ensure the health and well-being of families, including information and advice on family planning'. While it is not clear what is entailed in ensuring 'access', the general meaning of the word and the general intention of Article 10 would lead to the conclusion that States should not hinder free approach to, or obstruct admission of, information, but they may not be required to facilitate it. However, this rather restrictive meaning appears incongruous with the other terms of the provision (such as 'to help' and, especially, 'advice') which imply performance of some activity/ies.

For the same reasons as expounded above in relation to the right to

---

[171] See the views of the Committee in the case of *Hertzberg et al. v. Finland*, Communication No. R.14/61. UN, Report of the Human Rights Committee, General Assembly, Official Records, Thirty-seventh Session, Supplement No. 40 (A/37/40), pp. 161–165.

[172] *Ibid.*

[173] See: UN, *supra* note 43, paragraph 156; and UN, *supra* note 42, Recommendation 35.

decide the number and spacing of children, the right to health provided in Article 12 of the CESCR and Article 24(2)(f) of the Children's Convention can be invoked in relation to family planning information and education; the stipulation of 'guidance' in the Children's Convention also implies an actively conceived and implemented programme. However, it is less clear that the right to family planning education could be invoked pursuant to Article 13(1) of the CESCR. On the whole, Article 13 requires only that there be education, but it is quite limited in its treatment of the question of curriculum. Still, since Article 13(1) stipulates that 'education shall be directed to the full development of the human personality and the sense of its dignity', and insofar as family planning education may reasonably be necessary for individuals fully to develop their personalities and their senses of dignity, resort to the provision may be made. Article 10(h) of the Women's Convention is again the most helpful since it requires that educational information must be of such a nature as 'to help to ensure the health and well-being of families' (as opposed to other objectives which a State may wish to pursue).

In Europe, Article 10(1) of the ECHR secures the right 'to receive and impart information and ideas without interference by public authorities and regardless of frontiers'. As for several other rights in the Convention, Article 10(1) is followed by a limitations clause which permits restrictions on several grounds of which only 'the protection of health or morals' seems relevant to the subject at hand. But, since the object of the information to be received or imparted would be to serve an essentially private matter and/or would be to protect health, it would seem extremely unlikely that the restrictions of Article 10(2) would have much effect. Persons should thus be free to receive or impart virtually any and all information concerning family planning. Moreover, it is important to note that Article 10(1) specifically applies 'regardless of frontiers'. As such, there should be no interference with the importation or exportation of family planning information.

In recent years, case-law has helped to clarify the parameters of the right to family planning information in Europe. Following two Irish abortion-related cases before the European courts, consistent jurisprudence has been established regarding the right to information about medical services. In *Society for the Protection of Unborn Children Ireland Ltd v. Grogan*, the first case of this kind, the Court of Justice of the European Communities stated that Europe's open borders protect the free flow of information about medical services, including abortion clinics.[174] In *Open Door and Dublin Well Woman v. Ireland*, the European Court of Human Rights affirmed a right to free speech which included the dissemination of telephone numbers of British medical clinics, for medical information, including abortion information.[175] Since abortion is an extreme form of 'family planning', it may be deduced from these decisions that individuals living, respectively, in the European Union and States parties to the ECHR are equally entitled to seek and impart information on family planning methods and services.[176]

The right to access to family planning information appears to be well protected in the Americas and in Africa insofar as the right to information is protected with few if any restrictions in these regional systems. In the Inter-American system, Article 13(1) of the ACHR stipulates the 'freedom to seek, receive and impart information and

---

[174] The Supreme Court of Ireland upheld an injunction prohibiting the Irish Students' Union from publishing the telephone numbers of medical clinics in Great Britain that provide legal abortion services. The Court of Justice of the European Communities (ECJ) heard the case under Article 60 of the Treaty of Rome (regarding open borders within the European Economic Community for the provision of medical services). The ECJ ruled that it is not contrary to European Community law for a Member State in which medical termination of pregnancy is forbidden to prohibit students' associations from distributing information about the identity and location of clinics in another Member State where voluntary termination of pregnancy is lawfully carried out and about the means of communicating with those clinics (where the clinics in question have no involvement in the distribution of the said information); see the text of the decision in *Society for the Protection of Unborn Children Ireland Ltd. v. Grogan*, [1991] ECR I–4685, also reproduced in: 12 *Human Rights Law Journal* (1991), No. 11–12, pp. 455–471. The ECJ did not, however, directly confront Irish censorship of British telephone numbers accessing such information.

[175] The case originates in two applications lodged with the European Commission for Human Rights in 1988. The first application was brought by *Open Door Counselling Ltd.* and the second by *Dublin Well Woman Centre Ltd.* Both companies offered, *inter alia*, non-directive counselling to pregnant women in Ireland desiring information on obtaining abortions in clinics in Great Britain given that abortions are prohibited in Ireland. Following proceedings instigated by the Society for the Protection of Unborn Children Ireland Ltd., the Supreme Court found on 16 March 1988 that such counselling assisted in the destruction of the life of the unborn and was contrary to respect for the life of the unborn as expressly guaranteed by Article 40.3.3 of the Constitution of Ireland. An injunction was granted restraining the work of these companies, which then lodged applications with the Commission. The two applications were joined and declared admissible on 15 May 1990. The European Court of Human Rights held by fifteen votes to eight that there had been a violation of the right to receive and impart information guaranteed under Article 10(1) of the ECHR. See *supra* note 86.

[176] For an excellent review of the European jurisprudence on matters of information with influence on the right to family planning information, see Coliver, 'The Right to Information Necessary for Reproductive Health and Choice under International Law', 44 *The American University Law Review* (1995), No. 4, particularly pp. 1290–1294, as condensed from the author's chapter (*supra* note 84).

ideas of all kinds, regardless of frontiers, either orally, in writing, in print, in the form of art, or through any other medium of one's choice'. This seemingly absolute freedom is tempered only by slight restriction in the subsidiary paragraphs of Article 13. Indeed, Article 13(3) underlines the importance of the liberty by expressly precluding States even from 'indirect restrictions'. Aside from a prohibition on 'hate propaganda' and a restriction on 'public entertainments' for reasons of 'the moral protection of childhood and adolescence' (which could hardly apply to information on family planning), the only permissible restriction (in fact, an obligation) is the imposition of liability relating to the imparting of information and ideas. Thus, there should be no limitation on the flow of family planning information either within or between States Parties to the ACHR. Since the African Charter provides simply in Article 9 for an unqualified and unrestricted right 'to receive information', the same may be said for the freedom of information within and between States Parties to the African Charter.

For the reasons given above in relation to the right to decide the number and spacing of one's children, the right to health provided in the regional treaties may be invoked to obtain family planning information pursuant to the following provisions: Part I (paragraph 11) and Article 11 of the European Social Charter; Article 10(1) of the Additional Protocol to the ACHR; Article XI of the American Declaration; and Article 16 of the African Charter. However, it is to be noted here that Article 11 of the European Social Charter expressly secures the right to 'advisory and educational facilities for the promotion of health and the encouragement of individual responsibility in matters of health'. As such, this last treaty appears to require a much more active engagement on the part of States Parties.

2.4 The Scope of the Right to Access to Family Planning Services

Article 16(1)(e) of the Women's Convention combines access to family planning information and 'means' in unequivocal language. The ordinary meaning of the term 'means' would include material products and services. However, while the provisions for reproductive choice in the Women's Convention seek to ensure equal rights of men and women to the information and means necessary to exercise this right, they do not specify any particular form of family planning. As a result, States may claim that, as long as they do not obstruct individuals from seeking and receiving services, they are not infringing any rights. However, Fincancioglu argues that the obligation on States pursuant to Article 16(1)(e) is one of performance such that States must provide the means to exercise the decisions freely to be made.[177] Dixon-Mueller draws a similar conclusion of a positive *entitlement*, emphasizing that, since everyone effectively has the means to regulate their own fertility (by celibacy, periodic abstinence, coitus interruptus, herbal recipes, etc.), the right inevitably implies the use of 'modern' methods within the ordinary limitations of the State.[178] Cook and Dickens further reason that 'if the right to choice is admitted by legislation, an obligation is imposed upon administrative agencies to make that choice effective by provision of means for its exercise'.[179] International law (in the form of the Women's Convention) is not here concerned with whether compliance is by means of legislation, executive decree, or simple practice. The point is that when effective means for family planning are not made available, legitimate choice disappears and the 'right' becomes illusory, thus the 'means' in question must be concrete, practical and effective. However, this does not mean that the State is obliged to provide all kinds of family planning services nor any particular kind of service.

The link between the right to reproductive choice and the right to health is again underlined by the expressed inclusion of the right to access to family planning services in Articles 12(1) and 14(2)(b) of the Women's Convention. As such, this right appears unequivocal at least for persons within the jurisdiction of States Parties to the Women's Convention. Moreover, the *travaux préparatoires* of the Women's Convention in relation to Article 12(1) reveal that, while there was serious opposition to the inclusion of family planning services in the provision, it was retained with a view to future needs[180]—suggesting increasing importance over time.

Turning to the scope of the right to access to family planning services derived from provisions relating to the right to health in general at the universal and regional levels, it is to be recalled that provisions apply insofar as the absence of services *endangers* health.

2.4.1 Abortion as a Family Planning Service? Since no treaty defines 'family planning', the result is that every State, and even sub-units therein, deduces its own understanding of the methods of family planning which are to be permitted or made available. Laying at one

---

[177] Fincancioglu, *supra* note 147, p. 89.

[178] Dixon-Mueller, *supra* note 47, pp. 13 and 113.

[179] Cook and Dickens, *Abortion Laws in Commonwealth Countries* (1979), p. 58.

[180] Rehof, *supra* note 139, p. 45.

extreme is abortion which presents perhaps the thorniest problem of all with some commentators claiming it as a method of family planning and others proclaiming it another name for murder.

There is no doubt that family planning and abortion are connected. Unfortunately, *mortality* figures bear this out. In the developing world the inability to obtain safe and legal abortions is still the primary cause of maternal mortality.[181] Indeed, half of female deaths before the age of 45 are due to abortions performed under unsafe conditions.[182] Evidently, if effective contraception were more accessible, figures of maternal mortality owing to abortion would drop considerably. According to the WHO, the estimated 50 million abortions that occur each year are a significant indicator of the largely unmet need for more and better family planning services.[183] At least a third of these abortions are performed illegally and under poor conditions.[184] At present, one-third of all women in the developing world live in countries where abortion is essentially illegal on any grounds.[185] The horrible results of botched 'home-made' abortions in such countries are well known. Indeed, abortion recipes secretly passed among Romanian women during Ceausescu's pro-natalist campaign (complete with pregnancy police) are enough to convince many of the toughest pro-lifers that safe abortion services should be available as a matter of human rights law.[186] This confirms the *need* for effective family planning services. However, can abortion be considered a *method of family planning*?

Many go beyond the health-risk argument for legalizing abortion to say that a woman cannot truly have reproductive freedom if she is forced to continue an unintended or 'accidental' pregnancy against her will; in this view, the ability to terminate an unwanted pregnancy safely

---

[181] See Petchesky and Weiner, *supra* note 7, p. 2.

[182] *Ibid.*

[183] WHO, *supra* note 10.

[184] Figure cited in 'Nafis Sadik mobilise les énergies pour la 3e Conférence mondial sur la population', *Le Nouveau Quotidien—Journal Suisse et Européen (Supplément spécial)*, 31 May 1994, p. 4.

[185] See Dixon-Mueller, *supra* note 47, p. 172.

[186] Mueller ('Rumania: Pregnancy Police', *Connexions [Special Issue: Reproductive Rights—The Global Right]* [1989], No. 31) explains how women were instructed to begin with the least harmful method (e.g. douching with lemon juice or citric acid) and proceed in increasing desperation through to the very risky (e.g. taking various drugs in overdose twice a day for three days), see p. 23.

constitutes a core element of the right to reproductive choice.[187] While 'old-style abortions' may seem a particularly 'unacceptable' form of family planning, the debate over abortion has become much more complicated as the 'abortion pill' (RU–486) has become more widely available. Currently available in France, Britain and Sweden, and under trial in the United States[188], this abortifacient produces a nonsurgical termination and may be used up to the seventh week of pregnancy. The fact that it may be used quickly and discreetly, and resembles the contraceptive pill in its administration, renders it a somewhat more 'acceptable' form of abortion and blurs the traditional understanding of family planning as *preventive* care with techniques which have more in common with *curative* care. Interestingly, this view on RU–486 is compatible with the stance of Bangladesh, for example, which considers termination up to seven weeks as a 'menstrual regulation service' rather than an abortion.[189] However, the controversy stirred up in the United States concerning the clinical trials of RU–486 reportedly demonstrates that those who view it as a method of family planning are in the minority in at least that country.[190]

International instruments are generally vague[191] and unhelpful on

---

[187] For example, see Dixon-Mueller, *supra* note 47, p. 111.

[188] 'US Trials for French Abortion Pill Agreed', *The Times*, 17 May 1994, p. 12.

[189] See Dixon-Mueller, 'Innovations in Reproductive Health Care: Menstrual Regulation Policies and Programs in Bangladesh', 19 *Studies in Family Planning* (1988), No. 3, p. 129.

[190] 'Go-Ahead on Pill for Abortions', *International Herald Tribune*, 17 May 1994, p. 2.

[191] Part of the vagueness of the law derives from uncertainty over the precise notion of a 'human being', particularly the point at which a 'human being' may be said to exist and, therefore, enjoy rights.

In the context of the ECHR, the issue is more unclear because the right to life protected pursuant to Article 2(1) is to be enjoyed by 'everyone'. In considering this issue, the European Commission of Human Rights qualified its finding that 'both the general usage of the term "everyone" (toute personne) in the Convention . . . and the context in which this term is employed in Article 2 . . . tend to support the view that it does not include the unborn'. By expressly leaving it open 'whether Article 2 does not cover the foetus at all or whether it recognises a "right to life" of the foetus with implied limitations'; *X v. The United Kingdom*, *supra* note 169, paragraphs 9 and 23, respectively. Should the right to life in Article 2 of the ECHR pertain to the foetus at some stage of its development, then this would most probably constitute a limit to abortion.

Such a limitation on abortion presumably applies in States Parties to the ACHR pursuant to Article 4(1) which protects the right to life 'in general, from the moment of conception'. However, according to the Inter-American Commission on Human Rights, no such limitation applies in States Members of the OAS pursuant to the right to life protected by Article I of the American Declaration; see Resolution No. 23–81, Case 2141 (U.S.) 6 March 1981, OEA/Ser.L/V/II.54, doc. 9, rev. 1, 16 October 1981.

the issue of abortion, and international resolutions from the 1960s to the present have remained virtually silent with regard to abortion. Unfortunately, the Women's Convention sheds little light on the issue. Particular concern over this ambiguity was demonstrated by Malta which is one of only two States which have submitted reservations to the most significant provision protecting the right to reproductive choice (Article 16(1)(e) of the Women's Convention). According to the text of Malta's reservation, it

> ... does not consider itself bound by sub-paragraph (e) of paragraph (1) of article 16 in so far as the same may be interpreted as imposing an obligation on Malta to legalise abortion.[192]

It has been often observed that the drafting of the Women's Convention represented a constructive compromise, accommodating as many cultures as possible. Inevitably, specificity and clarity were sometimes sacrificed in order to appeal to as many parties as possible. As Boland et al. explain, although the Convention covers a wide spectrum of concerns, the 'fundamental ambiguities and conflicts have been glossed over in favour of political consensus'.[193] In his extensive review of the *travaux préparatoires* of the Women's Convention, Rehof comes to a similar conclusion, as follows:

> Some of these real considerations could not be expressed openly, but would nevertheless [be] determining factors. Some of them may therefore be cloaked in vague concepts and terms ... Diplomats often deliberately resort to so-called 'constructive ambiguity' to deal with such awkward situations. One thing is certain, the wording of such a convention is never the result of chance. It may be inconsistent and vague and it may create significant problems for lawyers trying to interpret and apply the Convention—but this may be precisely the effect envisaged by its framers.[194]

To say the least, therefore, the general nature of the terminology used in the family planning provisions in international human rights texts leaves us in considerable doubt as to whether the concept of reproductive choice includes the right to abort unwanted foetuses: there exists no explicit provision according such a right, but neither is it explicitly

---

[192] Rehof, *supra* note 139, p. 265.

[193] Boland et al., *supra* note 140, p. 89.

[194] Rehof, *supra* note 139, p. 3.

precluded.

Many use this ambiguity to argue that there is leeway in approaching the issue of abortion by means of interpretation. For example, some Members of the CEDAW interpret the Convention as including abortion rights and frequently ask States' delegates to comment on the situation of abortions in their countries when States' reports are reviewed.[195] In its recent review of major contraceptive methods in developing countries, the International Bank for Reconstruction and Development (IBRD), which is highly involved in funding family planning programmes, included three abortion methods under the category of *Other Fertility Regulation Methods*.[196] Cook uses another strategy and argues that, since safe abortion is the practice of medicine, women should be able to obtain a termination according to Article 15(1)(b) of the CESCR which provides for the right to 'enjoy the benefits of scientific progress and its applications'.[197]

Overall, international human rights bodies have been reluctant to address the question of abortion. Ongoing debate over abortion demonstrates the difficulty of attempting to establish international standards of practice on one aspect of reproductive choice among even western democracies where freedoms are assumed to be better secured.[198] The Cairo Programme of Action further demonstrates the sensitivity of the abortion issue with several States (mainly Muslim and Catholic) expressing their disapproval in relation to terms such as 'fertility regulation' and 'safe motherhood' used in the Programme—branding these as gateways for legal abortion.[199]

Bearing all of these considerations in mind, there are several reasons why it seems correct to conclude that international human rights law does not generally include abortion among the means to enable individuals to exercise reproductive choice. To begin with, abortion is not explicitly mentioned. Nor is it readily discernible from the plain meaning of any provisions that a right to abortion is implied. Secondly,

---

[195] For example, see UN, Centre for Social Development and Humanitarian Affairs, *The Work of CEDAW: Reports of the Committee on the Elimination of Discrimination against Women (CEDAW), Volume II* (1990), paragraph 330 (El Salvador).

[196] IBRD, *Effective Family Planning Programs* (1993), pp. 94-95.

[197] See Cook, 'International Human Rights and Women's Reproductive Choice', *supra* note 107, p. 82.

[198] See Blank, *supra* note 100, p. 7.

[199] See 'Population: Women Will be Taking More Control', *International Herald Tribune*, 27 July 1994, p. 5.

the absence of reservations similar to that of Malta relating specifically to Article 16(1)(e) does not necessarily imply that the remaining States Parties to the Convention interpret abortion as a method of family planning, only that they have not felt it necessary to make an explicit statement in this regard. Indeed, many developing countries have maintained strict laws against abortion (over 50 of such countries prohibit abortion entirely or permit it only *in extremis*).[200] The fact that almost all of these States, which are militantly against abortion and even have laws prohibiting it, have ratified the Convention without submitting reservations reveals a great deal. It implies that the great majority of the States Parties do not view abortion as a form of family planning or a form of exercising reproductive choice. Thirdly, it seems highly improbable that informed couples with access to a selection of contraceptive methods would choose abortion as a means of family *planning*, if not for ethical reasons at least on the grounds of health. Finally, abortion as a method of family planning might conceivably conflict with the right to life, depending upon the point of development of the foetus at the time of abortion.[201] Thus, Dixon-Mueller is correct in her conclusion that, 'many of the reproductive rights claimed by feminists . . . have been established at least indirectly in international standards *(with the exception of the right to terminate foetuses)*'.[202] In setting the extreme limit of methods of family planning as falling short of abortion (which is not to say that a right to obtain an abortion might not be derived from other human rights provisions), it is possible to conclude that all other safe methods should fall within the scope of 'family planning methods and services'. That a State is obliged to make available each and every method would, however, be an unsustainable conclusion. But, it may be concluded that the State must make available a reasonable selection of methods so as to make the choice meaningful.

---

[200] See Dixon-Mueller, *supra* note 47, p. 172.

[201] On the relation of abortion to the right to life protected by Article 6 of the CCPR, see Nowak, *supra* note 68, 'Article 6', pp. 122–124.

[202] Dixon-Mueller, *supra* note 47, p. 14 (emphasis added).

3. BENEFICIARIES OF THE RIGHT TO REPRODUCTIVE CHOICE

3.1 Introduction

According to general international law, individual human beings are not generally considered 'subjects of international law'.[203] However, they do enjoy legal recognition and capacity insofar as they are accorded both substantive and procedural rights and duties at the universal and regional levels, primarily (but not exclusively) through international human rights law. While the legal personality of individual human beings is not to be confused with that of States, it is clear that the evolving concepts of international relations and international law at the end of the twentieth century accord increasing importance to individuals.[204]

With regard to the right to reproductive choice, consideration of legal personality is relevant to clarification of the precise beneficiaries, or 'right-holders'. Discussions have arisen in this context regarding attribution of the right to reproductive choice or, phrased in a negative fashion, whether some individuals are not entitled to enjoy the right. The qualifying characteristics of the beneficiaries of the right are examined below according to categories of gender, marital status and couple. Also examined are the age at which a person may be entitled to exercise the right and whether adults incapable of comprehending the notions of 'consent' and 'responsible reproductive behaviour' may be deprived of the right.

3.2 Gender, Marital Status and Couples

Human rights treaties and the texts issuing from the Cairo and Beijing Conferences clearly situate the right to reproductive choice as belonging to *both women and men*.[205] While it is widely acknowledged that many women and girls have in reality limited decision-making power over their sexual and reproductive lives and often have unequal access to

---

[203] On 'subjects of international law', see: Brownlie, *supra* note 52, pp. 58–70, especially at p. 67; Detter, *supra* note 52, pp. 29–145; Harris, *supra* note 52, pp. 102–172, especially at pp. 102 and 135–137; and Shaw, *supra* note 52, pp. 135–186, especially at pp. 178–181.

[204] See Detter, *ibid*.

[205] See, for example, Cairo Programme of Action, paragraph 7.2, and Beijing Platform for Action, paragraph 97, reproduced in Appendices A and B, respectively.

health services,[206] women, men and adolescents have the right to be informed and make their own choices.[207] Thus, while not denying that 'reproductive freedom honestly confronts the fundamental point that the primary bearers of interests in human reproduction remain women, who generally carry the social, physical, psychological and practical burdens of child-bearing and rearing',[208] it must not be forgotten that the freedom has significance for both sexes. Tomaševski emphasizes the importance of this fact for one of several reasons:

> ... human rights norms relating to family planning address both parents rather than only the prospective mother. Reducing the discussion of family planning to women may indeed contribute to the tolerance of irresponsible fatherhood.[209]

Part of the problem, she explains, is that while 'proponents of reproductive rights often reinforce traditional attitudes which hold that procreation is the domain of women ... [t]his disregards the basic human rights principle that parenthood is not gender-specific but pertains to both women and men'.[210] This succinct explanation of Tomaševski is very important, implying not only a discrepancy in the evolution of social behaviour in the Western World and the laws which were created to protect 'the family' only a few decades ago, but also the apparent dichotomy between the Western (feminist) conception of relevant provisions and the 'traditional' views held by many in the remainder of the world.[211]

---

[206] See, e.g., Cairo Programme of Action, paragraph 7.3, and Beijing Platform for Action, paragraph 92.

[207] See Cairo Programme of Action, paragraph 7.2, and Beijing Platform for Action, paragraph 94.

[208] McLean, 'Women, Rights and Reproduction', in: McLean (ed.), *Legal Issues in Human Reproduction* (1990), p. 215. International Planned Parenthood Federation (IPPF) similarly declares that 'the right to family planning is first and foremost a right of women'; see IPPF, *supra* note 51, p. 14.

[209] Tomaševski, *Women and Human Rights* (1993), p. 17.

[210] Tomaševski, *supra* note 134, p. 281.

[211] In an excellent article, Oloka-Onyango and Tamale describe a form of two-track feminism occurring wherein representatives from the developing world have fewer opportunities to share their views on issues regarding the human rights of women—views which may ultimately contribute to the evolution of a *truly international* feminist theory. The authors cautiously explain that, at present, discussions on 'international' feminist theory are generally dominated by contributors from the north. Such discussions 'can only lead to the unfortunate conclusions that ... editors [and authors] ... presume a comity of perspectives

In reviewing each of the provisions in the universal human rights treaties which protect in some shape or form reproductive choice (the CCPR, CESCR, Children's Convention and the Women's Convention[212]), it is clear that they are not only non-gender specific, but expressly declare the equality of men and women as bearers of the stipulated rights. In the case of the Women's Convention, for example, annotations in the *travaux préparatoires* on the drafting of the provision regarding access to advice on family planning offer further explanation. Sweden, for example, did not want the Convention to make a specific link between women and family planning education since 'this should be a shared responsibility'.[213]

Conceptual and legal clarifications are still needed as concerns the marital status of the individual.[214] Only the Women's Convention (in Article 1) specifies that it is to apply irrespective of marital status. None of the other provisions for reproductive choice in the relevant treaties specify explicitly whether the persons entitled to the right must be married or not. This leaves the issue of entitlement somewhat ambiguous at the level of implementation. As a result, some States continue to provide contraceptive services only to married couples.[215] Some require a marriage certificate in order to obtain family planning services.[216] Certainly, a number of States felt it necessary to clarify in oral statements before the ICPD at Cairo that they understand the term *'couple'* in relation to reproduction means *'married couples'*.[217] However, the *travaux préparatoires* of the CCPR record that the UN Commission on Human Rights rejected a motion submitted by France that sought to restrict the definition of the family (as provided in Article 23 establish-

---

between the north and the south'; see Oloka-Onyango and Tamale, '"The Personal is Political" or Why Women's Rights are Indeed Human Rights: An African Perspective on International Feminism', 17 *Human Rights Quarterly* (1995), No. 4, particularly pp. 697–701.

[212] For example, the Women's Convention clearly leaves the choice to *both* men and women, using phrases such as 'men and women . . . shall have the same rights to decide freely'. Article 16(1)(e).

[213] See Rehof, *supra* note 139, p. 120.

[214] See, UN, *supra* note 170, p. 57

[215] In 1987, five States denied unmarried persons access to contraceptive services. See Fincancioglu, *supra* note 147, p. 93.

[216] *Ibid.*

[217] See, for example, 'reservations' made by Egypt (paragraph 25), the Holy See (paragraph 27), and the Islamic Republic of Iran (paragraph 28), UN, *supra* note 1, Chapter V: Adoption of the Programme of Action.

ing the right to marry and to found a family) to the marital couple.²¹⁸ The Human Rights Committee further clarified the issue in its General Comment No. 19 stating that:

> ... when a group of persons is regarded as a family under the legislation and practice of a State, it must be given the protection referred to in article 23 ... In view of the existence of various forms of family, such as unmarried couples and their children or single parents and their children, States Parties should also indicate whether and to what extent such types of family and their members are recognized and protected by domestic law and practice.²¹⁹

Thus, in the smaller scope of protection offered in the provisions in the CCPR, unmarried couples may also enjoy the right to found a family.²²⁰

As Tomaševski describes, the delinking of marriage and parenthood throughout Europe has given rise to increased demands for recognition of reproductive rights as held by individuals rather than couples.²²¹ However, this has so far not been recognized by the organs supervising implementation of the ECHR. To the contrary, the European Court of Human Rights has held that 'Article 12 [on the right to found a family] is mainly concerned to protect marriage as the basis of the family'.²²² Subsequent decisions of the European Commission of Human Rights have left the question open as to whether the right to found a family may be considered irrespective of marriage, although it has stated that '[t]he existence of a couple is fundamental'.²²³ While the European Commission has rejected the recognition of an individual's right to

---

[218] See Nowak, *supra* note 68, p. 413.

[219] See full text of General Comment No. 19 reproduced in Appendix D.

[220] Nowak (*supra* note 68, p. 413) comes to the conclusion that 'all other familial forms consistent with the legal and cultural peculiarities of the respective State' are protected by Article 23 and that it only 'presupposes at least that two persons of different sex and of marriageable age are living together.'

[221] See Tomaševski, *supra* note 131, pp. 1039–1040.

[222] *Rees*, judgment of 17 October 1986, Publications of the European Court of Human Rights, Series A, No. 106, p. 19. The judgment was founded on the reasoning that Article 12 stipulates 'the right to marry and to found a family' in conjunctive form as a single right.

[223] Application No. 6482/74, *X v. Belgium and the Netherlands*, Decisions and Reports 7 (1977), p. 75. For more on this issue, see van Dijk and van Hoof, *supra* note 128, p. 448.

parenthood in *same-sex* couples,[224] the European Parliament has stressed that 'family [population] policy cannot in any way stand in the way of progress towards ensuring that women have their own non-derivative rights'.[225] This being said, the European human rights bodies apply the same principles of equal rights expressed in the universal human rights instruments. In the Regional Platform for Action presented for the 1995 Beijing Conference on Women, the participating governments stressed the following:

> Human sexuality and gender relations are closely interrelated and together affect the ability of women and men to achieve and maintain sexual health and manage their reproductive lives. Equal relationships between women and men in matters of sexual relations and reproduction, including full respect for the physical integrity of the human body, require mutual respect and willingness to accept responsibility for the consequences of sexual behaviour . . .[226]

This statement strongly reinforces the notion that reproductive decisions must be made by the couple together, although the governments closed the statement by acknowledging that 'women's reproductive rights are often not respected and sometimes not yet recognized'.[227] As a means of correcting this problem, it was suggested that 'Governments and non-governmental organisations should, as appropriate, promote equal relationships between women and men in matters of sexual relations and reproduction'.[228]

The prevailing emphasis in hortatory international instruments since the mid-1970s has been upon a right to reproduce accorded to

---

[224] For example, in Application No. 15666/89, *Kerkhoven, Hinke & Hinke v. The Netherlands*, the European Commission of Human Rights decided on 19 May 1992 that a 'homosexual couple cannot be equated to a man and a woman living together' and that same-sex couples thus do not have a 'right to parenthood'.

[225] Council of Europe, Directorate of Human Rights, European Parliament Resolution of June 9, 1983, reprinted in: Human Rights Information Sheet No. 13, Doc. H/INF(83), April-October 1983, at p. 120.

[226] UN, Economic Commission for Europe, Regional Platform for Action—Women in a Changing World—Call for Action from an ECE Perspective, UN doc. E/ECE/RW/HLM/8, paragraph 27. It is evident that this same statement was carried over in the Beijing Platform for Action (paragraph 96) with the addition of a greater emphasis on shared responsibility.

[227] *Ibid.*

[228] *Ibid.*, paragraph 86.

'couples and individuals'.[229] This phrase, however, has not been incorporated into any human rights treaty. In referring to reproductive freedom as a right belonging to *'individuals and couples'*,[230] the hortatory instruments do not dictate how this 'freedom' is to be exercised.[231] Yet, in many (if not most) cultures women are susceptible to strong persuasion or even coercion to do what their husbands or partners want. For example, a Ghanaian study on the influence of one spouse over the other in reproductive decision-making found (not surprisingly) that men influence their wives' attitudes to contraception and rely on cultural norms that subjugate women to men.[232] Adjetey similarly describes the general pattern of reproductive decision-making in Africa: 'Women are often treated as minors, and thus considered incapable of making decisions in respect of their own reproductive lives'.[233] The reproductive decisions of African women 'are usually made under enormous pressures from family, community, and society to comply with prevailing gender and reproductive norm'.[234] Medina cites the similar problem of a deeply embedded culture of subordination of women in Latin America; to end this culture of subordination women must be educated on human rights and be encouraged to 'reclaim' them.[235]

In view of the serious cultural restrictions on women as independ-

---

[229] See, for example, the Cairo Programme of Action (paragraph 7.3) and the Beijing Platform for Action (paragraph 95).

[230] E.g., UN General Assembly resolution 21/2211 of 17 December 1966 refers to *'each individual family'*; 1974, 1984 and 1989 population conference documents refer to *'couples and individuals'*.

[231] This being said, several States participating in the Cairo ICPD felt it necessary to submit reservations with respect to the term *'individuals'*. See, UN, *supra* note 1, Chapter V: Adoption of the Programme of Action; for example, reservations by El Salvador (paragraph 9), Jordan (paragraph 11) and especially Egypt (paragraph 25) which called for 'the deletion of the word "individuals" since it has always been our understanding that all the questions dealt with by the Programme of Action . . . relate to harmonious relations between couples united by the bond of marriage'.

[232] See Ezeh, 'The Influence of Spouses Over Each Other's Contraceptive Attitudes in Ghana', 24 *Studies in Family Planning* (1993), No. 3, pp. 172–173.

[233] Adjetey, *supra* note 66, p. 1352.

[234] Correa and Petchesky, 'Reproductive and Sexual Rights: A Feminist Perspective', in: Sen et al. (eds.), *Population Policies Reconsidered: Health, Empowerment and Rights* (1994), p. 111.

[235] Medina, 'Toward a More Effective Guarantee of the Enjoyment of Human Rights by Women in the Inter-American System', in: Cook (ed.), *Human Rights of Women: National and International Perspectives* (1994), p. 261.

ent actors and free beneficiaries of their human rights, the criticism is made that international human rights law does not sufficiently protect women *in particular*—especially as the more vulnerable of the sexes in issues concerning reproduction. While such vulnerability is a matter of fact, cultural restrictions on independent action to claim and enjoy rights are exacerbated by inequalities in social independence (e.g. the absence of employment opportunities or social security) and failures to provide physical protection (e.g. against assaults including in the home). This is not, then, the failure of 'reproductive choice' *per se*, but rather a failure to secure other human rights pertaining to personal (physical) security and social independence (i.e. social security).

With regard specifically to the right to reproductive choice, States Parties with inequalities in laws which dictate who in the couple is entitled to decide or with laws which effectively limit the entitlement (such as those which allow husbands, but not wives, to obtain contraceptives[236] or that require a husband's authorization in order for his wife to obtain contraceptive services[237]) are in violation of their international obligations. Moreover, once a State ratifies the Women's Convention, all legislation and customary practices which create obstacles to this equality in decision-making must be repealed, as provided in Article 2(f) of the Convention. In this way, related concerns as referred to above are to be addressed.

The conclusion we can derive from the above is that both adult women and men are the beneficiaries of the right to reproductive choice. The choice may be made, ideally, by individuals forming a couple, regardless of their marital status. In the words of CEDAW, '[d]ecisions to have children or not, while preferably made in consultation with spouse or partner, must not nevertheless be limited by [these]'.[238] However, international law has so far not dictated how this private decision is to be made. However, it can go a long way to making it meaningful in practical terms by ensuring availability of information and services.

3.3 Adolescents

The status of young adults (legal minors) with regard to the right to

---

[236] See Dixon-Mueller, *supra* note 47, p. 95.

[237] See Cook, *supra* note 45, p. 13.

[238] CEDAW, General Recommendation No. 21, paragraph 22. *Supra* note 154. See also Appendix E.

reproductive choice merits special attention as a group. The lack of family planning counselling and services causes irreparable physical and social damage to adolescents, particularly girls.[239] It has been estimated that 40 per cent of all 14-year-old girls alive today will have been pregnant at least once by the time they are 20.[240] In Bangladesh, for example, four out of five adolescent girls are mothers; as are three out of five teenagers in Africa as a whole.[241] As discussed in Chapter I, the implications of teenage pregnancies are very negative in physical, emotional and socio-economic terms. Since the figures of such pregnancies are so high, it is absolutely critical to address the reproductive needs of adolescents. Yet, in many States, laws, regulations and clinical practices deny young persons access to family planning information and services.[242] Unmarried young people are a particularly vulnerable group whose access to contraceptive services is severely restricted in many societies. Concern for adolescent reproductive and sexual health education, particularly with regard to teenage pregnancy, has been raised in both the Cairo Programme of Action[243] and the Beijing Platform for Action.[244] It is of importance, however, that while both the Cairo and Beijing documents reaffirm a right to (and increased need for) information and education regarding reproductive health, neither acknowledge a right of adolescents to access to reproductive health

---

[239] Fincancioglu, *supra* note 147, p. 93.

[240] UNFPA, *supra* note 20, p. 12.

[241] *Ibid.*

[242] IPPF, *supra* note 51, p. 17.

[243] As stated in Chapter VI, paragraph 6.15 of the Cairo Programme of Action, which reads: 'Youth should be actively involved in the planning, implementation and evaluation of development activities that have a direct impact on their daily lives. This is especially important with respect to information, education and communication activities and services concerning reproductive and sexual health, including the prevention of early pregnancies, sex education and the prevention of HIV/AIDS and other sexually transmitted diseases. Access to, as well as confidentiality and privacy of, these services must be ensured with the support and guidance of their parents and in line with the Convention on the Rights of the Child.'

Chapter VII, paragraph 7.37, of the Cairo Programme of Action similarly reaffirms the need for 'integral sexual education and services for young persons, with the support and guidance of their parents and in line with the Convention on the Rights of the Child, that stress responsibility of males for their own sexual health and fertility and that help them exercise those responsibilities.'

[244] See, for example, paragraphs 93 and 95, reproduced in Appendix B.

(including family planning) *services*.²⁴⁵

It is not readily evident whether the scope of protection offered by the Women's Convention (as also with all the other human rights treaties with the exception of Children's Convention) extends to all women and men regardless of age. As Van Bueren explains:

> Although the Universal Declaration and the principal international and regional human rights treaties refer to 'everyone', this concept of inclusion seldom has been discussed with respect to the rights of the child . . . It is clear [for example] from the travaux préparatoires of the Universal Declaration of Human Rights and of the Civil and Political Covenant that the additional needs of children in exercising their right to freedom of expression were not considered.²⁴⁶

While the right to reproductive choice may apply to all humans irrespective of gender, portions of the right may be limited to persons of a certain minimum age. As the Women's Convention stands, it is unclear whether its provisions include young adults as beneficiaries.²⁴⁷ Had the phrasing in the Women's Convention read 'women and men of reproductive age' (rather than merely *'women and men'*) there would not have been any doubt that young adults fall under the protection of

---

²⁴⁵ The Beijing Platform for Action is particularly conspicuous in its silence on the subject. In its outline of specific actions, a call is made for increased information on reproduction while no mention is made regarding access to services to regulate reproduction, as follows:

'107 (e) Prepare and disseminate accessible information, through public health campaigns, the media, reliable counselling and the education system, designed to ensure that women and men, particularly young people, can acquire knowledge about their health, especially information on sexuality and reproduction, taking into account the right of the child to access to information, privacy, confidentiality, respect and informed consent, as well as the responsibilities, rights and duties of parents and legal guardians to provide, in a manner consistent with the evolving capacities of the child . . . of the rights recognized in the Convention on the Rights of the Child . . .

(g) Recognize the specific needs of adolescents and implement specific appropriate programmes, such as education and information on sexual and reproductive health issues and on sexually transmitted diseases, including HIV/AIDS, taking into account the rights of the child and the responsibilities, rights and duties of parents as stated in paragraph 107 (e) above.'

²⁴⁶ Van Bueren, 'The International Protection of Family Members' Rights as the 21st Century Approaches', 17 *Human Rights Quarterly* (1995), No. 4, p. 741.

²⁴⁷ As a general matter, Van Bueren (*ibid.*) reviews some of the conflicts between children's rights and 'parent's rights' along with the issue of consent in international and regional human rights texts.

the Convention.[248] This may, however, have been purposely omitted since many societies would question whether the choice would be 'responsible' (as Article 16(1)(e) stipulates) or, indeed, culturally acceptable. In fact, for the most part the problem is purposeful since the drafters of these treaties took special care not to intrude upon family privacy or over-regulate decision-making in the family, they also wished to have the texts adopted and eventually acceded to by as many States as possible.

Turning to the Children's Convention, it is apparent that the same care was taken not to dictate the process of decision-making within the family. A young person, like any adult, has two essential needs to ensure reproductive choice: a) information and education regarding family planning methods and services; and b) unrestricted access to the methods and services if the adolescent chooses to seek and use these.

An adolescent's right to information on family planning can be interpreted as guaranteed under Article 13 (which secures the right of a young person to seek information of his or her choice).[249] This interpretation appears to be secure on several fronts given: a) the consideration by the Committee on the Rights of the Child of the status of family planning information made available to adolescents in States Parties to the Children's Convention; and b) the consensus of this interpretation apparent in both the Cairo Programme of Action[250] and the Beijing Platform for Action.[251] While the phrasing of Article 24(f) of the Children's Convention leaves much to be desired, it provides only for parents (i.e. adults) to obtain family planning education and services. It could also be argued, therefore, that since access to family planning services is only mentioned in the context of parents (i.e adults), and this in the provision of the child's right to health (with health being the strongest link with which the right of the child to family planning services could be established), it is inferred that children are excluded from the right to access to family planning services under this treaty.

---

[248] The fact that the Cairo Programme of Action has a separate provision for reproductive health information and services for young persons (paragraph 6.15), situated in a separate section (Chapter VI) is possibly indicative of a consensus that adolescents are not considered the focus of general treaty law provisions.

[249] For the drafting history of Article 13 of the Children's Convention, see Detrick (ed.), *The United Nations Convention on the Rights of the Child: A Guide to the 'Travaux Préparatoires'* (1992), pp. 229–237.

[250] See paragraph 6.15, as reproduced in note 243 above.

[251] See paragraphs 107 (e) and (g), as reproduced in note 245 above.

In light of the above, it may be concluded that young persons are not guaranteed the right to access to family planning services—the second half of the equation of the right to reproductive choice. It would appear, therefore, that the only protection of an adolescent's reproductive choice would have to be derived from the interpretation of Article 13 regarding an adolescent's right to seek information. But to what degree is even this right protected?

The Children's Convention contains carefully phrased language which reinforces the notion of parental guidance regarding participation in decision-making. A balance is attempted: on the one hand, the child who is capable of forming his or her own views has the right 'to express those views in all matters' (Article 12), to seek the information and pursue the education of his or her choice (Article 13), and shall have freedom of thought, conscience and religion (Article 14), etc; on the other hand, however, it is cautioned that States Parties shall respect and take into account 'the rights and duties of the parents' (e.g. Articles 12, 14 and 18). Although Article 13 on the right to seek information is not accompanied by a clause recognizing parental authority and responsibility in family matters, it is understood that all choices and rights which may be exercised by the child must be considered in relation with those of the parents.[252] This being said, there is no statement of *exclusive* parental decision-making. These conclusions give rise to two further problematic issues: Whose right takes precedence in the event of conflict between parent and child? And at what point in life does the child become recognized as an adult with full capacities and unchecked rights?

In answer to the first question, the decision would have to be left to domestic courts and legislation, which would decide with the full knowledge of the rights of the child stipulated in the Children's Convention conditioned especially by the stipulation that the best interests of the child shall be a primary consideration (Article 3(1) of the Convention). Over the last decade a growing number of countries have implemented legislation to enforce the rights of children.[253] This being

---

[252] This is acknowledged in the Cairo (paragraphs 6.15, 7.8 and 7.37) and Beijing (107 (e) and (f)) documents which state that the 'support and guidance' and 'rights and duties' of parents must be considered in promoting information and education for adolescents on sexual and reproductive health.

[253] Norway, for example, has implemented the Children and Parents Act since 1981 and in the United Kingdom, children have had the protection of the Children Act since 1989. For more on such legislation and a review of the conditional clauses in the Children's Convention, see Van Bueren, *supra* note 246, especially pp. 740–747.

said, the question can also be partly answered by the response to the second question above. The Children's Convention does not stipulate an arbitrary age at which children may fully enjoy all the expressed rights, or at which their choices have prior consideration over those of their parents. Rather, the treaty establishes a wide margin of discretion regarding what exactly constitutes maturity, stating, for example, that 'the views of the child [shall be] given due weight in accordance with the age and maturity of the child' (Article 12) or 'in a manner consistent with the evolving capacities of the child' (Article 14). Specifying an age would have been heavily value-laden and essentially arbitrary since 'maturity' is case specific. Rather, the Convention has set broad parameters with some guidance and, one would imagine from the wording used, has established a gradient approach with the child benefitting from fuller rights as he or she grows older. The decision, therefore, is once again to be determined on a domestic basis, taking into consideration many factors including the socio-cultural environment.[254] This implies that the age at which young persons can enjoy their right to seek information (including family planning information) will be largely determined by the State, a determination which allows for a great range throughout the world.[255] Nonetheless, as a positive sign of active measures taken to improve the situation of family planning information to young persons worldwide, the Committee on the Rights of the Child frequently enquire into the situation at the time of reporting by States Parties.[256] Evidently, each State must be able to explain and defend its laws and policies with respect to its obligations under the Convention.

The European Court of Human Rights initially raised the issue of parents as the prior rights holder and the possibility of conflict with the

---

[254] As an example, the Norwegian Children and Parents Act of 1981 stipulates that parents must listen to their children's views before making a decision on their behalf and that by the age of twelve considerable weight should be given to the children's wishes (paragraph 31).

[255] For example, the Supreme Court of the United States had extended the right to obtain contraceptives to children under the age of 16 as early as 1977 following the decision in *Carey v. Pop. Services*, 431 U.S. 678 (1977).

[256] In 1995, for example, the Committee questioned Great Britain and Northern Ireland for 'the apparent insufficiency of measures taken to ensure the implementation of the general principles of the Convention' (paragraph 11) and specifically condemned the possibility for parents in England and Wales to 'withdraw their children from parts of the sex education programmes in schools' (paragraph 14); UN, Committee on the Rights of the Child, Concluding observations of the Committee on the Rights of the Child: United Kingdom of Great Britain and Northern Ireland, UN doc. CRC/C/15/Add.34.

wishes of the child in the case of *Kjeldsen, Busk Madsen and Pedersen v. Denmark*. In the opinion of the Court, the drafters of the Convention would not have intended to give parents dictatorial decision-making powers and it would be wrong for children who hold different views from their parents to have to abide by their parents' decision concerning educational matters.[257] From this decision it could be inferred, for example, that a child who wishes to attend sex education classes offered in school may attend the classes if he or she so chooses, despite the expressed decision of parents to withdraw their child from these classes.

3.4 Mentally Disabled Persons

Historically, although not so long ago, Western States had sterilization laws which allowed for the operation of 'the sort of people who should not be allowed to procreate'.[258] The targeted groups included criminals, the mentally impaired or 'feeble-minded' and the 'evil-minded'. Still today, mentally disabled persons as well as individuals with birth defects and/or hereditary diseases risk non-consensual sterilization.[259]

Mason describes very well the ethical problem faced in the consideration of the sterilization of this group of individuals. Mentally impaired persons are generally judged incapable of controlling their own reproductive behaviour by virtue of their reduced capacities of judgment. On the one hand, Mason explains, a person, incompetent or not, has a right to protection against invasion of his or her bodily privacy. Since the incompetent is, by definition, not competent to consent, there is a 'strong presumption that involuntary sterilization at the instigation of parent or guardian is an unacceptable violation of that privacy'.[260] It concurrently follows that the incompetent is unable to exercise his or her right to obtain information on, and methods of,

---

[257] *Case of Kjeldsen, Busk Madsen and Pedersen v. Denmark*, judgment of 7 December 1976, Publications of the European Court of Human Rights, Series A, No. 23.

[258] F. Pfafflin, 'The connections between eugenics, sterilization and mass murder in Germany from 1933 to 1945'. (1986 5 Med Law 1), as cited in Mason, *supra* note 104, p. 61.

[259] In the Cairo Programme of Action (paragraph 6.30), special attention was drawn to the situation of persons with disabilities stating that 'Governments should recognize needs concerning, *inter alia*, reproductive health, including family planning and sexual health, HIV/AIDS, information, education and communication. Governments should eliminate specific forms of discrimination that persons with disabilities may face with regard to reproductive rights'.

[260] Mason, *supra* note 104, p. 63.

family planning which could be desired were he or she capable of determinations.[261]

Upon examining practice today, it is evident that each case must be judged separately according to its particular facts. Despite the decision pronounced in the celebrated *Grady* case which took place in the United States in 1979 and introduced a 'substituted judgment' test allowing the full consideration of the parents' view over the incompetent's right to choose,[262] most States have chosen to adopt the 'best interests' (be it medical or social) rule.[263] As a result we have seen courts in recent times rendering conflicting decisions: Some favoured the preservation of the incompetent's fundamental right to procreation such as in the American case of *Skinner v. Oklahoma*[264] and the Canadian case of *Re Eve*[265]. Others have supported the right to choose; and yet others sought to authorize sterilization on the grounds that the incompetent was unable to care for herself or himself, was incapable of adequately caring for a child, or to preserve the physical and mental health of the mentally disabled person in question.[266]

International human rights treaties are completely silent on the issue of the specific rights of the mentally disabled.[267] This being said, the fundamental human rights to dignity, privacy and freedom of expression are guaranteed to all human beings and cannot be restricted by the inability of the individual to understand the meaning of these rights. In its General Comment No. 5, the Committee on Economic, Social and Cultural Rights has pronounced its interpretation of Article

---

[261] *Ibid.*, pp. 63–64.

[262] *In the matter of Lee Ann Grady* (1979), as cited in Mason, *supra* note 104.

[263] *Ibid.*, p. 64.

[264] *Skinner v. Oklahoma* (1942), as cited in Mason, *supra* note 104.

[265] *Re Eve* (1981) and (1987), as cited in Mason, *supra* note 104.

[266] As found, for example, in Canada in the case of *K and Public Trustee* (1985) and in the United Kingdom in *T v. T* (1988), as cited in Mason, *supra* note 104. A report by the WHO points out that the legislation of a number of countries considers induced abortion to be appropriate on these same grounds. See UN, *supra* note 108, paragraph 108. By extension, it could be concluded that general State practice worldwide demonstrates these as suitable grounds for sterilization.

[267] The only response to this issue by a UN body was in the form of the Principles for the Protection of Persons with Mental Illness and for the Improvement of Mental Health Care adopted by the UN General Assembly resolution 46/119 of 17 December 1991. However, like the ethical provisions issued by the Commonwealth Medical Association (arguably the authoritative figure in ethical research standards), sterilization is expressly prohibited on the mentally impaired as a treatment for mental illness.

10 of the CESCR with respect to persons with disabilities, stating that it implies the right of persons with disabilities, including mental disabilities, to marry and to have their own family, and that this right includes 'access to necessary counselling services'.[268] With reference to the Standard Rules on the Equalization of Opportunities for Persons with Disabilities, the Committee goes on to state that such persons should not be denied the opportunity to experience their sexuality 'in both the recreational and the procreational contexts . . . [and that b]oth the sterilization of, and the performance of an abortion on, a woman with disabilities without her prior informed consent are serious violations of article 10(2)'.[269]

In effect, the principle which should, and appears to, be applied in domestic courts is similar to that applied in the Children's Convention. As discussed above, the Children's Convention establishes a principle of gradated assessment, with the rights and choices of children given greater consideration as their capacities and maturity are judged to increase. A clause is attached to each of the provisions: any decision made for the child who is judged incapable of fully comprehending the implications of the decision shall always be taken with the best interests of the child in mind. The same appreciation of capacities of the mentally disabled person must take place on an individual basis and every decision taken regarding the need for sterilization should ultimately be in the best interests of the individual in the context of the environment in which he or she lives. Consequently, to the extent that mentally disabled persons are capable of exercising the right to reproductive choice, they are beneficiaries of this right.

3.5 Individuals with Hereditary Illnesses

A clearer case of violation of the right to reproductive choice arises in the event of forced sterilization of individuals born with birth defects or persons with hereditary diseases. While the Republic of China is not the only State to practice forced sterilization of the disabled, the State has recently come under close scrutiny, following the implementation of the Eugenics Law in June of 1994. As discussed earlier in this Chapter, the Chinese Eugenics Law bans marriage between couples likely to pass on genetic deficiencies and certain diseases, including

---

[268] General Comment No. 5. UN, Committee on Economic, Social and Cultural Rights, Report on the Tenth and Eleventh Sessions, Economic and Social Council, Official Records, 1995, Supplement No. 3 (E/1995/22), pp. 99–109.

[269] *Ibid.*, paragraph 31.

hepatitis, in view of the 'adverse effects on marriage and reproduction'; and those already married are forced to undergo sterilization. China is a Party to the Women's Convention which implies the right to found a family. Given that it is uncertain that these genetic deficiencies are passed on, that a great deal of these illnesses do not severely diminish one's ability to live a fulfilled life, and that the individual is in full possession of capacities to decide whether they desire a child and can responsibly care for it, this Law is strongly in violation of the right to reproductive choice and should be withdrawn. Indeed, at its darkest, this form of non-consensual sterilization may be used as a concealed method of genocide.

As another example, Gruskin highlights the special concerns of women with HIV/AIDS and their choice whether or not to bear a child. She argues that, although there is a 20 per cent risk that a baby born to a woman with the virus will also be infected, the woman's right to dignity and integrity is primordial. While it is the duty of the State to inform the woman of the risk and her choices, she alone has the right to make the difficult choice.[270] In short, while international human rights law does not offer a pre-determined solution in such a case, the fundamental human rights of the individual concerned must always be respected. Hence, the decision of any individual with hereditary disorders who is competent to understand the possible consequences of a pregnancy must have the right to choose notwithstanding the possible difficulties or costs to be incurred. Judging from domestic practice, particularly in Western States, this appears to be the generally accepted principle. To decide otherwise would be to take a step on a slippery slope towards sanctioned State interference in determining the value of any prospective child.

4. OBLIGATIONS OF THE STATE

4.1 Establishing State Responsibility

Article 2 of the CCPR obligates States Parties to *respect* and *ensure* (i.e. guarantee) individuals within their jurisdictions the rights proclaimed within the treaty. If a State fails to respect or ensure the enjoyment of the rights in this treaty, it violates Article 2 in conjunction with the

---

[270] See generally Gruskin, 'Negotiating the Relationship of HIV/AIDS to Reproductive Health and Reproductive Rights', 44 *American University Law Review* (1995), No. 4, pp. 1191–1206.

relevant substantive right.[271] According to general international law, States Parties are free to decide how they implement their international obligations;[272] as Nowak observes, '[o]f sole importance is the result of the implementation, i.e. the respect for and assurance of the rights of the Convention'.[273] By contrast, Article 2 of the CESCR does not contain an obligation to *respect* the rights provided in the Covenant but only to take steps towards their enjoyment.[274] However, while the Women's Convention similarly lacks the *respect* element, Article 2 does stipulate that States Parties must undertake 'to refrain' and 'ensure' non-discrimination through legislation and 'all appropriate means'. Discussions over the possible dichotomy of obligations (between 'to respect and ensure' and 'to take steps') is of less significance for the right to reproductive choice because the right to reproductive choice straddles both sets of rights, with some elements in one or other or both types of treaties. Still, it is of importance to understand the nature of obligations because only by clearly understanding obligations is it possible to establish State responsibility and, therefore, find a breach or violation—and only upon finding a breach may one legitimately consider remedies.[275]

---

[271] See Nowak, *supra* note 68, p. 37.

[272] For example, in a monistic system, such as in the Netherlands, international law ranks above domestic law. International human rights law can, therefore, be applied directly by the courts. Courts can declare void any domestic law or practice contrary to international human rights law. In a dualistic State, international law must be incorporated into domestic law in order for it to be applied. (For more on the two conceptions of international law, see generally Brownlie, *supra* note 52, pp. 32–37). The risk of violation of the right to reproductive choice is therefore greater in dualistic countries as these may fail to recognize interpretations of the right, or fail to implement legislation and other means to secure it within the jurisdiction. The fact that a large number of countries are dualistic (Nowak, *supra* note 68, lists among these Eastern and most Continental European States, and the United Kingdom and most Commonwealth States, p. 54 at paragraph 50) makes the application of the right to reproductive choice at the domestic level problematic in the many parts of the world which have not incorporated it.

[273] Nowak, *supra* note 68, p. 53.

[274] Because of the absence of a 'respect and ensure' clause, the Women's Convention, which arguably embodies the aspirational character of the CESCR, is criticized as a weak instrument without the foundation of 'entitlement' rights to strengthen the rights it proclaims. For specific descriptions of the differences between the Covenants, see: Nowak, *supra* note 68, pp. 56–57, and Romany, 'State Responsibility Goes Private: A Feminist Critique of the Public/Private Distinction in International Human Rights Law', in: Cook (ed.), *Human Rights of Women: National and International Perspectives* (1994), pp. 107–108.

[275] On the subject of State responsibility in international law, see: Brownlie, *supra* note 52, pp. 432–476; Harris, *supra* note 52, pp. 460–599; and Shaw, *supra* note 52, pp. 481–529.

4.2 Negative and Positive Obligations

4.2.1 Obligations of Forbearance. A 'negative' obligation on the part of a State implies that it must not interfere with the enjoyment of a person's right. In the specific context of reproductive choice, the right to found a family, the right to family planning information and freedom to choose 'means that the States Parties must *refrain* from restricting the exercise of these rights'.[276] This entails the commitment of a State to desist or forbear from interfering with an individual's choice on whether and when to have a child. It is precisely in this grey area that a national population policy may disguise a State's violation of the right to reproductive choice.[277] The status of population policies in this context is examined in Chapter IV.

4.2.2 Obligations of Performance. The flip-side nature of a State's obligation is to *ensure* an individual's enjoyment of a right. This 'positive' duty is inherent not only in economic, social and cultural rights but also in civil and political rights. States Parties are obligated to take positive steps to give full effect to the rights.[278] The great majority of the elements of the right to reproductive choice require positive (also known as 'active') acts by the State. The obligation of the State to ensure the realization of the right to reproductive choice 'through law and other appropriate means' (Article 2(a) of the Women's Convention) would imply, for example, taking active measures through the adoption of legislation and policies to make family planning information available and affordable in impoverished inner-cities, to render family planning services more readily accessible to rural populations, or to promote the open discussion of reproductive matters

---

[276] See Nowak, *supra* note 68, p. 36 at paragraph 18.

[277] The elements of the right to reproductive choice as posited in this book which are provided in the Women's Convention (the rights to family planning information and services and the freedom to choose the timing and spacing of births) are not backed by a negative obligation of the State to respect and *not interfere* with the enjoyment of rights (in this specific case) with the founding process of the family. This tandem duty to forbear and duty to perform precisely opens the way for States to employ coercive population policies which are difficult to claim as violations of the right to reproductive choice. Respect for the right to found a family is the 'minimum floor' while the ensuing 'how-to' right to family planning services is on a sliding scale of the State's ability to ensure. In light of this, a definition of the right to reproductive choice based solely on Article 16(1)(e) of the Women's Convention does not suffice to declare anti-natal population policies using incentives to be a violation of this right.

[278] Nowak, *supra* note 68, pp. 36–37 at paragraph 19.

between couples through advocacy campaigns. The Cairo and Beijing plans of action are precisely about this—i.e. States' positive obligations to *ensure* all women and men can enjoy their right to reproductive choice. In other words, the plans of action are not 'what-are books' creating new rights and legal standards, but 'how-to books' explaining ways to ensure their protection. They detail the content of specific agendas, in the form of programmes and policies, to ensure this and other long-existing rights. The conferences themselves are a means to develop consensus on the chapters and verses which should go into the 'how-to books'.

4.3 Reproductive Choice as a Private Matter Publicly Protected

The 'conservative' or 'doctrinal' approach to reading and interpreting international human rights law according to the 'ordinary meaning' of the provisions allows for a more effective protection of the right to reproductive choice because, if the right is spelled out within an international human rights treaty, States are bound to secure this right even if it involves the intimate issue of reproduction. However, some authors have felt it necessary to review the risk of conflict between human rights as situated in the public and private domain.[279] Discussions usually centre on disproving the limitations to certain rights because they fall within the 'private sphere' of the family unit or the couple in their intimacy. Such concerns and discussions are fundamentally misconceived because they misunderstand the nature of positive obligations relating to so-called 'horizontal effects'.

The notion of horizontal effect derives from the notion of vertical effect in which a State as duty-holder is bound to respect the rights of human beings who 'fall within' the State's jurisdiction; the State is conceived to be above and individuals below. According to vertical effects, the State (through its agents, i.e. executive, legislative or judicial branches including enforcement agencies) is to be held responsible for acts attributable to it. However, as in the case of domestic law, international law also holds the State responsible for its omissions. It is these omissions which are likely to have horizontal effects relating to relations between individual human beings. For example, the rights to life and personal security entail considerable obligations on the State to *ensure* (as opposed to 'respect') rights by protecting persons against assaults and possible homicide perpetrated by other individuals (i.e. not

---

[279] See, for example, Romany, *supra* note 274.

acting as or for the State). Concretely, the State is obliged to enact criminal legislation, establish a judicial system and place sufficient police protection in the streets. Failure to do so would be an omission which may have the horizontal effect of one private persons assaulting or murdering another.[280]

The duties of a State Party to the Women's Convention (as any other) to *ensure* the elements of the right to reproductive choice create horizontal effects. This implies that possible or actual interference with any of these rights by one individual against another requires action by the State. As established above, Article 2 of the Convention obligates the State to take the necessary steps to adopt legislative and other measures to ensure the individual's right to reproductive choice is protected or to create the necessary conditions for the enjoyment of this right. Hence, the individual's human right to reproductive choice does not only imply a positive obligation on the State to make family planning methods available to the best of its ability, it's horizontal effects also imply that a husband cannot veto his wife's choice to obtain a method of family planning, and *vice versa*. It similarly implies that a wife cannot appropriate a frozen embryo for implantation without her husband's knowledge and consent. In one case in Colombia, a court ruled in favour of a woman who was non-consensually sterilized after undergoing a caesarean operation and ordered the offending hospital to pay damages.[281] In other words, the State is obligated to create the space for freedom and to provide the possibility of a remedy (whether it be a penal sentence or payment for damage), when the human right of one individual has been interfered with by another.

However, the area which human rights law (and the State) cannot legislate is how couples make decisions on the number and spacing of their children. In this sense, the right to reproductive choice *does* become a private matter between two informed and consenting adults. So long as the couple has been able to obtain the information they desire and make a choice without coercion (whether by the State or by

---

[280] For more on horizontal effects (also referred to in its German equivalent as *Horizontalwirkung* or *Drittwirkung*), see Nowak, *supra* note 68, pp. 37–38, and van Dijk and van Hoof, *supra* note 128, pp. 15–20.

[281] The case *Aracelly Valencia Salazar v. Hospital General de Medellín*, No. 7795, Sala de lo Contencioso Administrativo, Santafé de Bogotá (1992) concerned a woman who while under anaesthesia for a caesarean section was sterilized by the physician without her knowledge or consent, on the argument that the operation was necessary to save her life owing to the presence of internal scar tissue found during the caesarean. The Court ruled on appeal that the doctor had exaggerated the urgency of risk and was wrong to have performed the permanent operation without the woman's consent.

any private party), the State has fulfilled its obligations issuing from the right to reproductive choice. For some, this free and informed choice may include a motivating stimulus, such as faith. For others, the choice may involve negotiating career goals. Certainly, the right does not imply the ultimate superiority of one individual's choice over the other in a couple. However, since coercion is to be precluded, the practical realities of reproduction and the use of family planning technologies may well dictate the relative importance of individual (i.e. the woman's) preferences.

TABLE 3. EXERCISING THE RIGHT TO REPRODUCTIVE CHOICE / IMPLICATIONS FOR THE STATE

	Affirmative choice Implications for the State	Negative Choice Implications for the State
Right to found a family	Free choice to have an initial child and thereby found a family. ***** State cannot interfere (coerce or impede) persons from having an initial child.	Free choice not to have any children and thereby 'found a family'. ***** State cannot interfere with this choice (e.g. by forcing someone to have a child).
Right to decide (freely and responsibly) the number and spacing of children	Freedom to have the number of children desired, provided one is able to care appropriately for them. ***** State cannot interfere in decisions with regard to the number of children desired or determine the number the persons may have (e.g. by employing compulsory sterilization after a certain number, or, theoretically, prescribing a determined number). However, it may question the ability of persons to care for the number of children they desire.	
Right to access to family planning information and education	Persons may access (seek and receive) the information they desire concerning family planning methods and services. Persons may also seek and receive counselling/advice. ***** State cannot impede individuals from seeking and receiving the desired information. State is also obliged to make such information accessible to the best of its abilities.	Persons may choose not to receive family planning information presented or available to them. ***** State cannot require persons to receive such information, even in the context of a preventive health care programme.
Right to access to the means for (methods/services of) family planning	Persons may access and use modern and effective methods of family planning. ***** State must not prohibit or obstruct persons from accessing family planning methods and services. State must provide, to the best of its abilities, access to the means of family planning.	Persons may choose, for whatever reason, to use a particular, or any, method of family planning. ***** State cannot forcibly or coercively enjoin persons to use a particular, or any, method of family planning (e.g. by inserting an IUD into a woman's uterus without her uncoerced consent).

CHAPTER IV

OBSTACLES AND CHALLENGES TO THE FULL REALIZATION OF THE RIGHT TO REPRODUCTIVE CHOICE

1. POPULATION POLICIES

1.1 State Interpretations of 'Responsible' Reproductive Choice

The full realization of the right to reproductive choice requires implementation at the domestic level based on the good will of States to respect their international obligations. This is essentially a matter of government policy. A population policy is a 'formal statement by a government of perceived national demographic problems, solutions and desired goals . . . together with an organizational plan of implementation'.[282] It is an explicit attempt by a State to influence the population growth rate. Some States maintain that there is no necessary conflict between a population policy and respect for the right to reproductive choice. While this may be true in some cases, a fragile balance must be struck to ensure the personal choices of individuals regarding their fertility is not coerced, obstructed or denied, as discussed in Chapter III. This requires avoiding too little or too much State intervention: both can infringe upon the individual's right to reproductive choice by failing to offer adequate family planning information and services or paying disproportionately large respect to the collective good of the community.

A significant success of the Cairo ICPD was in the recognition that population policies must become more 'human'. Although the sovereign right of States to establish their own population and development policies was reiterated, two important changes in the approaches of these policies were endorsed. The first appeal, launched by Algeria speaking on behalf of the Group of 77 and China, involved changing the focus of population policies so that these would be centred on human beings rather than numbers. This approach was widely

---

[282] Dixon-Mueller, *supra* note 47, p. 15.

recognized as essential. The second discussion resulted in a call for integration. In order to be fully effective, population policies and programmes would have to be amply integrated into the wider context of an overall strategy for sustainable development.[283] Germany, speaking for the European Union, said there were encouraging signs that States were moving 'away from the earlier emphasis on demography and population control to a focus on sustainable development including sustainable consumption and production patterns, mutual and individual rights and responsibilities, women's rights and the freedom to choose in particular with regard to child spacing and reproductive health'.[284] Whether this is true and will continue to be so depends again on the will of the State and the effective monitoring of national policies in the context of human rights.

Another important development in Cairo was that States acknowledged the risks of using social and economic incentives and disincentives in national family planning schemes. Consensus held that the overriding principle was that family planning programmes should aim to enable couples and individuals to exercise their right to reproductive choice, and it was stressed that experience demonstrated that programmes which respected this right were inevitably the most successful in reducing fertility.[285] This view was also expressed by the United Nations Population Fund, which has had decades of experience with population policy-making.[286] A population policy should, therefore, not only refrain from violating the right to reproductive choice, but expand the opportunities for its full enjoyment. Ghana's Population Policy serves as an excellent example. According to Article 5.14 of the State's policy, the Government of Ghana:

> ... emphasizes that the opportunity to decide the number and spacing of children is a basic human right and this includes right of access to relevant information, advice, and the means to prevent or postpone conception.[287]

However, despite acquired wisdom and the obligations of States Parties

---

[283] See Cairo Programme of Action, paragraphs 3.5–3.9 and 3.27.

[284] UN, *supra* note 226, p. 4.

[285] Cairo Programme of Action, paragraph 7.12. See also paragraph 13.1.

[286] According to its Executive Director, Nafis Sadik, coercion is 'not only incompatible with democratic values and human rights but it is ineffective in the long run'; Sadik, *supra* note 93, p. 34.

[287] Regional Institute for Population Studies, *Ghana Population Policy* (1969).

to the instruments securing the right to reproductive choice, a number of States resort to population policies which implement coercive methods to ensure the greatest number of users of modern contraceptives and, consequently, small family sizes.

The use of coercion worldwide in regard to fertility and reproduction has become more public in recent years. Coercion takes many forms. For example, in its General Recommendation No. 19, CEDAW called for States to take measures to prevent coercion by 'ensur[ing] that women are not forced to seek unsafe medical procedures such as illegal abortion because of the lack of appropriate services in regard to fertility control'.[288] In its General Recommendation No. 21, CEDAW condemned 'coercive practices which have serious consequences for women, such as forced pregnancies, abortions or sterilization'.[289] Other charges of coercion have been made describing violations of the right to reproductive choice of individuals who are 'persuaded, tricked or coerced into accepting contraception or sterilization by over-zealous family planning promoters in the absence or truly informed consent'.[290] The most well-documented of these have been in Asia and involve such allegations as:

— mass sterilization camps established by the government of India (financial incentives are offered to both sterilization recruiters and the potential clients, mostly women, and village sterilization quotas must be filled). Millions of people in the country (many allegedly rounded up by police against their will) were sterilized in a six-month period;[291]

— NORPLANT 'safaris' in Indonesia, operations in which family planning personnel, accompanied by soldiers, enter a village, gather the populace and expound the virtues of family planning, often with an implied threat that the village would be punished if family planning methods were not adopted. These safaris typically

---

[288] General Recommendation No. 19, paragraph 24 (m); for full text of the recommendation see UN, Report of the Committee on the Elimination of Discrimination against Women, Eleventh Session, General Assembly, Official Records, Forty-seventh Session, Supplement No. 38 (A/47/38), pp. 1–6.

[289] General Recommendation No. 21, paragraph 22; for full text of the recommendation see *supra* note 154.

[290] Dixon-Mueller, *supra* note 47, p. 19.

[291] See Boland et al., *supra* note 140, p. 100. Also Bok, *supra* note 101, p. 21.

resulted in village women's mass acceptance of NORPLANT.[292]

By far the greatest criticism has been levelled against China's population policy. Despite official denials, coercion plays an even greater role in family planning programmes in China. Confronted with a huge population (22 per cent of the world's total population), a limited amount of arable land and unbalanced economic development, the Chinese Government made family planning a fundamental national policy in 1979.[293] Chinese officials feared that, without the policy, the population could reach 1.2 billion by the year 2000.[294] Much of the coercion reported to be used to enforce this policy is psychological: women are monitored, usually on a monthly basis, at the workplace and in community clinics to ensure that the contraception used remains effective and to monitor early signs of pregnancy; and couples must seek the permission of their watchful *danwei*s (units composed of older women from the community) to have a child.[295] The coercion is coupled with implicit or explicit threats of physical force.[296] Such pressure ensures that women use contraceptives (primarily intra-uterine devices [IUDs] which they are forbidden to remove[297] and evidently cannot remove on their own), are sterilized, or if they are pregnant and already have a child, undergo an abortion.[298]

In view of these multiple forms of coercion which have been documented, coercion could best be defined as the imposition of force by pressure or threat and incentives or disincentives that may compromise voluntary choice in matters of reproduction.

---

[292] A report issued by the National Family Planning Co-ordinating Board in 1993 indicated that most acceptors were not told that NORPLANT could be removed before five years, while only half received a physical examination before insertion; see Boland et al., *supra* note 140, p. 99.

[293] China Population Information and Research Centre, 'The Population of China: Problems and Strategies', 9 *China Population Today* (1992), No. 4, p. 1.

[294] *Ibid.*, p. 3.

[295] See Kane, *The Second Billion: Population and Family Planning in China* (1987), particularly p. 41.

[296] For more discussion, refer to Chapter VII below on asylum cases based on physical threats to control reproduction.

[297] Doctors found removing IUDs may face fines and incarceration; see Boland et al., *supra* note 140, p. 98.

[298] *Ibid.*

1.2 The Use of Incentives for 'Responsible' Decision-Making

Incentives and disincentives used to encourage responsible reproductive decision-making have been adopted the world over to reinforce pro- or anti-natalist policies. A spectrum of incentives and disincentives exist and it is worthwhile questioning whether some are more 'human-rights-friendly' (i.e. compatible with international human rights law) than others. Incentive programmes which have been employed include:

(a) direct and immediate payments in cash or in kind (e.g. clothes or food) to acceptors, doctors, recruiters or communities;
(b) expanded maternity benefits;
(c) priorities in housing and medical care;
(d) first choice in the selection of schools.

These are generally employed in Asia, particularly in China.[299] Disincentives, or 'negative incentives', penalize those who engage in fertility behaviour beyond a specified limit.[300] Examples include:

(a) docking of wages;
(b) deferral of promotions;
(c) denial or withdrawal of paid maternity leave or allowances;
(d) imposition of levies on family income for unauthorized children.[301]

In implementing these programmes, recruiters who do not meet their quotas often risk being fired from their jobs, forfeiting promotions or losing income; not surprisingly, they are sorely tempted to pressure clients or falsify reports.[302]

Although not immediately obvious, positive incentives exist in much of the developed world with low fertility, both as a social and economic package supporting individuals during and after the child is

---

[299] Freedman and Isaacs, *supra* note 51, p. 25.

[300] Lieberson, *supra* note 50, p. 81.

[301] (a), (b), and (c) are particularly employed in China. See Salaff, 'The Right To Reproduce: The People's Republic of China', in: Spicker et al. (eds.), *The Contraceptive Ethos* (1987), p. 124. Also *ibid.*, p. 79.

[302] As evidenced in India; see Warwick, *Bitter Pills* (1982), p. 198.

born and as an incentive to bear children.[303] In States which have made the demographic transition to low fertility, pro-natalist population policies are often adopted on the reasoning that the absence of population replacement poses a threat to the socio-economic standards of the State—an increasingly smaller population of labourers are unable to pay for the needs of a growing aging population.[304] However, given the general wealth of individuals living in these countries, positive incentives are less likely to influence their choice of the number of children they wish to have,[305] and certainly not to the extent disincentives would influence very poor individuals to not have more children. While it is more difficult in the circumstance of wealthier States offering positive incentives for larger families to reason that the incentives are based on the individual's 'responsibility' to the community, this may be only tenable in the extreme where the survival of the community is at stake. However, even in this case, such a political or moral responsibility could never become a legal obligation. In this case, the 'incentive' would be coercive.

Opposition to incentives to encourage 'responsible' family planning has increased in recent years. As one author states, incentive and disincentive schemes are 'inevitably discriminatory in societies characterized by unequal distribution of resources because they appear coercive to some individuals or groups but trivial or beneficial to others'.[306] When incentives such as food and clothing are of such importance to survival for very poor individuals, 'free' choice becomes an illusion.[307] This opinion is reaffirmed by Hartman who recognizes that, although incentives are ostensibly voluntary (people can choose to accept or reject them), 'such views display a fundamental ignorance of the social context in which incentives are introduced . . . For people

---

[303] As an example, in Finland the payment of the maternity allowance begins even before a child is born. It continues as 'parenthood allowance', which may be followed by the 'child home care allowance', payable until the child is three. A further child care allowance is also available from this point onwards, depending on the individual situation. KELA (Social Insurance Institution, Government of Finland), *A Guide to Benefits* (1994).

[304] For a more detailed discussion, see Meredith and Thomas, *Planned Parenthood in Europe: A Human Rights Perspective* (1986), particularly p. 15.

[305] However, persons living at or below the poverty line in States where social security systems provide larger homes and/or more social benefits according to the number of children they have may well be influenced in their reproductive decision-making.

[306] Dixon-Mueller, *supra* note 47, p. 20.

[307] LC Working Group on Human Resources, *Women, Human Rights and Reproduction* (1990), p. 9.

who are desperately poor, there is no such thing as free choice'.[308] Incentives, she adds, not only do very little to change people's basic attitudes to family planning, they make it a negative experience.[309]

Lieberson, on the other hand, concludes that positive incentives are morally permissible, provided that other means of solving the population problem have been tried and failed. He and others contend that, in poor areas, payments in cash or kind enable individuals to exercise choices that would have otherwise been beyond their means, effectively enhancing their right to reproductive choice.[310]

In conclusion, it seems evident that any form of disincentive is intimidating and ultimately coercive, leaving individuals with no real choice in their fertility matters. Population policies which employ such methods to promote family planning are clearly contrary to international human rights law. However, it is extremely difficult to conclude that incentives are inherently coercive and, therefore, it becomes difficult to claim that such policies are in violation of human rights. Much turns on the specific facts. In any case, if we truly want to promote human rights and grapple with the population explosion, policies must confront the issues facing individuals when they make their choice. Offering incentives alone and ignoring the bigger issues such as absence of social security or employment not only renders the individual's right to choose illusory but also raises the spectre of other negative effects on the quality of life.

2. CULTURAL AND RELIGIOUS NORMS

The Women's Convention condemns traditional customs and practices,[311] and socio-cultural norms[312] which maintain discrimination against women, the superiority of one sex over the other and stereotyp-

---

[308] Hartman, *supra* note 46, pp. 65–66.

[309] *Ibid.*, p. 67.

[310] Lieberson, *supra* note 50, pp. 80–81.

[311] Article 2(f) of the Convention provides that States Parties shall undertake '[t]o take all appropriate measures, including legislation, to modify or abolish existing laws, regulations, customs and practices which constitute discrimination against women'.

[312] Article 5 provides 'States Parties shall take all appropriate measures: (a) To modify the social and cultural patterns of conduct of men and women, with a view to achieving the elimination of prejudices and customary and all other practices which are based on the idea of the inferiority or the superiority of either of the sexes or on the stereotyped roles for men and women'.

ing of social roles. Yet customary beliefs in male privilege and female inferiority are prevalent in many societies.

Custom and culture are of particular concern with respect to reproductive choice as the reproductive behaviour of individuals and couples has traditionally been shaped by implicit (if not explicit) societal signals and rules.[313] Social prescriptions or proscriptions which create conditions for, even if they do not require, high fertility, include those which:

— disapprove of certain forms of sexual expression or family planning methods;
— encourage early or universal marriage for girls;
— attribute greater social status to women and men who have children;
— accord a greater degree of respectability and wisdom to men in the community according to their number of children;
— assess the wealth of individuals according to the size of their families;
— restrict social roles for women and men;
— support patriarchal traditions which limit women's choices and access to family planning methods and services;
— encourage polygyny;
— promote the birth of sons.[314]

Such cultural requirements can be psychologically coercive and frustrate the individual's reproductive freedom and choice.

The manner in which these beliefs influence reproductive decisions can be so deeply rooted that many consider it unrealistic to believe that

---

[313] Demeny, 'Human Rights in a Changing Political and Socio-Economic Environment', in: UN, *Population and Human Rights: Proceedings of the Expert Group Meeting on Population and Human Rights, Geneva, 3–6 April, 1989* (1990), p. 75.

[314] For an excellent description of cultural norms which negatively impact upon the reproductive choice of women (including some of these listed) in the particular context of African society, see Adjetey, *supra* note 66, particularly pp. 1355–1364. It is important to note that, while most studies on the influence of socio-cultural norms on reproduction have focused on women as the 'victim' of socially-incited discrimination, men also are socially 'coerced' into culturally-prescribed patterns of reproductive behaviour, some of which are apparent in the present list. However, the starting point must be to abolish customary practices which prejudice women as the 'inferior sex'. For a broad discussion on the negative impact of culturally-stereotyped roles for women, see generally Chapter IV, Cairo Programme of Action, and paragraph 4.1 specifically for a discussion on reproduction and gender relations.

the ratification of a treaty such as the Women's Convention would lead to changes in these customary traditions.[315] The extent to which a *free* decision can truly be made in light of the economic, social and religious pressures which come into play is a valid concern. As one sociologist explains, the impact of contraceptive use or controlled fertility on a woman's relations with her kin is often significant: a woman whose reproductive behaviour is seen as 'deviant' may have her position within her new-found family threatened.[316] Seeking contraceptive services, failing to produce children, or failing to produce the appropriate number of children (particularly sons) can cause stress within the family, while fulfilling the reproductive expectations of the kin group may bring support and satisfaction—a feeling of 'belonging'.[317] Correa and Petchesky also recognize this influence, pointing out that a 'social model of human behaviour does not assume that individuals make decisions in a vacuum or that reproductive "choices" are equally "free" for everyone'.[318] A study of customs in the Sahel similarly found that women have minimal choice as to whether or when to bear a child. In this culture, large families are highly esteemed, and the social and religious pressures to bear children are great.[319] In such circumstances, many women who might choose to use family planning methods do not seek services out of fear for social stigmatization.[320]

Khushalani examines the role of human rights in the traditional communities and customs of Asia and Africa. In his view, traditional cultures do not view the individual as autonomous or possessed of rights superior to society; the individual is conceived as a part of a greater whole, a 'group' within which one has a defined role and status.[321] In traditional Asia and Africa there is no dichotomy between

---

[315] Indeed, even in instances where women and men have equal status before the law, custom holds firm. An example of this is Bangladesh where, although the Constitution ensures equality of the sexes, custom shapes the lives of men and women according to a patriarchal, patrilineal and patrilocal social system: a woman's reproductive role is thus strongly prescribed by social, cultural and religious traditions. See World Bank, *Poverty Reduction Handbook* (1992), pp. 2–13.

[316] Dixon-Mueller, *supra* note 47, pp. 113–115.

[317] *Ibid.*, p. 120.

[318] Correa and Petchesky, *supra* note 234, p. 111.

[319] Boye et al., 'Marriage Law and Practice in the Sahel', 22 *Studies in Family Planning* (1991), No. 6, pp. 347–348.

[320] *Ibid.*, p. 348.

[321] Khushalani, 'Human Rights in Asia and Africa', in: Snyder and Sathirathai (eds.), *Third World Attitudes Toward International Law* (1987), p. 322.

individual and society—in contrast with the Western emphasis on individual rights vis-à-vis the State. This, he and others claim, is the source of conflict in Western-oriented international standards which deal with human rights, presumably including the right to reproductive choice.[322]

Another survey of human rights in Africa cites a view held by many African leaders that the notion of human rights is incompatible with the very essence of African cultures.[323] Indeed, some leading African politicians (notably male) denounce internationally established norms of gender equality rights as 'un-African' and claim that 'phenomena such as authority and equality for women are alien to African cultures'.[324] Such views are, of course, difficult to reconcile with international undertakings. Sullivan expresses the same concern and points out the difficulty in altering discriminatory cultural norms in such societies where the political and social processes in which 'cultural' values are articulated often exclude women.[325]

Conservative interpretations of various religious doctrines proclaim the sanctity of the act of sexual intercourse as an act of love between a husband and wife, and a pregnancy resulting from this act to be the will of God. Attempts to prevent pregnancy are, therefore, against God's will, since the purpose of the marital union is to bear children and raise them in the faith. Those who strictly abide by the teaching of the faith can use only natural methods of family planning—methods which carry a high risk of pregnancy. This leaves the individual with little control regarding the planning of family size or spacing of children. In many instances, religious and cultural beliefs are so closely linked so as to become indistinguishable. This is particularly so when the institutions of government and religion combine. Inevitably in many of these cases 'constraints on reproductive choice are a function of state politics rather than a reflection of religious doctrine', but leaders 'use' interpretations of the doctrine to justify positions on gender and reproduction.[326]

In brief, therefore, culture and religion are sources of behavioural

---

[322] *Ibid.*

[323] Jensen and Poulsen, *Human Rights and Cultural Change: Women in Africa* (1993), p. 6.

[324] *Ibid.*

[325] Sullivan, 'Women's Human Rights and the 1993 World Conference on Human Rights', 88 *American Journal of International Law* (1994), No. 1, pp. 157–158.

[326] Obermeyer, 'Reproductive Choice in Islam: Gender and State in Iran and Tunisia', 25 *Studies in Family Planning* (1994), No. 1, p. 44.

codes which may well conflict with the norms of international human rights. The conflict has been debated in academic, philosophical and spiritual circles for many years. Some progress occurred at the June 1993 World Conference on Human Rights where the resultant Vienna Declaration reaffirmed the international community's commitment to the universality of human rights and condemned religious and cultural practices which restrict the human rights of women. According to the Vienna Declaration, the influence of 'national and regional particularities and various historical, cultural and religious backgrounds must be borne in mind', but it is 'the duty of States, regardless of their political, economic and cultural systems, to promote and protect all human rights and fundamental freedoms'.[327] With this understanding, the Vienna Declaration's Programme of Action regarding violence against women calls for the 'eradication of . . . certain traditional or customary practices, cultural prejudices and religious extremism' which violate the human rights of women.[328] It includes a specific reference to the rights of women to health and expressly reiterates women's equal rights to the 'widest range of family planning services'.[329]

Although cultural and religious barriers to reproductive choice are significant, they are not insurmountable. Declines in population growth have demonstrated that family planning and religion can exist in symbiosis. A host of secular States have experienced successful national family planning programmes despite their traditionally strong social norms supporting large families and the significant role of religious institutions. Cultural and religious (as well as socio-economic) conditions in East Asia, for example, were not particularly favourable to fertility transition. Yet in Korea, where Confucian traditions stress the centrality of the family and the patrilineal family structure allows parents to influence their children's reproductive decisions, family planning programmes have resulted in the decline of fertility.[330] Opposition to family planning based on religious doctrine also appeared in the form of Islamic fundamentalism in Indonesia and Roman Catholicism in the Philippines, yet these barriers were successfully overcome.[331]

---

[327] UN, Vienna Declaration and Programme of Action, World Conference on Human Rights, Vienna, 14–25 June 1993, UN doc. A/CONF.157/23, Part I, paragraph 5.

[328] *Ibid*, Part II, paragraph 38.

[329] *Ibid.*, Part II, paragraph 41.

[330] IBRD, *supra* note 196, p. 18.

[331] *Ibid.*

As An-Na'im rightfully advances, one cannot escape one's culture. Yet it is important to remember *whose* view of cultural and religious values it is that is being propagated.[332] Ultimately, he concludes, religion is human made, i.e. secular, and we *choose* to make it political.[333] The question should then revolve around how to take charge and use (not to be interpreted as 'manipulate') religion as a vehicle of change in attitudes towards reproductive choice with a view to enhancing respect for this right. Religious values and cultural norms which influence reproductive choice may be freely accepted by individuals but cannot be imposed on those who choose not to act according to them. To conclude otherwise would violate the freedom of thought, conscience and religion. But to ensure this choice is real, cultural and religious tolerance on the part of the community is essential. States must recognize their part in ensuring this tolerance and in modifying any laws which effectively support coercive and discriminatory norms. This is particularly so for States Parties to the Women's Convention, given its special emphasis on the need to abolish cultural and religious-based discrimination according to Articles 2(f) and 5(a).

Ultimately, from the perspective of positive international law, the above-mentioned views and difficulties are of virtually no material relevance: if the State has accepted to be bound by human rights treaties, it must respect its obligation. Cultural relativist arguments are, in this sense, possible explanations for sentiments and policies, but they do not constitute permissible excuses for non-compliance with obligations. Moreover, such arguments appear to ignore the regional standards which have been elaborated by States of differing socio-cultural experiences on their own initiatives and under the auspices of their own regional organizations.

---

[332] The diversity of views on family planning under Islam is examined in Chapter V.

[333] Abdullahi An-Na'im, remarks made following a panel discussion on religious and cultural rights at the Conference on the International Protection of Reproductive Rights held at the American University, Washington D.C., 10–11 November 1994.

3. THE COST OF REPRODUCTIVE CHOICE

3.1 State Obligations: The Principle of Relativity

The family of social rights, of which the right to reproductive choice is a part, have often been criticized as 'wishful' rights, or rights reserved to wealthier States. The argument is that social (and cultural and economic) rights require the use of resources whereas civil and political rights do not require resources.[334] Although the indivisibility of all categories of rights are continuously reaffirmed,[335] '[r]egrettably, adherents of opposing schools of thought resort more to catchwords and political sloganism than to serious analysis of . . . social . . . rights as individual, enforceable rights'.[336]

---

[334] Eide, 'Economic, Social and Cultural Rights as Human Rights', in: Eide et al. (eds.), *Economic, Social and Cultural Rights: A Textbook* (1995) reviews this reasoning and correctly declares it 'a gross oversimplification', pp. 37–38.

[335] The interrelationship between civil and political rights on the one hand, and economic, social and cultural rights on the other is clearly demonstrated in the textbook. *Ibid.*

[336] Eide and Rosas, 'Economic, Social and Cultural Rights: A Universal Challenge', in: Eide et al. (eds.), *Economic, Social and Cultural Rights: A Textbook* (1995), p. 17. In fact the Women's Convention is stronger than the CESCR in terms of binding States to a commitment of fulfilling the social rights it enumerates so far as several provisions require States Parties 'to ensure' the stipulated rights. It has been advanced that the obligation on States in Article 2(1) of the CESCR 'to take steps . . . to the maximum of [their] available resources . . . to achieve progressively the full realization of the rights recognized in the . . . Covenant' provides an excuse for States to renege on their obligations on the grounds of 'unavailable resources' (see Eide, *supra* note 334, pp. 35–40 for a description of views on the obligation). This argument, however, does not hold firm in the case of both the CESCR and Women's Convention. The first reason being that in its General Comment No. 3 (*supra* note 121), the Committee on Economic, Social and Cultural Rights discredits this interpretation stating that the 'full realization of . . . social . . . rights will generally not be able to be achieved in a short period of time. In this sense the obligation differs significantly from that contained in article 2 of the International Covenant on Civil and Political Rights which embodies an immediate obligation to respect and ensure all of the relevant rights. Nevertheless, [this provision] . . . should not be misinterpreted as depriving the obligation of all meaningful content . . . [Rather, it] . . . imposes an obligation to move as expeditiously and effectively as possible towards that goal . . . [with the] full use of the maximum available resources' (paragraph 9).

It follows that a State Party invoking an economic excuse must: a) demonstrate a 'lack' of available resources; and b) demonstrate how the lack of available resources prevents it from meeting the minimum core of its obligations.

The same reasoning would apply in the case of obligations in the Women's Convention. Moreover, operative Article 2 in the Women's Convention does not even introduce the notion of a 'progressive realization' and can, therefore, even be said to be firmer in its obligations than the CESCR.

Social rights, however, are not luxury. Composed of both negative and positive obligations on the part of the State, some are certainly more easily enforceable than others, and indeed cost-free. A delicate balancing act between negative and positive duties of the State must be struck, minimizing extremes at both ends of the spectrum of duties. Nowak describes this as the 'principle of relativity', explaining that all duties of performance to give effect to the rights in a convention are to be commensurate with their financial and socio-economic abilities.[337] At the same time, this principle of 'relativity' or 'reasonableness' does not allow States to plead 'inability' owing, for example, to financial constraints. Rather, the specific character (negative or positive) of the obligations must be considered: negative duties not to interfere with a right, for example, generally bear little or no financial cost and cannot, therefore, be easily disrespected.[338] Specifically, the negative obligation of the State not to restrict access to information on family planning methods or to forbear from interfering with an individual's choice to found a family carries with it no pecuniary cost, and thus no excuses on these grounds can be maintained. However, not every State has the wealth to guarantee free family planning supplies and services to all individuals within its territory. It can therefore be deduced that, no matter the level of natural endowment of a State, the obligation of that State to forbear implies a minimum level of obligation to ensure the right, while the positive obligation to perform has no maximum ceiling (e.g., a wealthy State should ensure access to high-technology methods of monitoring fertility). In short, while there is no valid excuse for failure to forbear, judging compliance with obligations of performance is a much more difficult matter since it is relative to wealth.

3.2 Examining the Real Costs

Deliberate government action to restrict reproductive choice may be less of an impediment than the cost of providing the means for reproductive choice.[339] In most countries, the demand for family planning has

---

[337] Nowak, *supra* note 68, p. 37 at paragraph 19. It is to be noted that even ensuring freedom from torture in relation to horizontal effects is necessarily relative since no State can absolutely guarantee that one will never be tortured by a private party performing a criminal act.

[338] For a detailed review of the principle of relativity, see Buergenthal, 'To Respect and to Ensure State Obligations and Permissible Derogations', in: Henkin (ed.), *The International Bill of Rights: The Covenant on Civil and Political Rights* (1981).

[339] Fincancioglu, *supra* note 147, p. 88.

outstripped supply. This gap must be narrowed if reproductive choice is to be meaningfully enjoyed and huge increases in populations avoided.[340] Compared generally with other development expenditures, population assistance represents a small fraction of the development dollar.[341] It has been estimated that the cost of implementation of programmes related to family planning, based on projections on the number of couples and individuals who are likely to be using family planning information and services, will amount to $10.2 billion in the year 2000, and $13.8 billion in 2015.[342] Accepting the figure of 535 million couples using family planning services,[343] this would translate into an annual cost of approximately $20 per couple. While family planning information and services are a major component of population programmes, other components such as data collection, demographic research, policy formulation, population and development planning, etc., must also be included in the total budget, resulting in an expensive 'family planning package'. The above figures underscore the formidable challenge to the international community to muster the essential resources to ensure the right to reproductive choice throughout the world. It is not too surprising, therefore, to find governments in developing countries uneasy with this time bomb. Such funding is not easily found. However, governments and donor organizations must make larger investments and place the population crisis further up on their list of priorities, joining this problem with others such as a clean environment and sustainable development.[344] As one of a number of practical suggestions made at the Cairo ICPD to tackle this economic vortex, international technology cooperation efforts could be made to promote national capacity-building so that 'the local production of contraceptives of assured quality and affordability' could occur.[345]

Overall, government spending on family planning may be double or triple that provided by donors, yet the proportion of overall government budgets going to family planning ranges merely between 0.01 to just over one per cent.[346] Critics are quick to argue that the lack of

---

[340] UNFPA, *supra* note 20, p. 13.

[341] IBRD, *supra* note 196, p. 31.

[342] Figures presented in the Cairo Programme of Action, paragraph 13.15 (a).

[343] UNFPA, *Population Issues, supra* note 6, p. 6.

[344] This link was firmly established in the 1987 report by the World Commission on Environment and Development, *supra* note 22, pp. 95–117, especially at p. 97.

[345] Cairo Programme of Action, paragraph 14.4.

[346] IBRD, *supra* note 196, p. 33.

funding for reproductive health care and choice reflects the marginal position of women in many societies; such gender bias, they rightfully claim, constitutes an enormous stumbling block on the road to a sustainable economy.[347] While successful programmes have been achieved on seemingly shoe-string budgets, it is nonetheless evident that sufficient funding is required if the means to modern (and thus effective) family planning are to be guaranteed.[348] The personal cost to users in many developing countries is so high as to be dissuasive. To pay for contraceptive pills, for example, users in 15 of 24 Sub-Saharan African countries would need five per cent or more of average annual income, and users in six others would pay 20 per cent or more.[349] It is evident, therefore, that public provision of, or subsidies towards, contraceptive methods must be made if individuals are to truly exercise reproductive choice in much of the developing world. Moreover, given the state of financial accounts and available resources in these countries, most of the money is going to have to come from wealthier States if any effect is really to be had.

For the eighteen leading donors,[350] population assistance constituted 1.18 per cent of official development assistance (ODA) in 1990, the last year for which data have been compiled.[351] This was roughly the same figure in the 1980s but lower than the proportion for the 1970s, which was just under two per cent.[352] According to UNFPA estimates, any impact on spiralling population growth will require an increase in donor funding to at least four per cent of ODA by the end of the dec-

---

[347] UNFPA, *supra* note 20, p. 39.

[348] As an example of what this could imply, India, recognizing that it had an obligation to provide maternal health services to the 26 million women who become pregnant each year, set a goal to offer all women a minimum, but essential, package of maternal health services, rather than providing more services to fewer women; The Population Council, *Safe Motherhood Partners: Emphasizing Action* (1992), p. 4. If such a package of family planning services was to be devised, care would have to be taken to offer a variety of low-cost modern methods to ensure individuals were still able to choose effective methods which suited them best.

[349] IBRD, *supra* note 196, pp. 33–34.

[350] Most donor assistance in population comes from 18 countries, ten of which provide 96 per cent of the funds. In descending order of their 1990 contributions, these were the United States, Japan, Norway, Germany, Canada, Sweden, the United Kingdom, The Netherlands, Finland, and Denmark. See UNFPA, *Population Issues, supra* note 6, p. 6.

[351] *Ibid.*

[352] IBRD, *supra* note 196, p. 33.

ade.[353] Not surprisingly, the Cairo Programme of Action calls on donors 'to increase substantially their contribution, in order to meet the needs of . . . family planning and other activities by the year 2000'.[354]

Spurred possibly by the population conference in Cairo, donor agency funding has increased. Leading up to the conference, for example, the United States Government gave $13.2 million to the International Planned Parenthood Federation (IPPF, one of the largest family planning agencies in the world), which was reported to represent only the first instalment of a five-year, $75 million commitment to IPPF; the United States also resumed funding to the United Nations Population Fund (UNFPA) in 1993.[355] Nonetheless, funding still remains relatively small, as expenditure on family planning must increase along with population growth.

In conclusion, States Parties should not be allowed, on the one hand, to claim that they do not have adequate finances or resources to ensure family planning information, counselling and services while, on the other hand, refuse donor assistance for these precise purposes. Sen et al. share this view, firmly believing that States should be 'obliged to provide the enabling conditions'[356] with respect to empowering individuals to make informed, safe and effective decisions about their own fertility. This would be the case in law for those States Parties to the relevant conventions discussed above. Finally, given the realities we face today, there is also a critical need to convince governments and assistance agencies to provide the necessary resources, by demonstrating the cost-benefit value of investment in population programmes both for receiving and donor States.

---

[353] UNFPA, *Population Issues, supra* note 6, p. 6.

[354] Cairo Programme of Action, paragraph 14.8.

[355] 'Family Planning for All', *International Herald Tribune*, 2 December 1993, p. 4.

[356] Sen et al., 'Reconsidering Population Policies: Ethics, Development, and Strategies for Change', in: Sen et al. (eds.), *Population Policies Reconsidered: Health, Empowerment, and Rights* (1994), p. 7.

CHAPTER V

SECURING RESPECT FOR THE RIGHT TO REPRODUCTIVE CHOICE THROUGH THE WOMEN'S CONVENTION

1. IMPLEMENTATION IN GENERAL

The Convention on the Elimination of All Forms of Discrimination against Women is the most significant of the human rights treaties in the protection of the right to reproductive choice. The Convention was drafted, adopted and entered into force in a period of under ten years, placing it among the quickest of all United Nations human rights treaties to be generated.[357] To date, it has been ratified by 151 States and signed by approximately a dozen others.[358] The specific provisions of the Convention are legally enforceable against those States which have ratified it, representing an express undertaking to ensure the right to reproductive choice. States which have only signed the Convention still bear a legal obligation to show good faith by not acting or permitting action so as to frustrate the objects of the treaty.[359] The Women's Convention gives the right complete protection. Specifically, Article 2 of the Women's Convention details the various undertakings of a State Party. However, as Tomaševski explains:

> [a] mere ratification of a human rights treaty does not necessarily mean that human rights norms become operative in a country, but it demonstrates the willingness of the government to accept human rights obligations, adjust its laws and practice to international standards ... At least this is how it should be.[360]

---

[357] Tomaševski presents a succinct chronology of the drafting of the Women's Convention in table form; see *supra* note 209, p. 106.

[358] Information received from UN, New York, Division for the Advancement of Women, 10 January 1996. The listing of the States Parties to the Women's Convention as at 1 January 1996 can be found in Appendix C.

[359] As expressed in Article 18 of the Vienna Convention on the Law of Treaties.

[360] Tomaševski, *supra* note 209, p. 108.

2. THE SYSTEM OF SUPERVISION

2.1 Weaknesses in the Reporting System and Efforts Towards Improvement

The mechanism for supervision of the Women's Convention has many weaknesses. To begin, the number of States which have failed to submit reports to CEDAW is a serious problem. States are required to submit their initial report one year after they have ratified the Convention. Periodic reports are due every four years thereafter. States are reminded of their duty to report one year before the due date. As at 3 February 1995,[361] 135 reports were overdue. Forty-one of the 130 States Parties had never yet presented their initial reports—five of these being due in 1982.[362] Nearly all those received were submitted late. Apparently, this duty is even less respected by earlier ratifying States Parties: non-submissions of third periodic reports outnumber submissions 55 to 29, with only six of the 29 reports received on time. A good number of States are late with two or more reports.[363] Many of the responsible governments claim the reporting procedure to be a burden, yet reporting is one of the few ways by which CEDAW can monitor State compliance with respect to ensuring protection of the right to reproductive choice and all other rights contained in the Convention. To remedy this problem, States which hold poor records in relation to submission of their reports should be made firmly aware of their intolerable lack of compliance. Records of submissions should be distributed as widely as possible[364] to encourage public pressure.[365]

---

[361] All figures cited were counted from the Committee's report of the fourteenth session, Annex IV 'Status of submission and consideration of reports submitted by States parties under article 18 of the Convention on the Elimination of All Forms of Discrimination against Women'; UN, Report of the Committee on the Elimination of Discrimination against Women, UN doc. A/50/38 (1995).

[362] These are: Bhutan, Cape Verde, Dominica, Haiti and Lao People's Democratic Republic.

[363] For example, Brazil, which ratified the Convention on 1 February 1984, has never yet submitted a report despite the fact that three (initial for 1985, second periodic for 1989 and third periodic for 1993) are due.

[364] For example, tables of submissions records could be circulated and discussed at the annual session of the Commission on Human Rights and press releases made upon the meetings of CEDAW.

[365] Cases of non-submissions to the Committee on the Rights of the Child are equally numerous and the fact that most States have still not submitted their reports after three reminders from the Committee shows that alternative, *more public*, actions should be used to encourage submissions. For the listing of States Parties to the Children's Convention

To make matters worse, CEDAW's examination of the reports received has been further delayed.[366] In the past, CEDAW has been limited to a meeting time of two weeks.[367] As a result, CEDAW has been unable to review all the reports submitted:[368] given the large number of Parties to the Convention, it is practically impossible to thoroughly review and discuss each State's report.[369] The information contained in all the reports is thus likely to be already outdated and any action taken by CEDAW possibly too late to be effective. Such a tight restriction on a monitoring committee is found in no other international human rights instrument, and represents the shortest duration of meeting time of all human rights treaty bodies.[370] Moreover, while it is commendable to see new ratifications to the Convention each year, this also translates into an increased workload for CEDAW. The result has been an impressive backlog in the review of reports. After ongoing criticism,[371] and faced with the near futility of the task, CEDAW issued a General Recommendation in 1995 to amend Article 20 'in respect of the meeting time of the Committee, so as to allow it to meet annually for a duration as is necessary for the effective performance of its functions'.[372] Approval is still to be given by the General

---

with late submissions and the number of reminders sent by the Committee, see UN, Committee on the Rights of the Child, Provisional Agenda and Annotations, UN doc. CRC/C/47, pp. 4–6.

[366] For more ample discussion, see Meron, 'Enhancing the Effectiveness of the Prohibition of Discrimination against Women', 84 *American Journal of International Law* (1990), No. 1, p. 214.

[367] According to Article 20 of the Convention, the Committee is only to assemble for a duration of 'not more than two weeks annually' to consider States' reports.

[368] Reports are considered by CEDAW an average of three years after they are received.

[369] At its annual meeting in 1995, CEDAW considered the reports of 13 States. As a comparison, the Committee on the Rights of the Child was scheduled to review seven, the Human Rights Committee five, and the Committee on Economic, Social and Cultural Rights four, each within a duration of over two weeks. If States Parties were to report on schedule, CEDAW would be expected to consider 30 reports each session. See UN, *supra* note 361, p. 15.

[370] See Meron, *supra* note 366, p. 214.

[371] Meron, for example, suggested extending the duration of sessions already in 1990; see Meron, *supra* note 366, p. 214.

[372] CEDAW, General Recommendation No. 22 to amend article 20 of the Convention, in: UN, *supra* note 361.

Assembly.[373]

A third weakness of the system lies in the fact that the supervisory body relies primarily on information from governments which are no doubt reluctant to report on violations for which they may be condemned. Silence or denial, therefore, are frequent. For example, when CEDAW members questioned the limited freedom and sanctions imposed under China's population policy,[374] the representative of the government of China simply recalled the positive role of incentives.[375] In the past, human rights NGOs have been requested by the supervisory bodies of human rights treaties to make informal submissions on the situation of human rights in certain States.[376] Indeed, several monitoring groups are already in place and may serve as excellent sources of information on the general situation of human rights[377] or on population-related legislation and practices in particular.[378] This should be encouraged with respect to the Women's Convention as reporting by relatively non-biased external sources would not only reduce the gap in information on States with long overdue reports, but also reduce the likelihood of government 'cover-up' of human rights

---

[373] Criticism of the General Assembly has been growing for a number of years. CEDAW's final reports are submitted to the Economic and Social Council and then to the General Assembly for consideration. Critics claim that the response of the General Assembly is 'cursory at best' (Jacobson, 'The Committee on the Elimination of Discrimination against Women', in: Alston [ed.], *The United Nations and Human Rights* [1992], pp. 452–453), and that the body does not do enough to support CEDAW's conclusions and initiatives especially in regard to 'failures to abide by the obligation to report, the submission of inadequate report, or evidence of treaty violations by States Parties'. Bayefsky, 'Making the Human Rights Treaties Work', in: Henkin and Hargrove (eds.), *Human Rights: An Agenda for the Next Century* (1994), p. 250. Criticism of this obstructionist approach of the General Assembly was again raised since CEDAW's recommendations to revise the Convention's provision and extend the meeting time as well as to move the treaty-body's place of servicing to Geneva have so far gone unheeded by the General Assembly.

[374] See UN, Centre for Social Development and Humanitarian Affairs, *The Work of CEDAW: Reports of the Committee on the Elimination of Discrimination against Women (CEDAW), Vol. I* (1989), paragraphs 138, 148, 149 and 152.

[375] See *ibid.*, paragraphs 161 and 162.

[376] See Tomaševski, *supra* note 209, p. 109.

[377] One such endeavour would be the preparation of compilations of country-specific situations; for example, see generally Andreassen and Swinehart (eds.), *Human Rights in Developing Countries: 1990 Yearbook* (1991).

[378] The reviews of national population legislation by independent institutes would provide excellent background information. For example, see generally Boland (ed.), *Annual Review of Population Law, 1989* (1989).

violations. The absence of an individual petition procedure allowing the CEDAW to consider individual complaints against States Parties (similar to that provided in the Optional Protocol to the CCPR) is also a major shortcoming of the Convention.[379] Until such a protocol is adopted,[380] the only option left is for CEDAW to seize the opportunity to obtain greater clarification on State performance from the States' delegates at the annual CEDAW assembly.

2.2 *CEDAW's Monitoring of the Right to Reproductive Choice*

Prior to the ICPD in Cairo, the reports of CEDAW demonstrated that Committee members did occasionally take note of references concerning the accessibility of family planning methods and services and the level of reproductive freedom in any particular State. Most commonly, CEDAW members requested further clarification and information on national population policies and family planning programmes.[381] Reports also demonstrated that in a few instances specific questions were directed at States regarding their protection of the right to reproductive choice. In the case of Mexico's report, at the Second Session, for example, the Committee stated that:

> [t]here were other areas that required additional clarification and amplification, such as health . . . No reference was found in the report to family planning, whether a woman had an option in the spacing of the births of her children and whether abortion was legalized.[382]

Nevertheless, the overall quality of reporting on the implementation of the provisions for the right to reproductive choice under the Convention has been unsatisfactory, and CEDAW's monitoring of compliance with the relevant provisions has been poor.

Since the Cairo ICPD, however, the quality of reporting and CEDAW's questioning of State representatives have improved dramatically. At the fourteenth session in 1995, the first session held since the

---

[379] Meron, *supra* note 366, p. 216.

[380] A draft protocol was submitted and reviewed by CEDAW at its meeting in 1995. While CEDAW did not recognize this to be the official draft optional protocol, the document was used as a source of identifying the elements which should be included in a draft; see UN, *supra* note 361.

[381] For example, see UN, *supra* note 374, paragraphs 242 and 255 (Ecuador) or 320 and 330 (El Salvador).

[382] *Ibid.*, paragraph 72.

Conference, nearly every State reported and/or was questioned on some element of reproductive choice.³⁸³ The Committee also issued at this session 'Suggestion 8 on the Follow-up to the International Conference on Population and Development' which, in 'recalling the provisions of articles 10(h), 12 and 16(1)(e) of the Convention . . . with respect to . . . the right of access to family health and family planning education, the right to equality in health care services . . . and the right to equality in deciding freely and responsibly on the number and spacing of children [reaffirmed in Cairo]', requested coordination among all the human rights bodies to promote the effective exchange of information to facilitate the follow-up to the Cairo Programme of Action.³⁸⁴

In light of the above, it is apparent that the ICPD has been a catalyst for action by CEDAW. The improvements in the monitoring system represent a significant move towards ensuring respect for the right to reproductive choice, potentially making CEDAW an effective treaty body for its protection.³⁸⁵

3. THE PROBLEM OF RESERVATIONS AFFECTING REPRODUCTIVE CHOICE

3.1 Introduction

International law allows for certain reservations to be made in certain circumstances;³⁸⁶ reservations are expressly permitted pursuant to the

---

³⁸³ See generally UN, *supra* note 361, pp. 25–120.

³⁸⁴ *Ibid.*, pp. 11–12.

³⁸⁵ Unfortunately, the tide of enthusiasm may be already waning as witnessed at the fiftieth session of the UN General Assembly in 1995. Part of the blame for the historical ineffectiveness of CEDAW lies in the fact that the servicing of the Committee has always been separated from the servicing of other treaty bodies (the Commission on the Status of Women, which services CEDAW, was first placed in Vienna and more recently New York while all other treaty bodies have been serviced by the Centre for Human Rights in Geneva). However, although CEDAW requested the Secretary-General to relocate the Committee and its servicing to Geneva to centralize its efforts with the other treaty bodies (UN, *supra* note 361, p. 13 at paragraph 1), no action was taken either by the Secretary-General or the General Assembly. The Committee, it appears, will therefore remain in New York for an unspecified length of time, despite the fact that Article 20(2) of the Convention allows the Committee to determine the place of meeting it deems 'convenient'.

³⁸⁶ On reservations in general, see: Brownlie, *supra* note 52, pp. 608–611; Harris, *supra* note 52, pp. 751–761; and Shaw, *supra* note 52, pp. 570–576.

Vienna Convention on the Law of Treaties.[387] While Article 2 of the Vienna Convention defines a reservation, 'this definition begs the question of validity'.[388] Reservations are thus considered to be everything from a blight to a blessing in international law.

The Women's Convention distinguishes itself as possessing the greatest number of reservations by States Parties of any international human rights treaty. This is no doubt owing to the fact that it deals with a highly sensitive issue for many States: the position and role of women in society. Although there is evident consensus on some substantive provisions and despite its large number of adherents, so many States have submitted reservations to the Convention that its true success may be questioned.

The problem of reservations came to the forefront in 1986 when the Secretary-General was led to request views on the matter from all States Parties to the Convention. The study proved futile with less than 20 per cent of the States presenting their views.[389] This was undoubtedly attributable to the volatility of the subject matter of the Convention.[390] Pronouncements on the subject by CEDAW created such ill-feeling[391] that by 1988 the CEDAW all but abandoned the idea of taking firm action on reservations to the Women's Convention.[392] In what seems

---

[387] Specifically in Part II, Section 2 on reservations (Articles 19–23).

[388] Brownlie, *supra* note 52, p. 608.

[389] See description of the study in Clark, 'The Vienna Convention Reservations Regime and the Convention on the Elimination of Discrimination against Women', 85 *American Journal of International Law* (1991), No. 2, pp. 283–284.

[390] The approach of CEDAW towards the issue of the human rights of women in Islam gave rise to a hardened atmosphere and unwillingness on the part of some States Parties to discuss the issue of their reservations; see *ibid.*, p. 289.

[391] In 1987, CEDAW requested that: '[T]he United Nations system as a whole, in particular the specialized agencies of the United Nations, and the Commission on the Status of Women, . . . promote or undertake studies on the status of women under Islamic law and customs and in particular on the status and equality of women in the family . . . taking into consideration the principle of El Ijtihad in Islam.' UN, Report of the Committee on the Elimination of Discrimination against Women, Sixth Session, General Assembly, Official Records, Forty-second Session, Supplement No. 38 (A/42/38), Decision 4, p. 80. A number of States, outraged at what they saw as an attack on Islam, and ECOSOC and the General Assembly responded with hostility. The General Assembly even issued a resolution requesting CEDAW to reconsider its decision; see paragraph 9 of UN General Assembly resolution 42/60 adopted 20 November 1987 in: UN doc. E/1987/SR.10–SR.14 (1987). Bayefsky is particularly critical of the General Assembly's absence of support for CEDAW in this and other cases, see *supra* note 373, pp. 249–251.

[392] Bayefsky, *supra* note 373, p. 288.

a meagre attempt to once again tackle the issue of reservations, CEDAW issued a second General Recommendation concerning reservations in 1992 which suggested the introduction of a procedure in the Convention to examine the validity and legal effect of reservations.[393]

With regard more to the subject at hand, several States have submitted reservations to various provisions in international human rights treaties which negatively impact, to varying degrees, on the right to reproductive choice. Those which have not yet been withdrawn are listed in Tables 4 and 5 below. CEDAW, aware of the negative impact of many of the reservations to equality in marriage and family relations, in particular to Articles 2 and 16, tried to resolved the matter in its General Recommendation No. 21 issued in 1993. The General Recommendation contains detailed guidelines on the review and gradual withdrawal of these reservations.[394]

As Table 5 below clearly demonstrates, the interpretive declarations on provisions in the Children's Convention relating to reproductive choice focus primarily on the religious concerns of one Islamic State and three Catholic States regarding the content of family planning information and education. In making these declarations, they clarify the content of education which is acceptable to the morality of the majority. Their compatibility is valid to the extent that the morality they represent is truly that held by the majority of their people and to the extent that the State does not use this declaration to infringe upon the core of the right of individuals to seek and impart the information they desire.

The reservations to the Women's Convention listed in Table 4 all introduce a risk, to varying degrees, to the full enjoyment of the right to reproductive choice.[395] While they are relatively few in number, the grounds on which they are made are cause for considerable concern. For this reason, and because of the importance of the Women's Convention in securing reproductive choice, the content and grounds of this particular group of reservations are examined below. Given that a number of the reservations concern fundamental provisions and appear to be incompatible with the aims of the Convention, the general admissibility of certain reservations is first reviewed. The special matter

---

[393] CEDAW, General Recommendation No. 20, in: UN, *supra* note 288, pp. 7–8.

[394] See the relevant text of General Recommendation No. 21 reproduced in Appendix E, paragraphs 41–49, and in particular paragraphs 43 and 48(a).

[395] As described in CEDAW's General Recommendation No. 21, paragraphs 42 and 43, and in greater detail below.

TABLE 4. RESERVATIONS TO PROVISIONS IN THE WOMEN'S CONVENTION AFFECTING REPRODUCTIVE CHOICE*

Article (content)	Reserving State	Objecting State(s)
2 (non-discrimination in general)	Bangladesh 'does not consider itself bound by the provisions . . . as they are in conflict with Sharia law based on Holy Quran and Sunna'	Germany Mexico Netherlands Sweden
	Egypt 'is willing to comply . . . provided that such compliance does not run counter to the Islamic Sharia'	Germany Mexico Netherlands Sweden
2(f) (abolition of discriminatory customs and practices)	Iraq 'is not bound by the provision . . . reservation . . . shall be without prejudice to the provisions of the Islamic Sharia according women rights equivalent to the rights of their spouses so as to ensure a just balance between them'	Germany Mexico Netherlands Sweden
	Malaysia 'does not consider itself bound by the provision . . . [as it] conflict[s] with the provisions of the Islamic Sharia law'	**

Article (content)	Reserving State	Objecting State(s)
5(a) (modification of socio-cultural gender inequalities)	Malaysia *'does not consider itself bound by the provision . . . [as it] conflict[s] with the provisions of the Islamic Sharia law'*	**
16 or 16(1) in general (equality in matters of marriage and family)	Egypt *'will comply . . . provided compliance is without prejudice to the Islamic Sharia's provisions whereby women are accorded rights equivalent to those of their spouses so as to ensure a just balance between them'*	Germany Mexico Netherlands Sweden
	Iraq *'is not bound by the provision . . . reservation . . . shall be without prejudice to the provisions of the Islamic Sharia according women rights equivalent to the rights of their spouses so as to ensure a just balance between them'*	Germany Mexico Netherlands Sweden
	Israel *'laws on personal status which are binding on various religious groups do not conform with provisions . . .'*	— — —

Article (content)	Reserving State	Objecting State(s)
16 or 16(1) in general (equality in matters of marriage and family)	Malaysia *'does not consider itself bound by the provision . . . [as it] conflict[s] with the provisions of the Islamic Sharia law'*	**
	Thailand *'does not consider itself bound by the provision'* (no explanation)	Germany Mexico Netherlands Sweden
16(1)(e) (equality in reproductive choice)	Malta *'does not consider itself bound . . . in so far as the same may be interpreted as imposing an obligation on Malta to legalise abortion'*	– – –
29(1) (dispute settlement regarding interpretation)	Argentina, Bahamas, Brazil, China, Cuba, Czech Republic, Egypt, El Salvador, Ethiopia, France, India, Indonesia, Iraq, Israel, Jamaica, Kuwait, Mauritius, Morocco, Poland, Romania, Thailand, Trinidad and Tobago, Tunisia, Turkey, Venezuela, Viet Nam, Yemen	– – –
General Reservations	Libya *'. . . accession cannot conflict with the laws on personal status derived from the Islamic Sharia'*	Denmark Finland Germany Mexico Netherlands Norway Sweden

****

(*) Reservations submitted to relevant Articles based on grounds which do not concern reproductive choice are excluded. The information is current up to 3 January 1996, as received from the United Nations, New York, Division for the Advancement of Women.
(**) Reservation by Malaysia entered in 1995; status of objections not yet clear.

TABLE 5. INTERPRETIVE DECLARATIONS ON, AND RESERVATIONS TO, PROVISIONS AFFECTING REPRODUCTIVE CHOICE IN OTHER UNIVERSAL HUMAN RIGHTS TREATIES*

Article (content)	Reserving State	Objecting State(s)
Convention on the Rights of the Child**		
13 (information)	Algeria '... national and foreign periodical and specialized publications, whatever their nature or purpose, must not contain any illustration, narrative, information or insertion contrary to Islamic morality, national values or human rights ...'	− − −
24(2)(f) (family planning services for parents)	Argentina 'considers that questions relating to family planning are the exclusive concern of parents in accordance with the ethical and moral principles and understands it to be a State obligation, under this article, to adopt measures providing guidance for parents and education for responsible parenthood ...'	− − −
	Holy See 'interprets the phrase "family planning education and services" ... to mean only those methods of family planning which it considers morally acceptable, that is, the natural methods of family planning'	− − −

Article (content)	Reserving State	Objecting State(s)
24(2)(f)	Poland *'considers that family planning and education for parents should be in keeping with the principles of morality . . .'*	– – –

****

(*) Reservations submitted to the noted Articles which are based on grounds not concerning reproductive choice are excluded. No substantive reservations were made to the Articles relating to reproductive choice in either the International Covenant on Civil and Political Rights or the International Covenant on Economic, Social and Cultural Rights. Information current up to 1 January 1996.
(**) Only interpretative declarations were made regarding the relevant Articles in this Convention.
(– – –) Denotes absence of objection.

of reservations to the settlement of disputes regarding interpretation is also considered.

3.2 Admissibility of Reservations in General

Reservations to the Women's Convention are permitted so long as they are not 'incompatible with the object and purpose of the Convention' (Article 28(29) of the Women's Convention). CEDAW, however, has expressed its concern that a 'number of reservations appeared to be incompatible with the object and purpose of the Convention'.[396] Yet, how is incompatibility assessed, and, more importantly, can some of the reservations in Table 4 be deemed incompatible with the object and purpose of the Women's Convention?

There are a number of sources which strongly affirm the inadmissibility of the reservations which affect reproductive choice, on the precise grounds that they are incompatible with the object and purpose of the Women's Convention, in particular reservations to Articles 2 and 16, among others. To begin, CEDAW has asserted that, since the *raison d'être* of the Convention is to eliminate discrimination on the basis of

---

[396] CEDAW, General Recommendation No. 4, in: UN, Report of the Committee on the Elimination of Discrimination against Women, *supra* note 391, p. 78.

gender, any general clause on equality of genders are to be considered core provisions which cannot be renounced and, upon reviewing reservations and subsequent reports submitted by States which have placed reservations to Articles 2 and 16, the Committee has pronounced such provisions to be essential to the object and purpose of the Convention and requested related reservations to be withdrawn.[397] No State has so far heeded this request.

According to Article 21 of the Vienna Convention on the Law of Treaties, objections to reservations by States merely preclude the legal effects of the provision as between the reserving and objecting State and do not serve as authoritative interpretation as to what are or are not core provisions of a treaty. However, they inevitably shed some degree of light on States' interpretations of core obligations. Although there are only four States which officially object to the reservations to Articles 2 and 16, this is relatively indicative in the specific case of the Women's Convention since these four States seem to have consistently aimed their objections to the same reservations, indicating a pattern of particular concern and effectively implying a special character to these provisions. The fact that relatively few objections have been made to these reservations overall does not particularly imply that these are not core provisions. As explained in General Comment No. 24 of the Human Rights Committee with respect to the CCPR:

> . . . because the operation of the classic rules on reservations is so inadequate for the Covenant, States have often not seen any legal interest in or need to object to reservations. The absence of protest by States cannot imply that a reservation is either compatible or incompatible with the object and purpose of the Covenant.[398]

Reservations to Articles 2 and 16, as well as the remaining reservations affecting reproductive choice listed in Table 4, can be considered as

---

[397] For example, CEDAW asked Bangladesh to withdraw its reservation to Article 2, considering this reservation to such a vital provision to indicate an absence of genuine adherence to the treaty (CEDAW/C/SR.96, paragraphs 63–101). Also, before, the Republic of Korea withdrew its reservations to Article 16(1), CEDAW stressed that Article 16 was essential to the Convention's object and purpose, and that the reservation was thus incompatible (CEDAW/C/SR.87, e.g. paragraphs 22–25). This view is confirmed in the reading of CEDAW's General Recommendation No. 21 (reproduced in part in Appendix E) particularly condemning States that have entered reservations in whole or in part to Article 16 together with Article 2, thus maintaining the inequality of women in the home and the family.

[398] UN, General Comment No. 24 of the Human Rights Committee, CCPR/C/21/Rev.1/Add.6, paragraph 1, as reproduced in part in Appendix F.

incompatible with the object and purpose of the Women's Convention by a careful reading of binding international law texts and relevant authoritative interpretative instruments. The clearest guidance of this kind can be achieved by reading the provisions on reservations in the Vienna Convention on the Law of Treaties together with General Comment No. 24 of the Human Rights Committee regarding reservations. Basing itself on the reservations clauses in the Vienna Convention, the Human Rights Committee issued this particular General Comment in response to the 46 States Parties to the CCPR which had issued a total of 150 reservations of varying content and scope between them.[399] The General Comment arose out of the Committee's concern that 'the number of reservations, their content and their scope, may undermine the effective implementation of the Covenant and tend to weaken respect for obligations they, and other State Parties, have in fact undertaken'.[400] The arguments invoked by the Human Rights Committee in its General Comment No. 24 can be said to apply generally to the other international human rights treaties given that the reasoning used in forming the views in this Comment can be easily transposed to the other instruments.[401] This is certainly the case with regard to the Women's Convention, especially in light of the fact that the latter vaunts an even greater number of reservations, many of which quite clearly touch the very object and purpose of the Convention.

In General Comment No. 24 it is observed that reservations, when phrased in clear and specific terms, may serve a useful function, enabling States which consider that they have difficulties in guaranteeing all the rights in the treaty to accept the generality of obligations its upholds (paragraph 7). The Human Rights Committee, basing itself on the Vienna Convention on the Law of Treaties has concluded as incompatible:

a) reservations that offend peremptory norms representing customary international law;[402]

b) reservations affecting non-derogable rights;[403]

---

[399] *Ibid*. The figure cited is valid as of 1 November 1995.

[400] *Ibid*.

[401] Indeed, the essence of the arguments put forth represent the logic in the nature of an agreement (treaty) as stipulated in the Vienna Convention on the Law of Treaties.

[402] UN, *supra* note 398, paragraph 8.

[403] *Ibid.*, paragraph 10.

c) reservations to supportive guarantees, given that these then 'evade that essential element in the design of the [convention], which is also directed to securing the enjoyment of the rights';[404] and

d) 'widely formulated reservations which essentially render ineffective all [convention] rights'. General reservations to the entirety of a treaty are particularly incompatible with the object and purpose of a treaty since the State has not accepted any real international rights or obligations.[405]

For the most part, the above 'rules', when applied to the reservations to the Women's Convention in question, equally indicate that the latter are inadmissible. Beginning with the first rule (evidently the strongest and therefore least contestable) it would be difficult, if not impossible, to argue that any of the reservations at issue conflict with peremptory norms of customary law. Indeed, this would be difficult to establish in many instances.[406] It could, however, be easily argued that the right to non-discrimination on the basis of gender (Article 2) is a non-derogable right. Should this right be derogated the entire foundation on which the Women's Convention is built collapses, rendering it impotent.[407] The third 'rule' is perhaps the principal basis by which to condemn the reservations to Article 16 as incompatible given that equality in all aspects of family and marriage are essential supportive

---

[404] *Ibid.*, paragraph 11.

[405] *Ibid.*, paragraph 12.

[406] It is interesting to note, however, that in describing peremptory norms which could theoretically not be the subject of reservations, the Human Rights Committee included the right to marry as one such norm (paragraph 8). This same right is equally secured in Article 16 of the Women's Convention, a fact which possibly lends support again to CEDAW's assessment that the provisions in Article 16 are core provisions which cannot be subject to reservation. Thus, according to the description by the Human Rights Committee of what constitutes customary international law, there may be some manner in which to argue that provisions on the right to marry and, as an extension of the provision, the right to reproductive choice represent such norms (although the reasoning in the General Comment would no doubt be challenged).

[407] It is also interesting to note that the Women's Convention does not expressly provide for derogation. This may be understandable insofar as human rights treaties are so fundamental (pronouncing 'inalienable rights') as to infer some contradiction in admitting any derogation.

guarantees for the general right to non-discrimination.[408] Cook neatly sums up the risk arising from reservations to Article 16, as follows:

> [a] state party that proposes not to be bound by this provision would seem to leave its women in jeopardy of suffering discrimination in the most personal and pervasive aspects of their lives. Accordingly, an unexplained reservation seems to strike at the heart of the Convention's purpose.[409]

Many States have questioned the reasonableness of reservations to Article 16 arguing that it places in doubt the credibility of the commitment of reserving States to eliminate discrimination against women in an area where they are most vulnerable. Others are harsher in their criticism, qualifying a reservation to Article 16 as a substantive derogation from the fundamental object and purpose of the Convention (i.e. to eliminate discrimination against women sustained in family laws) and thus a threat to the integrity of the instrument.[410] Bangladesh's reservation to Article 16(1)(c) and (f), based on the *Sharia* (Islamic law), was a particular source of conflict.[411] As a result, CEDAW expressed its concern that Islamic law discriminated against Muslim women in Bangladesh, with Bangladesh responding by urging 'the greatest caution in using the Convention as a pretext for doctrinaire attacks on Islam'.[412] Egypt and others supported Bangladesh's criticism, accusing CEDAW of demonstrating cultural imperialism and religious intolerance.[413] Finally, Libya's broadly formulated reservation to the entire Convention is clearly contrary to the fourth rule on

---

[408] More specifically in relation to the right to reproductive choice, it should be noted that a number of States have submitted reservations to a few or almost all sub-paragraphs of Article 16(1) *except* sub-paragraph (e) securing reproductive choice. While this is fortunate for the protection of reproductive choice, it also raises the question of whether equal rights to reproductive choice can effectively be guaranteed without the other 'supporting' rights in Article 16 regarding equality in family life and marriage, let alone the general principle of non-discrimination on the basis of gender as secured in Article 2.

[409] Cook, 'Reservations to the Convention on the Elimination of Discrimination against Women', 30 *Virginia Journal of International Law* (1990), p. 703.

[410] *Ibid.*, pp. 706–707.

[411] See UN, Status of the Convention on the Elimination of All Forms of Discrimination against Women; Report of the Secretary-General of 12 September 1985, UN doc. A/40/623.

[412] UN, Provisional Summary Record of the Eleventh Meeting of ECOSOC (Concerning the Convention on the Elimination of All Forms of Discrimination against Women) (1990), UN doc. E/1987/SR.11, paragraph 13.

[413] Clark, *supra* note 389, p. 288.

inadmissible reservations since it is not at all clear what obligations it has in fact accepted.[414]

While this argumentation has not been exhaustive, it should adequately demonstrate that a large majority of the reservations affecting reproductive choice (listed in Table 4) are incompatible with the object and purpose of the Women's Convention and are, therefore, inadmissible as contrary to international law. The only way for this to be rectified is for the reservations to be withdrawn *in grosso modo*. However, requests for withdrawals have met with consternation and firm rejection on the part of most reserving States, as briefly described in the introduction to this section. What then would be the next step, other than passive acceptance of the *status quo*? It would seem to this author that the most appropriate starting point would be to examine the details of the arguments based on *Sharia* law and custom and assess their validity.

3.3 Reservations on the Grounds of Religion

Few States are truly secular. In many societies religion still determines the way in which couples consider their reproductive and sexual capacities, gender roles and fertility. How then does international law deal with the influence of religion upon the actions of the State and, more specifically, upon State action concerning reproduction?

Most of the States which have entered reservations to the provisions listed in Table 4 (as well as many others which have submitted reservations to other provisions in the Women's Convention) specifically invoke *Sharia* law as their reason for the reservations, stating precedence of, or preference for, this law over treaty law in the event of incompatibility or a general conflict with *Sharia* law. However, the fact that the reservations vary somewhat and that States have submitted their reservations to slightly different provisions within the Articles,[415] serves as a first indication that the broadly applied reservation based on *Sharia* law is extremely misleading, with variations in each State's interpretation of Islamic *Sharia* and its codification in domestic law. In the case of Article 2, for example, Bangladesh has made a reservation because the provision 'conflicts with *Sharia* law based on the Holy

---

[414] It is not surprising, therefore, that Libya's reservation drew the largest number of objections—seven in total. Six of these objections cited incompatibility with the Convention.

[415] For a brief discussion, see Lijnzaad, *Reservations to UN-Human Rights Treaties: Ratify and Ruin?* (1995), p. 321.

Quran and *Sunna*'; Egypt because it may 'run counter to the Islamic *Sharia*'; and Iraq because it may bring 'prejudice to the provisions of the Islamic *Sharia*'. Conversely, Egypt and Iraq present a broader view of the *Sharia* in their reservations to Article 16 in its entirety, presenting the argument that their national legislation is more protective of the human rights of women regarding family and reproductive matters than is the Women's Convention: both reason that the reservations based on *Sharia* fall within the scope of Article 23 of the Women's Convention which provides in part as follows:

> [n]othing in the present Convention shall affect any provisions that are more conducive to the achievement of equality between men and women which may be contained:
> a) In the legislation of the State Party.

CEDAW has considered this matter. A reservation based on 'equal' rights as already existing in *Sharia* law, it found, would accord women rights equivalent to the rights of their spouses so as to ensure a just balance between them, in which case the reservation would not be incompatible.[416] However, determination of incompatibility set aside, the logic of these reservations is not evident, since they proclaim, on the one hand, that these rights are already secured in domestic law, while on the other hand, that the provisions for equality are in conflict with *Sharia* law. In attempting to look at such reasoning in a positive light, one can only read an implication that *Sharia* law provides for greater equality between women and men than the provisions offered in the Women's Convention. Yet, this would not cause any conflict: many States provide broader protection of human rights than international instruments confer.[417] But, such reservations demonstrate bad faith on the part of the reserving States because they imply both that the protection offered by the Convention is unsatisfactory and because they place domestic laws above international law. Hence, the conclusions of CEDAW in this respect are disappointing: while these may not be strictly *incompatible* (in the traditional understanding of rules of incompatibility) with the Convention, they are certainly illogical and appear contrary to the spirit of the treaty and of international law in general.

---

[416] For the considerations of CEDAW on the issue, see the discussion in Cook, *supra* note 409, pp. 704–705.

[417] If this were the case, interpretive declarations would have been more appropriate in this respect and would not nullify the legally binding nature of the provision.

Judging from the previous experiences of tackling these sweeping reservations on the grounds of religion, the best, and very likely the most appropriate, solution may be to focus on the lack of specificity of the reservation rather than the issue of religion as the point of contention to be resolved.[418] A reservation based on a religious doctrine in general is, as a whole, not sufficiently specific. Even if every State Party has full knowledge of the Islamic *Sharia*, it is difficult to assess the effect of such a reservation. As Clark points out, this leaves States with 'considerable scope for different judgments about the nature and extent of conflict between the *Sharia* and the law, as there would be in determining the extent of conflict between the Bible and the law'.[419] Indeed, Islamic scholars even hold contrasting views regarding reproductive choice under Islamic law. One author's in-depth review of Islamic Holy literature and the writings of Islamic philosophers leads him to the conclusion that 'there is no verse in the *Quran* . . . which forbids the husband or wife to space pregnancies or reduce their number according to their physical, economic or cultural abilities, i.e. there is no text prohibiting . . . methods of contraception'.[420] In her study of interpretations of Islamic law and their implications on reproductive rights, Obermeyer presents a number of scriptures which emphasize mutual consent and participation in reproductive matters.[421] Muslims of the conservative approach, on the other hand, view reproductive choice as contrary to Islam and retort that standards of rights and choice are being imposed on Muslims by secular and

---

[418] Challenges to the reservations based on Islamic *Sharia* have inevitably given rise to seemingly irreconcilable views over the purported cultural relativism of international human rights, freedom of religion, and the relationship between religion and the State. The following are excellent readings on one or more aspects of these views: An-Na'im, 'State Responsibility Under International Human Rights Law to Change Religious and Customary Laws', in: Cook (ed.), *Human Rights of Women: National and International Perspectives* (1994), for a discussion on the legitimacy of religious and cultural laws within a universal human rights approach; and Bielefeldt, 'Muslim Voices in the Human Rights Debate', 17 *Human Rights Quarterly* (1995), No. 4, for a succinct overview of diverse Muslim views on the human rights rhetoric as compared to Western philosophy and ideology. The latter also makes a relevant point regarding the importance of remembering the timeframe of the ideology portrayed in these historical scriptures (which, for example, traditionally assumes unequal rights between women and men) which differ from the modern idea of universal human rights (p. 596). A study of the Christian spectrum would likely demonstrate a similar variation in views. However, these are not discussed because no reservations have been made on the ground of Christian tenets.

[419] Clark, *supra* note 389, p. 310.

[420] Omran, *Family Planning in the Legacy of Islam* (1992), p. 85.

[421] See Obermeyer, *supra* note 326, specifically pp. 377–378.

powerful States.⁴²² Yet another author concludes that the principles enshrined in Islamic religious texts are beyond the law: no legislative body (including international law) can revise the *Quran* or the *Sunna* since legislation is restricted within the limits prescribed by the *Sharia*.⁴²³

Effectively, the problem lies in the variations of interpretations arising from different schools of thought and religious sects that follow different codes. As there is no central authority or divinely ordained clergy that can declare official doctrine (as in Christianity), there is no such thing as *the* Islamic law.⁴²⁴ Despite the potential richness of interpretation of Islamic law, many observers have found that politically active fundamentalists in the Muslim World make selective use of *Sharia* to legitimize practices which subjugate women. Female genital mutilation, for example, is not found in, or required by, Islamic law, yet it is maintained in many Muslim countries as *religious* custom.⁴²⁵ Obermeyer concludes somewhat differently that constraints on reproductive choice are a function of State politics rather than a reflection of religious doctrine and that leaders often use Islam to justify views on gender and reproduction.⁴²⁶

What one may conclude from all of these diverse Islamic views on reproductive choice is that reservations in a general and thus unspecific manner on the grounds of an extremely broad religious stance are hardly sufficient or acceptable: accepting 'this kind of reservation entails accepting an inappropriate degree of uncertainty about the treaty'.⁴²⁷

What is lacking in the Women's Convention is a provision which ensures the eradication of discrimination based expressly on religion. This being said, both the Preamble and Article 1 of the Women's Convention strongly imply that discrimination based on religious reasons would not be compatible with the object and purpose of the treaty. The international community has also condemned discrimination in this guise by way of the 1981 Declaration on the Elimination of All

---

⁴²² As summarized by Obermeyer, *supra* note 326, p. 41.

⁴²³ Khushalani, *supra* note 321, p. 328.

⁴²⁴ See: Freedman and Isaacs, *supra* note 51, p. 27; and Obermeyer, *supra* note 326, p. 42.

⁴²⁵ See Shaheed, 'The Cultural Articulation of Patriarchy: Legal Systems, Islam and Women', 6 *South Asia Bulletin* (1986), No. 1, pp. 38–44.

⁴²⁶ See Obermeyer, *supra* note 326, pp. 44–49.

⁴²⁷ Clark, *supra* note 389, p. 311.

Forms of Intolerance and of Discrimination Based on Religion or Belief.[428] According to Article 4 of the Declaration, States have expressed their willingness to:

> take effective measures to prevent and eliminate discrimination on the grounds of religion or belief in the recognition, exercise and enjoyment of human rights and fundamental freedoms in all fields of civil, economic, political, social and cultural life.

3.4 Reservations Concerning Discrimination Rooted in Culture

Reservations to Articles 2(f) and 5(a) of the Women's Convention (the only treaty which deals directly with the eradication of discriminatory cultural practices and the enjoyment of reproductive choice) maintain the *status quo* in States which condone cultural norms infringing upon women's reproductive choice. While it may be encouraging to note in Table 4 that only one State has submitted a reservation to Article 5(a) concerning discriminatory customs, the relative absence of reservations is misleading. This is because some States have made broader reservations relating to another provision which effectively includes these more limited provisions. For example, three States (Bangladesh, Egypt and Iraq) refuse to modify legislation which legally permits discriminatory customs to exist by submitting reservations to Article 2 or, more specifically, 2(f). By making these reservations these States can still maintain measures which interfere with access to, or provision of, family planning services, in the name of 'culture'. In each of these States, customs regarding fertility (whether they are truly socially or religiously influenced) are strongly pro-natalist and reproductive choice can hardly be described as 'free'. In this light, the objections by States such as Germany, Mexico, the Netherlands and Sweden (arguing against such sweeping reservations based on Islamic *Sharia* law to articles which seek to eradicate customary discrimination in areas which have a stronghold over women's private lives) seem well-founded and put in doubt the validity of the reservations. The incompatibility of such reservations with the object and purpose of the Convention may be clearly established for the same reasons as described above with regard to religion.

---

[428] Proclaimed by UN General Assembly resolution 36/55 of 25 November 1981; for the full text of the Declaration, see UN, *Human Rights: A Compilation of International Instruments, Volume I (First Part)* (1994), pp. 122–125.

3.5 Reservations Concerning Settlement

There remains the issue of reservations to the settlement of disputes as provided in Article 29(1) of the Women's Convention. An astonishing 27 States (nearly 20 per cent of all States Parties to the Convention) have submitted a reservation to Article 29(1), effectively refusing to negotiate any difference in interpretation with another State or to submit such a dispute to arbitration or, subsequently, to the International Court of Justice. Such a reservation in this particular convention is cause for concern as it offers the ultimate 'escape hatch' since a dispute will essentially remain unsettled and, therefore, entitlements will remain unclarified.[429] While Article 29(1) appears to confer a procedural right, the non-respect of this procedure may well result in a substantive right remaining unclarified and, therefore, possibly not respected. As such, the incompatibility of reservations on settlement can be questioned insofar as they suggest bad faith on the part of the reserving States. Clearly, the large number of reservations attest to the fact that many States Parties to the Women's Convention are not prepared to settle on precise definitions or methods of conduct regarding such fundamental issues as the right to reproductive choice. Lijnzaad astutely points out the lack of consistency in reservations with States Parties placing reservations to certain provisions in the Women's Convention and not to other treaties with identical provisions. As an example, Brazil, Jordan and Tunisia have submitted reservations to Article 15(4) of the Women's Convention but not to Article 12(1) of the CCPR which equally deals with freedom of movement and the right to choose residence. An even stronger example is Brazil's reservation to Article 16(1)(a) of the Women's Convention stipulating the right to enter into marriage, a provision which can also be found in Article 23(2) of the CCPR which Brazil has not placed under reservation, despite the fact that the texts of these provisions are identical.[430] Such inconsistencies strongly suggest discriminatory intentions on the part of the reserving State in clear contradiction of the very object and purpose of the Women's Convention.

While it is easy to state now that an error was probably made in allowing such an important provision to the effective application of the Convention to be subject to reservation, this and the points made above

---

[429] In the case of the Women's Convention, the problem of treaty interpretation *per se* may be even more serious given that disagreement about the compatibility of reservations may imply an underlying absence of accord on treaty interpretation.

[430] See Lijnzaad, *supra* note 415, pp. 318–319.

do not help to solve the problem at hand. As a result of these reservations, CEDAW's hands are somewhat tied and there is relatively little room to manoeuvre in this respect, as evidenced by the cold response to CEDAW's call to certain States to withdraw their reservations. Ironically, however, the body best placed to resolve the problem of reservations to settlement is CEDAW. Therefore, another attempt must be made by CEDAW, with the full support of all States Parties to the Convention together with the UN Secretary-General and the General Assembly, to address the issue of reservations in a serious manner, as difficult as this exercise may prove.[431]

3.6 Strengthening the Women's Convention

One can certainly appreciate that the drafters of the Women's Convention had a particularly difficult task in accommodating all cultures and traditions on such a private and sensitive matter as reproductive choice. However, all these reservations definitely demonstrate a lack of political will to protect and promote the right to reproductive choice. Furthermore, the framework of the Convention as it stands leaves much to be desired and the weaknesses of the Convention resulting therefrom have not gone unnoticed. Nevertheless, and insofar as the Women's Convention remains the best instrument to address the subject, delegates at the 1993 World Conference on Human Rights called for the universal ratification of the Women's Convention by the year 2000,[432] thereby empowering the campaign to eliminate discrimination generally and broadening the protection of the right to reproductive choice specifically. The Programme of Action which resulted from the Conference also made three important recommendations essential to strengthening the implementation of the Women's Convention:

a) encouraging CEDAW to continue its review of the reservations to the Convention;

b) urging States to withdraw reservations deemed contrary to the object and purpose of the Convention or otherwise incompatible

---

[431] Lijnzaad is very critical of CEDAW members regarding their knowledge of reservations and the law of treaties, and suggests a number of practical steps for improvement such as a yearly update on reservations, declarations, notifications and objections relating to the Women's Convention as an essential Committee document. See Lijnzaad, *supra* note 415, p. 368.

[432] UN, *supra* note 327, Part II, paragraph 39.

with international treaty law [the cases of Libya coming especially to mind];

c) directing CEDAW to quickly examine the possibility of preparing an optional protocol creating a complaints procedure under the Women's Convention.[433]

Regrettably, however, the Conference did not advance measures by which CEDAW could be assisted in carrying out these recommendations. Nor did it recognize the need to extend CEDAW's annual period of assembly, provide improved secretariat support or ensure the exchange of information between CEDAW and other human rights treaty bodies.[434]

---

[433] *Ibid.*, Part II, paragraphs 39 and 40.

[434] See Sullivan, *supra* note 325, p. 160.

CHAPTER VI

SECURING RESPECT THROUGH OTHER MEANS

1. OTHER LEGAL MEANS

Although CEDAW has the greatest potential to secure the right to reproductive choice at the international level, other treaty bodies can also oversee compliance by States Parties. The Committee on the Rights of the Child, established under the Children's Convention, is one such body. Under this Committee, the rights of parents to obtain family planning services and of children to information on family planning may be secured through a procedure of State reports similar to that under the Women's Convention. The reporting system under the Children's Convention is somewhat weaker than that of the Women's Convention to the extent that States Parties are only required to report every five years. However, Article 44(2) stipulates that the information supplied must be sufficient to provide a comprehensive understanding of implementation, thus reducing the likelihood of the submission of poor (and effectively useless) reports seen so frequently by CEDAW. As noted in Chapter III, the Committee on the Rights of the Child does keep an eye on the availability and accessibility of family planning information for children.

Turning to the two Covenants, the Economic and Social Council maintains the competence to supervise the rights to health and to education for the full development of the individual in States Parties to the CESCR. This is also principally achieved through a procedure of periodic State reports which are examined by the Committee on Economic, Social and Cultural Rights. The Human Rights Committee, established under the CCPR, is also mandated to monitor the general compliance of States Parties with regard, *inter alia*, to the rights to found a family, to privacy and to obtain information. Unfortunately, there is relatively little information relating to the right to reproductive choice as generated through the supervisory Committees under either Covenant. This may be attributed to three reasons: 1. States generally do not include such information in the reports they submit; 2. expert

Members of the Committees generally do not put questions to reporting States in concern of this subject; and 3. there are very few, if any, non-governmental organizations which actively encourage inclusion of reproductive matters in State reports or Committee examinations. Consequently, good opportunities for supervision of relevant elements of the right to reproductive choice are missed.

The Optional Protocol to the CCPR offers another (and perhaps more effective) mechanism to secure implementation in the form of an individual communications procedure. Due to the controversial nature of such a procedure at the time of the elaboration of the CCPR, it was decided to make the Human Rights Committee's competence over individual communications optional.[435] Still today less than two-thirds of the States Parties to the CCPR have accepted the individual communications procedure by becoming a party to the Optional Protocol. According to Articles 1 and 2 of the Optional Protocol individuals within the jurisdiction of a State Party to the Protocol 'who claim to be victims of a violation by that State Party of any rights set forth in the Covenant' may make a petition to the Human Rights Committee once they have exhausted all domestic remedies. This allows the Committee to consider a concrete case and to render its 'views' with regard to the compliance (or otherwise) of obligations by the State concerned. While such 'views' are not legally binding they have two significant effects. First, in the instant case, the publication of the views creates significant pressure on the State to correct its specific practice by making restitution to the specifically injured applicant and by amending any related laws or practices. Second, it establishes a sort of 'case-law' through which all States may better know the extent of their obligations vis-à-vis similar cases; this encourages all States to amend any laws or policies which would most probably not be viewed by the Committee as in compliance with obligations. Although no claim of violation of the right to found a family or to obtain family planning information has ever been made and, therefore, no helpful views have been rendered through this procedure, the possibility remains open.

While the treaty bodies to universal human rights instruments provide authoritative interpretation and monitoring of the stipulated rights, they meet only occasionally (two to three times a year), for very short periods of time (two to three weeks), and only one has an individual complaints procedure (which is optional). Moreover, their determinations are not legally binding. In comparison, the regional

---

[435] See Nowak, *supra* note 68, pp. 647–648.

treaty bodies have more strengths. Indeed, in several respects it is preferable to seek decisions within the regional frameworks for individual cases or for general issues. The European Court and Commission of Human Rights have been particularly effective in overseeing compliance with the ECHR, particularly with regard to the right to information[436]—which is very relevant for family planning. Indeed, decisions issuing from both bodies are held in high respect and influence understandings within other regional bodies. A system of collective complaints has also recently been introduced under the Additional Protocol to the European Social Charter.[437] The Additional Protocol, adopted 9 November 1995, provides in Article 1 that 'international non-governmental organisations which have consultative status with the Council of Europe and have been put on a list established for this purpose by the Governmental Committee' may 'submit complaints alleging unsatisfactory application of the Charter'. In light of this provision, any NGO with consultative status concerned with health, or more specifically family planning, issues could group similar complaints of violations of the right to reproductive choice and submit a complaint to the Committee of Independent Experts.[438] As more States join the Council of Europe and accede to the ECHR and the European Social Charter and its Additional Protocol, the provisions will apply to more people and there will be greater opportunities to use the human rights monitoring and protection mechanisms. The same is true for the regional systems of the Americas and Africa, although neither is as developed or experienced as the European system.[439]

---

[436] See van Dijk and van Hoof, *supra* note 128, pp. 407–428, particularly at pp. 413–419.

[437] Council of Europe, Additional Protocol to the European Social Charter Providing for a System of Collective Complaints and Explanatory Report (Provisional Version), Council of Europe, Directorate of Human Rights, Social Charter Section, H95_ 8E, 5 July 1995.

[438] According to Article 2, any Contracting State could further recognize 'the right of any other representative national non-governmental organisation within its jurisdiction . . . to lodge complaints'. Consequently, as a purely theoretical example, the United Kingdom could recognize the right of International Planned Parenthood Federation to lodge a collective complaint alleging the inaccessibility of family planning services as a form of non-compliance with the right to health.

[439] For comprehensive examinations of the systems of protection of human rights in each of the three regions, see and compare: van Dijk and van Hoof, *supra* note 128; Buergenthal et al., *Protecting Human Rights in the Americas: Selected Problems* (1990); and Ouguergouz, *La Charte Africaine des Droits de l'homme et des Peuples* (1993).

2. NON-LEGAL MEANS

2.1 Extra-Conventional Mechanisms

Those concerned with legal matters involving reproduction awaited with anticipation the first report of the newly mandated Special Rapporteur of the UN Commission on Human Rights on violence against women[440] to see if forms of coercion in reproductive choice would be considered under the rubric of gender-based 'violence'[441] such as forced female sterilization or the practice of female genital mutilation (FGM).[442] According to the conditions of the mandate, the Special Rapporteur has the competence to receive communications from individuals and to examine their cases. The Special Rapporteur is also mandated to conduct visits to countries where violations are alleged to have occurred and effectively to investigate reports of violations of the right to reproductive choice which constitute a form of violence against women. Having adopted the basic approach of other 'special procedures' of the Commission on Human Rights,[443] and respecting the principle of *audi alteram partem* (i.e. to hear the other side; to hear both sides), the Special Rapporteur may confront States about their laws, policies and practices. This is a particularly attractive form of supervision of State compliance with human rights treaty obligations. Individ-

---

[440] The mandate was created pursuant to Commission on Human Rights resolution 1994/45 of 4 March 1994, as approved by Economic and Social Council decision 1994/254 of 22 July 1994.

[441] For the resolution creating the mandate, see UN, Commission on Human Rights resolution 1994/45, UN doc. E/CN.4/1994/132, pp. 140–145.

[442] Infibulation, practised in regions of Asia and North Africa, is considered a particularly violent form of genital mutilation. Usually at menarche, girls undergo this ceremonial circumcision of the entire genital area (i.e. the clitoris, vulva and inner and outer labia) to prevent penetration and maintain virginity. In rural areas, crude instruments such as unwashed glass and tin-can tops are used. The wound is opened only upon marriage. This practice impacts negatively on reproductive choice when infection or bleeding lead to infertility. For further discussion, see: WHO, *Female Genital Mutilation (Information Kit)* (1994); and Robson, 'Torture, not Culture', *Amnesty International (British Section) Journal*, No. 63 (1993), pp. 8–9.

[443] For information on the work of the 'special procedures' of the Commission on Human Rights, see: UN, Joint Declaration of the Special Rapporteurs/Representatives/Experts and Chairmen of Working Groups of the Special Procedures of the Commission on Human Rights', UN doc. A/CONF.157/9; and the reports of the 1994 and 1995 meetings of the Special Rapporteurs/Representatives/Experts and Chairmen of Working Groups of the Special Procedures of the Commission on Human Rights, UN docs. E/CN.4/1995/5 and E/CN.4/1996/50, respectively.

uals are able to make themselves heard in a direct fashion and action can be swift on the part of the Rapporteur. This mechanism also has the advantage of not being restricted to a specific legal instrument, but addressing general issues on a global scale in a public report and forum.

In her preliminary report, the Special Rapporteur dealt with two important issues affecting reproductive choice: reproductive technologies[444] and the violation of the right to reproductive choice by one person in a couple in the privacy of their homes.[445] The Special Rapporteur also acknowledged allegations of rape and forced pregnancy in wartime.[446] It is of great importance that the Rapporteur has

---

[444] Paragraph 56 reads:
'The area which is particularly relevant to the problem of violence against women in the context of technology is the issue of reproductive technology. Though reproductive technology has allowed women greater freedom and greater choice with regard to the important function of childbirth, it has also created innumerable health problems for women, problems which are often ignored by the medical establishment. These health problems have resulted in female deaths which in other circumstances might have been avoided. Women's access to adequate health care becomes a crucial factor in this regard. In addition, reproductive technology which allows for preselection of the sex of the child has resulted in the killing of female foetuses and selective abortion. The practice of surrogate motherhood which has developed recently has also resulted in the exploitation of the bodies of women from the third world. Modern technology has been the means of liberation and choice for many women, but for others it has resulted in death and exploitation.'
UN, Preliminary report submitted by the Special Rapporteur on violence against women, its causes and consequences, Ms. Radhika Coomaraswamy, in accordance with Commission on Human Rights resolution 1994/45, UN doc. E/CN.4/1995/42.

[445] *Ibid.*, paragraph 70 reads:
'Doctrines of privacy and the concept of the sanctity of the family are other causes for violence against women to persist in society. In the past, the State and the law intervened with regard to violence in the home only when violence became a public nuisance. Otherwise, the doctrine of privacy allowed for violence to continue unabated. The public/private distinction, which has been at the root of most legal systems, including human rights law, has created major problems for the vindication of women's rights. However, in recent times the approach to law has changed. States are increasingly reaching into the privacy of the home. In developing countries the regulation of reproductive rights has become an important concern. States are now increasingly being held responsible for human rights offences committed within the home. States are required, by standards of due diligence, to prevent as well as punish crimes of violence which take place in the private domain.'

[446] 'A further characteristic of this atrocious practice is the use of rape as a method to terrorize civilian populations in villages and to force ethnic groups to leave. An escalation in the atrocities committed against women during armed conflicts is the practice of forced pregnancy and maternity. After being subjected to deliberate attempts to impregnate them, women are detained until it is too late for them to obtain an abortion, in an attempt

recognized in her very first 'ground-setting' report violations of the right to reproductive choice as forms of violence against women. In subsequent reports, it may thus be expected that specific practices will be evaluated in this regard.

As another positive development, the Inter-American Commission on Human Rights appointed in 1994 a Special Rapporteur, Claudio Grossman, to assess the observance by member States of human rights and freedoms, focusing on women alone. The Special Rapporteur is mandated to examine domestic laws that inhibit women's full and equal enjoyment of their human rights as provided in the ACHR. Like Special Rapporteurs in the UN system, this Rapporteur is able to receive individual petitions or complaints which will make it easier to assess alleged violations of the right to reproductive choice against an individual or a smaller group of persons who may find it more difficult to bring a complaint before the Inter-American Commission (which is a more passive and responsive monitoring mechanisms than is a Special Rapporteur).

2.2 The Role of International Assistance

International development organizations, such as the International Bank for Reconstruction and Development and the World Bank, are potentially important players in securing human rights, including the right to reproductive choice, in developing countries.[447] Linking international donor funding (whether governmental, inter-governmental or non-governmental) with State compliance with human rights treaty obligations can be a very effective recipe for the protection of human rights. This can be achieved through both 'positive' and 'negative' linkaging. Positive linkage would be achieved through a wider concept of 'development' where such matters as reproductive health and choice would be included in overall planning such that specific projects would be eligible for funding. By contrast, 'negative' linkage would be achieved through placing conditions on the receipt of aid, trade or participation. In this last case, respect for the right to reproductive choice could be one such condition. Certainly, the promise of the benefits of aid and/or trade constitute powerful incentives to comply.

An-Na'im, a representative of Africa Watch and well-known

---

humiliate the ethnic group of the victim and to "dilute" it'.; *Ibid.*, paragraph 279.

[447] It is worthy to note that one human rights treaty even refers to the possibility of States calling upon international assistance to achieve respect for the rights it sets forth: see Article 2(1) of the CESCR.

advocate of human rights in Africa, reflects on financial aid dependency and equally suggests that aid should be used to ensure compliance with human rights treaties.[448] At the same time, however, many like An-Na'im also criticize the involvement of 'Western' agencies in the formulation and implementation of population policies in the developing world. Specifically, An-Na'im warns that aid should not be related to the cultural or religious views of the donor State where they differ from that of the receiver State. To get around this problem, it would be legitimate for aid, trade and participation to be conditioned with specific reference to the evaluation of an independent third party of universal representativeness, e.g. CEDAW.

The whole issue of conditionality clauses attached by States and NGOs remains contentious. This being said, it is ultimately the free choice of the donor as long as the conditions are not contrary to international law. At the ICPD, the diversity in views regarding the involvement of Western donor organizations in poorer States became more acute: Muslim fundamentalists battled against the 'pharaohs of the *new family order*'[449] and the Vatican sounded the alarm against the promotion of 'cultural imperialism' and the adoption of concepts which 'have been written in a very small geographic area between New York and Washington', concepts which 'reflect the life-style mentality of a certain, small region of the world'.[450] Whatever the validity of these arguments, they clearly represent strongly held perceptions which strike at the legitimacy of standards. In order to respond to these perceptions, it would be best to use an independent third party to supervise the implementation of *positive* international law. Some donor agencies have checkered pasts; clandestine aid and pressure tactics have been accused of contributing to a feeling of distrust within developing countries.[451]

These arguments set aside, international donor organizations are 'ready-made' mechanisms for regulating implementation, although standards must be acceptable to all those involved. Freedman and Isaacs see such standards as already required by international law, stating that:

---

[448] An-Na'im, *supra* note 333.

[449] As described in 'Family, Population, AIDS and Abortion', 25 *Impact International* (1994), No. 5, p. 15.

[450] 'Cardinals Dive into the Population Fray', *International Herald Tribune*, 15 June 1994, pp. 1 and 6.

[451] Warwick, *supra* note 302, pp. 203–204.

> ... if a multilateral institution such as the World Bank is to be guided by any legal or ethical standards when it engages in 'population dialogues' such standards should be fashioned by the international community according to international law, including human rights law.[452]

While such funding would effectively have strings attached, at least the 'strings' would be derived from provisions in international standards and would therefore already be widely accepted. As a consequence, international donor organizations could offer funding on the condition that population policies be implemented in a manner which respects the right to reproductive choice. Care would have to be taken where NGOs are the donor. NGOs, because of the very nature of their existence, are free to formulate the mandate and conditions they desire. The issue becomes hazy, however, when their policies clash with that of a possible receiving State. An example An-Na'im cites is that of the organization Catholic Relief Services which attaches conditionalities to the distribution of financial aid which are based on Catholic principles of contraceptive practices, hence the conditioning of money to comply with certain norms which may not even be those shared by the receiving State. Donor States, of course, do the same thing: Bangladesh's 'menstrual regulation services'[453] were threatened when US AID sought to stop funding, declaring these services to be a disguise for abortion.[454]

Certainly, the idea of conditionality in general is not a new one.[455] For example, since the 1975 Tom Harkin Amendment to the International Development and Food Assistance Act, the U.S. prohibits economic assistance to States with records of gross violations of human rights.[456] In 1986, the European Union (then Community) similarly declared that, henceforth, respect for human rights would be a required element of European development funding for third world countries. If funding by these States were linked specifically to the respect of standards set out in international treaties as *independently* supervised,

---

[452] Freedman and Isaacs, *supra* note 51, p. 26.

[453] For a description of what menstrual regulation services involve, see Dixon-Mueller, *supra* note 189.

[454] An-Na'im, *supra* note 333.

[455] On the subject of conditioning aid or trade on compliance with human rights standards in general, see Kumado, 'Conditionality: An Analysis of the Policy of Linking Development Aid to the Implementation of Human Rights Standards', *The Review of the International Commission of Jurists*, (1993) No. 50, pp. 23–30.

[456] *Ibid.*, p. 25.

then criticisms that conditionality is 'just a way of judging others by one's own standards' could be quelled.

Independent grass-roots assistance by NGOs has so far been the principal way of improving the enjoyment of the right to reproductive choice. International NGOs have been pioneers in the population and development fields. In many instances, the planning and carrying out of population and development programmes have involved NGOs. They have also served as advocates in various States, reminding governments of the human rights issues involved.[457] NGOs should be encouraged to remain active, particularly in the monitoring of population programmes. One NGO, the International Women's Rights Action Watch (IWRAW), serves as a perfect example of the potential monitoring role of NGOs. IWRAW reviews and monitors law and policy changes throughout the world in accordance with the principles of the Women's Convention. Every year it publishes the list of States' reports scheduled for review at the CEDAW meetings and calls for information from individuals on the major problems of women, including limitations on the right to reproductive choice, within those States. It thus offers an indirect individual complaints framework for hearing and monitoring the situation of reproductive choice as provided in the Convention.[458]

---

[457] Sadik, *Population Policies and Programmes* (1991), pp. 245–246.

[458] See, for example, International Women's Rights Watch, *The Women's Watch*, No. 5, Issue 2 (1991), p. 5.

Chapter VII

Expanding the Reach of the Right to Reproductive Choice

1. EXPANDING THE RECOGNITION OF SERIOUS VIOLATIONS OF THE RIGHT TO REPRODUCTIVE CHOICE

1.1 The Recognition of Forced Pregnancy as a Serious Violation

The issue of the right to reproductive choice becomes linked with rape when the rape results in a pregnancy. In this event, a woman's right to reproductive choice is clearly violated, not only because she is faced with an unwanted pregnancy, but also because she has been coerced into a sexual relation which has resulted in pregnancy by physical violence without her consent. In other words, forced pregnancy resulting from rape is an extremely severe violation of a woman's right to reproductive choice as provided, *inter alia*, under Article 16(1)(e) of the Women's Convention. This connection has been established in recent years both in the contexts of armed conflict[459] and marital relations.

---

[459] In his treatment of cases, the Special Rapporteur on the situation of human rights in Yugoslavia specifically referred to the Women's Convention, among others, as a pertinent international human rights instrument which should be considered in this context. See UN, Report of the situation of human rights in the territory of the former Yugoslavia, UN doc. E/CN.4/1993/50, paragraph 74 (Annex II).

At a later date, CEDAW expressed its concerns to the Special Rapporteur and reiterated that rape constituted a violation of international human rights guarantees. This argument was made on the basis of rape *in general*, as follows:

'The Committee emphasizes that rape and other attacks on women's physical and mental integrity and their security of person violate international human rights guarantees, including the norms stated in the Convention on the Elimination of All Forms of Discrimination against Women. In its general recommendation No. 19 on violence against women, the Committee stated that such violence is a form of discrimination prohibited by the Convention and that such violence breaches the duty to ensure the equal protection of humanitarian norms in time of international or internal armed conflict or civil strife.' UN, Rape and abuse of women in the territory of the former Yugoslavia: Report of the Secretary-General, UN doc. E/CN.4/1994/5, paragraphs 20–22, in particular paragraph 21.

1.1.1 The Context of Armed Conflicts. The issue of forced pregnancy through rape as a tactic of warfare and as a war crime has been addressed extensively in the context of the recent war in the former Yugoslavia[460] and in the conflict in Rwanda.[461] In both the cases of the conflicts in the former Yugoslavia and Rwanda, rape is expressly considered as a breach of international humanitarian law and a crime against humanity in certain circumstances.[462]

In order to prove a violation of the express right to reproductive choice in the circumstance of rape, it would appear necessary to prove that pregnancy resulted from rape. The team of experts created to investigate allegations of rape in the territory of the former Yugoslavia was subsequently able to identify 119 pregnancies resulting from rape during 1992,[463] although a strong argument was made that the number of rapes resulting in pregnancy was considerably higher due to under-reporting.[464] A large majority of these pregnancies ended in abortion. In at least one case the verbal intention of the aggressors was to forcibly impregnate their victim, and ensure that she would not seek to abort the foetus,[465] leaving her no choice but to bear the child

---

[460] See UN doc. E/CN.4/1994/5, *ibid.*, paragraphs 16–17.

[461] The international war crimes tribunal for Rwanda likewise includes rape among offenses over which it has competence. For the mandate of this tribunal, see: UN Security Council resolution 955 (1994) adopted at its 3453rd meeting on 8 November 1994, particularly Articles 2 (on the definition of genocide) and 6 (on individual criminal responsibility), as well as: UN, Security Council, Final Report of the Commission of Experts Established Pursuant to Security Council Resolution 935 (1994), UN doc. S/1994/1405 generally.

[462] See: reports on former Yugoslavia, UN doc. E/CN.4/1994/5, *supra* note 459, paragraphs 16–17; and report on Rwanda, UN, *supra* note 461, paragraphs 137–143.

[463] UN doc. E/CN.4/1993/50, *supra* note 459, paragraph 9.

[464] According to the report, 'Virtually all interviewed physicians and health workers felt that the reporting of rape resulting in pregnancy would be far lower than its actual occurrence due to the profound emotional pain and stigma associated with rape. Indeed, it had become express policy for some medical personnel not to inquire of women requesting abortions whether they had been raped'; *ibid.*, paragraphs 22–24, and particularly paragraph 29. Moreover, the team of experts found a significant rise in the number of total abortions performed in the territory of the former Yugoslavia, an increase which may be attributed to the rise in the number of pregnancies resulting from rape; see *ibid.*, paragraphs 15–21.

[465] One ethnic Croat woman who was detained in a Serb-controlled camp reported that, while raping her, the men shouted 'you will have a Serbian child' and they then told her that, if she were pregnant, she would be 'forced to stay until six months pregnancy': see *ibid.*, paragraph 41. The only intention which can be clearly deduced from this is that the aggressors sought to prevent her from obtaining an abortion.

against her will. Some captors allegedly said their intention was to impregnate the women in their camp to make 'Chetnik babies' (an allusion to the Serbian partisans in World War II), while some women were allegedly periodically examined by gynaecologists with the result that, if found to be pregnant, they were set apart and given special privileges until their seventh month (when it was too late to obtain an abortion) only then to be released.[466]

The physical, psychological and social impact of the act of rape itself already bears serious consequences on the victim. Severe traumatization and clearly misplaced but real feelings of guilt and shame are often accompanied by the fear of rejection by spouse or family. These concerns become even more serious when a woman becomes pregnant and is forced to carry the pregnancy to term. A great majority of the 119 women found by the Special Rapporteur's experts to have become pregnant following rape in the former Yugoslavia delivered babies, most having been denied abortions: in certain cases followed up by the team of investigating experts, the infants were rejected by the women following their birth.[467]

It has yet to be seen whether the International Criminal Tribunal for the Former Yugoslavia established to prosecute war crimes in the region will deal with alleged systematic sexual assault as a crime against humanity.[468] Certainly, a number of NGOs and individuals are urging forced pregnancy achieved as a result of such rapes to be prosecuted as a war crime.[469]

1.1.2 The Context of Marital Relations. In many societies, 'girls are taught to be ready for sex with their husbands at all times and never to say no to his advances'.[470] A possible result of this conditioning and behav-

---

[466] UN, Security Council Final Report of the Commission of Experts Established Pursuant to Security Council Resolution 780 (1992), UN doc. S/1994/674, Annex 241, No. 65.

[467] See, UN doc. E/CN.4/1993/50, Annex II, *supra* note 459, paragraph 43.

[468] To date, no indictment before the former Yugoslavia War Crimes Tribunal includes charges of rape. For the texts of the indictments, see 16 *Human Rights Law Journal* (1995), No. 4–6, pp. 217–238.

[469] For example, the Women's Rights Project of the NGO Human Rights Watch is working to further this view and supply evidence; see Human Rights Watch, *Human Rights Watch World Report 1995* (1994), pp. 335–339.

[470] Beatrice Akua Duncan, *Marital Rape as a form of Domestic Violence and the Needs for Law Reform in Ghana*, (1994) (unpublished LL.M. dissertation, Georgetown University Law Center, Washington, D.C.), as cited in Adjetey, *supra* note 66, at footnote 21.

iour is that a woman may find herself pregnant when she may not have desired it. In almost all Latin American countries abortion in the case of rape remains a criminal offense.[471] In light of both types of rape, and the pregnancy which can result, what protection does international law provide in the event that a *wife* is forced by her husband to bear a child? While this situation occurs throughout the world, it would be difficult to establish conjugally forced pregnancy as a violation of international human rights treaties. As discussed above, international human rights law texts are generally vague with regard to the reproductive decision-making process between couples. While the texts from recent international conferences affirm that a woman should have the *individual* and prior right to reproductive choice (since it is really only her health which is placed at risk), binding international law texts appear to confer the right to *couples*, with the understanding that they make the choice responsibly together. How exactly the decision is finally made remains an uncertain matter. However, the element of force raises the issue of assault in violation of the woman's (including wife's) personal security rights which the State is obligated to ensure. Failure by the State to take adequate steps[472] to protect a woman/wife against such assaults would constitute a violation on the part of the State by virtue of horizontal effects.

A ruling by the European Court of Human Rights in application of the ECHR, does concomitantly provide a degree of recognition of a woman's right not to be subjected to forced impregnation by her husband. In two cases examined together, the European Court unanimously held that the United Kingdom's decision that the husbands could not invoke immunity to escape conviction and sentence for rape and attempted rape upon their wives was in line with the ECHR.[473] Drawing from these conclusions, it could be argued that where forced impregnation was the result of rape, husbands should be charged with a criminal offence, just as rape and forced impregnation by anyone who is not directly tied with the person would be charged: husbands should not be privileged in this respect. Effectively, however, recognizing *forced impregnation* arising from both marital and non-marital rape as a criminal offence and a violation of a woman's right to

---

[471] Medina, *supra* note 235, p. 260.

[472] 'Adequate steps' would, at a minimum, include protective (i.e. criminal) legislation.

[473] Judgments pronounced on 22 November 1995 for *S. W. v. The United Kingdom* (47/1994/494/576), and *C. R. v. The United Kingdom* (48/1994/495/577). To be reproduced as Publications of the European Court of Human Rights, Series A, No. 335–B and No. 335–C.

reproductive choice may be a largely academic exercise offering little protection since it would be very difficult to establish that the intention of the rape was to forcibly impregnate the woman and because the woman would likely be faced with an interminable pregnancy by the time the courts decided the matter—and this even more likely if the State prohibits abortion on the ground of rape. The fundamental offence is that of sexual assault (irrespective of result) constituting a possible violation of personal security rights with pregnancy representing an aggravation of the assault/violation in terms of damage.

1.2 The Right to Asylum as a Result of Serious Violations of the Right to Reproductive Choice

There is evidence that the violation of the right to reproductive choice of individuals has implications which stretch beyond national borders, and that such violations are being taken more seriously. In recent years a number of individuals who have sought asylum have based their claims on coercive population practices as representing a form of persecution.

In 1990, the Executive Committee of the Office of the High Commissioner for Refugees affirmed the linkage between a violation of the rights guaranteed under the Women's Convention and persecution on grounds recognized in the 1951 United Nations Convention relating to the Status of Refugees[474] (hereafter the Refugee Convention). Severe discrimination prohibited by the Women's Convention could thereby be invoked as the basis for the granting of refugee status.[475] Widely reputed to be the most developed domestic guidelines for the determination of refugee status on this basis, the *Women Refugee Claimants Fearing Gender-Related Persecution* guidelines[476] issued by Canada's Immigration and Refugee Board broadened the interpretation made in

---

[474] Adopted on 28 July 1951 by the United Nations Conference of Plenipotentiaries on the Status of Refugees and Stateless Persons convened under General Assembly Resolution 429 (V) of 14 December 1950. For the full text of the Convention, see 189 UNTS 150. Also reproduced in: UN, *Human Rights: A Compilation of International Instruments, Volume I (Second Part)* (1994), pp. 638–654.

[475] UNHCR, Executive Committee, Note on Refugee Women and International Protection, EC/SCP/59, p. 5.

[476] Immigration and Refugee Board, Canada, *Guidelines Issued by the Chairperson Pursuant to Section 65(3) of the Immigration Act: Women Refugee Claimants Fearing Gender-Related Persecution* (1993).

the statement by the UNHCR Executive Committee[477] and affirmed that 'severe discrimination on grounds of gender' could contribute to a finding of persecution if 'it leads to consequences of a substantially prejudicial nature for the claimant and if it is imposed on account of any one, or combination, of the statutory grounds for persecution'.[478] The Guidelines have already prompted action. Just a few years after being adopted, the Canadian Federal Court of Appeal ruled in the case of *Cheung v. Canada*[479] that the compulsory sterilization of a woman who violated China's one-child policy could be recognized as 'persecution' and asylum was duly granted.[480]

In this case, the claimant (Ms. Cheung) desired a second child despite her full understanding of the repercussions she could suffer in violating China's one-child policy. In this knowledge, Ms. Cheung was forced to have her second child in hiding and could not register the birth. When she returned to her husband's home, the Family Planning Bureau (alerted about the second child) came and forcibly took her away to a clinic in order to be sterilized. However, the doctor could not proceed with the operation because she had an infection which would impede him from operating for another six months. Before the six months were up, the claimant fled her province to avoid being sterilized against her will. After some years of hiding and movement, the claimant went to Canada. It was accepted by the Board that the claimant would be sterilized if she were forced to return to China. The Federal Court of Canada ruled that women in China such as Ms. Cheung, who have more than one child, and are faced with forced sterilization on this account, form a *particular social group* with a well-founded *fear of persecution* so as to come within the meaning of the definition of a Convention refugee.[481]

---

[477] For a detailed review of provisions for refugee status on grounds of gender discrimination, particularly with reference to the Canadian Guidelines, see generally Macklin, 'Refugee Women and the Imperative of Categories', 17 *Human Rights Quarterly* (1995), No. 2.

[478] Immigration and Refugee Board, Canada, *supra* note 476, p. 3.

[479] *Cheung v. Canada*, (Minister of Employment and Immigration), 2 FC 314 (FCA), 1 April 1993.

[480] Macklin describes the connection stating that 'while the goal of population control [of the People's Republic of China] may be entirely defensible, one may contend that forced abortions and forced sterilization of women are each persecutory means of accomplishing the objective'; see, *supra* note 477, p. 231.

[481] Justice Linden, in his contribution to the judgment, declared, 'Brutality in furtherance of a legitimate end [to control population growth] is still brutality', as cited in *supra* note

This decision in favour of the claimant was not the first in Canada.[482] In 1989, a Chinese citizen had similarly claimed, and was granted, refugee status after giving testimony on the forcible State control over her reproductive choice. The woman and her husband were aware that, according to the one-child policy enforced in the region where they lived, they should not have a second child. However, their first born being a girl, it was considered essential that the woman bear a male child as the family practised an ancestral form of worship which required that a son perform the daily ritual of maintaining the family shrine and perform graveside rituals. After refusing orders from the Birth Control Office that she have an abortion, officers forcibly took her to the hospital and the baby was aborted six months into pregnancy. While in hospital, a long-acting contraceptive intra-uterine device was implanted into her womb. She and her husband further received a fine as punishment for the second pregnancy. Soon after, the woman and her husband left China to come to Canada and seek asylum. The Refugee Division granted the woman and her husband asylum as it found the claimant's fear of persecution to be well-founded on the basis that the beliefs and values of her family were being eroded by the State through the enforcement of the one-child policy. While the deciding factor in this case was not the violation of her right to reproductive choice forming a basis of persecution, it was a significant one.[483]

While the above cases demonstrate positive action at the domestic level in the recognition of serious violations of reproductive choice, decisions to the contrary have also demonstrated that not all States are prepared to give the violations the attention they deserve. In the United States, for example, the Board of Immigration and Appeals submitted three cases to the Attorney-General for review which called for a decision on the validity of asylum claims based on enforcement of the People's Republic of China's 'One Couple – One Child' population

---

479, paragraph 323.

[482] Disappointingly, another panel on the Federal Court of Appeal came to the opposite conclusion in the case of a male claimant, even though the same form of persecution was suffered; see *Chan v. Canada* (Minister of Employment and Immigration) 20 Imm.LR 2d 181, 1993. The ruling in *Chan* has gone to appeal before the Supreme Court of Canada.

[483] See Cases Nos. C89–00036 and C89–00037, 1989, Convention Refugee Determination Decisions No. 30, Immigration and Refugee Board, Canada.

policy. All three cases and their appeals were dismissed.[484] The next few years will hopefully lead to consistent practice on the issue among States, fuelled by the recommendations and promises made at the Cairo and Beijing Conferences, and hopefully moving favourably towards wider acceptance of refugee claims from individuals suffering persecution owing to their opposition to coercive national population policies. At the very least, States which practice such coercion should be condemned more frequently and publicly[485] and encouraged to modify their policies.

2. EXPANDING IMPLEMENTATION THROUGH THE WORK OF INTERNATIONAL ORGANIZATIONS

UN specialized agencies such as the United Nations Population Fund (UNFPA), World Health Organization (WHO), the International Labour Organisation (ILO), the United Nations Children's Fund (UNICEF), the United Nations Development Fund for Women (UNIFEM), and most recently the Office of the United Nations High Commissioner for Refugees (UNHCR) are becoming increasingly involved in the promotion and protection of the right to reproductive choice, providing the weight of professional authority. Such agencies either directly or indirectly assist in fulfilling the right through educational and assist-

---

[484] The claims were dismissed on the grounds that no reasonable fear of persecution could be established due to inconsistencies in their stories and the inability to situate the form of persecutions suffered within the five grounds (i.e. race, religion, national origin, political opinion or membership in a particular group) specified in the U.S. Immigration and Nationality Act (INA). A report by the State Department's Bureau of Human Rights and Humanitarian Affairs was also considered which noted that in the province from which two of the applicants came the population policy was somewhat more relaxed than in others. Also a disadvantage to the claimants was the report's statement that their province was a major source of legal and illegal immigration and that 90 per cent of Chinese asylum applicants from that region had based their claims on opposition to China's family planning policies. For more information on these cases, refer to Interpreter Release (No. 70) of 22 November 1993 at section 9, pp. 1558–1561. For more ample discussion on the particular case of the *Matter of Chang* and consideration of recommended changes in the US INA, see generally Shiers, 'Coercive Population Control Policies: An Illustration of the Need for a Conscientious Objector Provision for Asylum Seekers', 20 *Virginia Journal of International Law* (1990), No. 4.

[485] For example, the documentary televised on Channel 4 (U.K.) in January of 1996 regarding the ill-treatment and deaths (alleged as murders) of children in orphanages in China caused great public outcry and consequently the British government applied pressure on China to improve the situation; as reported by Higgins, 'Mystery of the "Missing" Orphans', *The Guardian*, 10 January 1996, p. 3.

ance programmes, and in facilitating the practical availability of family planning services.

As an example among these organizations, the UNFPA seeks to ensure that governments supply sufficient and reliable information and counselling in order that family planning decisions can be made with free and informed consent. This is done by devoting considerable resources (human and material) to communications efforts designed to broaden knowledge regarding reproductive choice and contraceptive methods. According to its mandate, funds appropriated to States must be used in a manner which respects the right to reproductive choice.[486]

As a different example, the ILO's mandate includes promoting educational activities on population and family planning questions through information programmes within enterprises, co-operatives and rural institutions, and encouraging participation by medical services within enterprises in the promotion of family planning services.[487] The ILO's population programme has developed and applied an effective system of monitoring and evaluation, comprised of monthly project progress reports, tripartite project reviews and independent *ad hoc* evaluations.[488] Although no single instrument guides the population programme, a number of ILO conventions are highly relevant. Population programmes are thus strengthened by the existence of such conventions as the 1919 Maternity Protection Convention (and its 1952 Revised Convention), the 1975 Human Resources Development Convention and the 1981 Workers with Family Responsibilities Convention.[489] States Parties to these Conventions undertake to report on the action they have taken to implement the treaties and independent panels regularly review the application of the instruments.[490]

---

[486] UNFPA, *Population Issues, supra* note 6, pp. 8 and 18.

[487] See International Labour Organisation, *International Labour Standards and ILO Population Programmes* (1992), p. 1.

[488] *Ibid.*, p. 32.

[489] See generally, *ibid.*

[490] In the case of the 1981 Convention, for example, a general survey was carried out by the ILO in 1993 to examine the progress of each State Party to the Convention in fulfilling its obligations under the instrument. The survey demonstrated that, in some States, information and education campaigns on family planning and family life are carried out in the work place. According to the survey, the government of Mexico, for example, supports programmes to introduce and expand family planning services at work which stress the need for shared responsibility between parents; see ILO, *Workers with Family Responsibilities* (1993), paragraph 95.

Taking promotion of reproductive health and family planning in the work place one step further, the ILO held a joint workshop with UNFPA on population policy and development planning strategies, enlarging the scope of its current work.[491]

As a final example, UNHCR, in its guidelines aimed at assisting refugee workers confronting cases of sexual violence, reasserts the human right to reproductive choice, which refugees, as any individuals, hold and shall have respected.[492] The office recently took steps to enlarge the scope of its protection of refugees and displaced persons to make available basic reproductive health care in refugee situations.[493] Most refugees and displaced persons do not have access to even the most basic elements of reproductive health care, including access to family planning services to plan and space pregnancies. Together with UNFPA, UNHCR organized a workshop in June 1995 which brought together over 50 international organizations and NGOs involved in reproductive health. Based on discussions at the workshop and surveys of current reproductive health activities in refugee sites, the *Field Manual on Reproductive Health in Refugee Situations* was drafted to help individuals working with refugees understand the issues and tackle them in a practical manner. As a result, concerted efforts will be made to provide supplies of family planning methods along with family planning education and counselling in refugee situations.[494]

3. THE WAY FORWARD

Securing the right to reproductive choice could have a significant impact on some of the greatest problems we face today. As such, governments and international organizations must view population,

---

[491] ILO/UNFPA Technical Workshops on Population Policy and Development Planning Strategies, Geneva, 25 October–1 November 1994; see generally papers presented at the workshop including Jon Bongaarts' presentation on policy options in population and Christine Oppong's paper on ILO standard-setting.

[492] See generally UNHCR, *Sexual Violence against Refugees: Guidelines on Prevention and Response* (1995).

[493] In light of the well-documented prevalence of high fertility rates, unsafe abortion, sexual violence, and other threats to reproductive health in refugee populations, the first call for action met with consensus at the ICPD; See the Cairo Programme of Action, paragraph 10.25.

[494] See generally UNHCR, *Proceedings of the Inter-Agency Symposium on Reproductive Health in Refugee Situations: Palais de Nations, Geneva, 28–30 June, 1995* (1995).

environment, development and resource issues as intimately connected and place all of these on their list of priorities. Population stabilization must be sought with respect for individual choice, without coercion. To do so, States must invest in poverty alleviation, universal access to health care, education and other aspects assisting human development.

Ultimately, protections offered by treaties depend on what people are willing to make of them. There are a number of ways to make sure these protections are used and respected. First, we must seek to redress the barriers to the enjoyment of the right to reproductive choice (such as restrictive policies, national laws, lack of practical family planning alternatives, etc.) by enforcing the relevant provisions in the Women's Convention and other treaties. This would be achieved by enhancing the mechanisms for supervision of compliance with the treaties as they stand. These could be improved by facilitating the tasks of monitoring bodies to investigate individual complaints, censuring States which fail to observe their obligations (including submission of reports) and demanding States to account for their failure to perform according to the relevant instruments. On their own initiatives, the UN treaty bodies could elaborate further general comments and recommendations which would offer authoritative interpretations to guide both States and individuals in understanding the full extent of stipulated rights.[495] Furthermore, bodies established by the treaties, CEDAW in particular, should be used more effectively and frequently as tools for argument and persuasion to change violative and abusive national legislation and population policies. They should be used as a means of mobilizing grassroots advocacy by giving the right to reproductive choice a clear point of focus on standards that have internationally recognized legitimacy. Advocates and NGOs could play an important role in improving enjoyment of the right to reproductive choice by raising public and even governmental awareness, scrutinizing the compatibility of domestic legislation and practices, encouraging ratification of all relevant instruments, and helping to bring more cases before the supervisory bodies at both the universal and regional levels. In any event, the challenge of implementation lies in the translation of internationally recognized standards into domestically enforceable laws; States must be urged to alter domestic laws and practices so that they conform with international standards and grant domestic procedural capacity and remedies. International humanitarian agencies and NGOs

---

[495] One important example of this would be a General Comment by the Committee on Economic, Social and Cultural Rights in relation to the right to health.

can assist by gathering, publishing and monitoring data relative to reproductive choice and seeking explanations from States with poor performance records. These and other donor organizations can also stress respect of the right to reproductive choice as a condition to furnishing financial assistance.

It is clear that population policies have become a necessity in developing countries to meet the challenge of high population growth, economic hardship and the depletion of resources. However, policies based on principles of coercion or disincentives to enforce 'responsible' planned parenthood effectively nullify free choice. The use of force also breaches other human rights—personal security rights in particular. As more and more States take serious action to reduce population growth, the risk of abusive interpretations of 'responsible' reproductive choice rises. Several measures can be taken to reduce this risk. First, governments could condition their bilateral relations (especially trade) on compliance with international obligations. Second, as donor agencies step up their funding, so the ability to discourage violations of this right by States increases: donor agencies could withhold funding for population programmes which employ disproportionately coercive measures to enforce 'responsible' reproductive behaviour on parts of their populations.

The universality of human rights is one of the cornerstones of international human rights law. Yet even States which have subscribed to this principle by ratifying international instruments continue to plead cultural and religious relativism to justify the continuation of discriminatory practices. This is particularly so for the reservations to the Women's Convention. Such reservations undermine respect for the right to reproductive choice and should be considered contrary to international treaty law as they defeat the purpose of the Convention. The States which have entered reservations to these provisions on grounds of conflict with religious norms should be urged to take immediate action to withdraw the reservations and eradicate any form of violation of the right to reproductive choice maintained by cultural and religious norms. The fact that the influence of discriminatory cultural traditions and customs regarding reproduction permeate society to such an extent should not excuse inaction at the level of law. To the contrary, prying open the 'citadel of privacy' we may challenge the claims of 'religion' and 'local culture' used to defeat domestic application of international human rights norms,[496] not only in the case of reserving States but

---

[496] Boland et al., *supra* note 140, p. 91.

any State Party which does not abide by its treaty obligations. International agendas for action such as the Cairo Programme of Action and the Beijing Platform for Action offer additional concrete steps which should be taken in this respect.

While this study does not purport to have offered definitive solutions to the problems of implementing the right to reproductive choice, it has hopefully drawn attention to the importance of discussion of the issues involved and the challenges we face in securing its protection. Its entire purpose has been to show individuals that international human rights law belongs to *people*—women and men—and is not just a dark labyrinth of standards and recourses inaccessible to the common person. To the contrary, there is a rich body of established legal norms which may be invoked before or through a variety of bodies and mechanisms. As such individuals must start to make these their own, become aware of what international law can do for them and how they can effectively use it to have the number of children they want, if they want and when they want—a choice which paves the way for full, healthy and productive lives for them and their families.

APPENDIX A

EXCERPTS FROM THE PROGRAMME OF ACTION OF THE 1994 INTERNATIONAL CONFERENCE ON POPULATION AND DEVELOPMENT[1]

United Nations
INTERNATIONAL CONFERENCE ON POPULATION AND DEVELOPMENT

Cairo, Egypt
5–13 September 1994

Annex

Programme of Action of the International Conference on Population and Development

. . .

Chapter VII

REPRODUCTIVE RIGHTS AND REPRODUCTIVE HEALTH

7.1 This chapter is especially guided by the principles contained in chapter II and in particular the introductory paragraphs.

A. *Reproductive rights and reproductive health*

Basis for action

7.2 Reproductive health is a state of complete physical, mental and social well-being and not merely the absence of disease or infirmity, in all matters relating to the reproductive system and to its functions and processes. Reproductive health therefore implies that people are able to have a satisfying and safe sex life and that they have the capability to reproduce and the freedom to decide if, when and how often to do so. Implicit in this last condition are the right of men and women to be informed and to have access to safe, effective, affordable and acceptable methods of family planning of their choice, as well as other methods of their choice for regulation of fertility which are not against the law, and the right of access to appropriate health-care services that will enable women to go safely through pregnancy and childbirth and provide couples with the best chance of having a

---

[1] UN, Report of the International Conference on Population and Development, Cairo, 5–13 September 1994, UN doc. A/CONF.171/13, 18 October 1994.

healthy infant. In line with the above definition of reproductive health, reproductive health care is defined as the constellation of methods, techniques and services that contribute to reproductive health and well-being by preventing and solving reproductive health problems. It also includes sexual health, the purpose of which is the enhancement of life and personal relations, and not merely counselling and care related to reproduction and sexually transmitted diseases.

7.3 Bearing in mind the above definition, reproductive rights embrace certain human rights that are already recognized in national laws, international human rights documents and other consensus documents. These rights rest on the recognition of the basic right of all couples and individuals to decide freely and responsibly the number, spacing and timing of their children and to have the information and means to do so, and the right to attain the highest standard of sexual and reproductive health. It also includes their right to make decisions concerning reproduction free of discrimination, coercion and violence, as expressed in human rights documents. In the exercise of this right, they should take into account the needs of their living and future children and their responsibilities towards the community. The promotion of the responsible exercise of these rights for all people should be the fundamental basis for government- and community-supported policies and programmes in the area of reproductive health, including family planning. As part of their commitment, full attention should be given to the promotion of mutually respectful and equitable gender relations and particularly to meeting the educational and service needs of adolescents to enable them to deal in a positive and responsible way with their sexuality. Reproductive health eludes many of the world's people because of such factors as: inadequate levels of knowledge about human sexuality and inappropriate or poor-quality reproductive health information and services; the prevalence of high-risk sexual behaviour; discriminatory social practices; negative attitudes towards women and girls; and the limited power many women and girls have over their sexual and reproductive lives. Adolescents are particularly vulnerable because of their lack of information and access to relevant services in most countries. Older women and men have distinct reproductive and sexual health issues which are often inadequately addressed.

7.4 The implementation of the present Programme of Action is to be guided by the above comprehensive definition of reproductive health, which includes sexual health.

Objectives

7.5 The objectives are:

(a) To ensure that comprehensive and factual information and a full range of reproductive health-care services, including family planning, are accessible, affordable, acceptable and convenient to all users;

(b) To enable and support responsible voluntary decisions about child-bearing and methods of family planning of their choice, as well as other methods of their choice for regulation of fertility which are not against the law and to have the information, education and means to do so;

(c) To meet changing reproductive health needs over the life cycle and to do so in ways sensitive to the diversity of circumstances of local communities.

Actions

7.6 All countries should strive to make accessible through the primary health-care system, reproductive health to all individuals of appropriate ages as soon as possible and no later than the year 2015. Reproductive health care in the context of primary health care should, *inter alia*, include: family-planning counselling, information, education, communication and services; education and services for prenatal care, safe delivery and post-natal care, especially breast-feeding and infant and women's health care; prevention and appropriate treatment of infertility; abortion as specified in paragraph 8.25, including prevention of abortion and the management of the consequences of abortion; treatment of reproductive tract infections; sexually transmitted diseases and other reproductive health conditions; and information, education and counselling, as appropriate, on human sexuality, reproductive health and responsible parenthood. Referral for family-planning services and further diagnosis and treatment for complications of pregnancy, delivery and abortion, infertility, reproductive tract infections, breast cancer and cancers of the reproductive system, sexually transmitted diseases, including HIV/AIDS should always be available, as required. Active discouragement of harmful practices, such as female genital mutilation, should also be an integral component of primary health care, including reproductive health-care programmes.

7.7 Reproductive health-care programmes should be designed to serve the needs of women, including adolescents, and must involve women in the leadership, planning, decision-making, management, implementation, organization and evaluation of services. Governments and other organizations should take positive steps to include women at all levels of the health-care system.

7.8 Innovative programmes must be developed to make information, counselling and services for reproductive health accessible to adolescents and adult men. Such programmes must both educate and enable men to share more equally in family planning and in domestic and child-rearing responsibilities and to accept the major responsibility for the prevention of sexually transmitted diseases. Programmes must reach men in their workplaces, at home and where they gather for recreation. Boys and adolescents, with the support and guidance of their parents, and in line with the Convention on the Rights of the Child, should also be reached through schools, youth organizations and wherever they congregate. Voluntary and appropriate male methods for contraception, as well as for the prevention of sexually transmitted diseases, including AIDS, should be promoted and made accessible with adequate information and counselling.

7.9 Governments should promote much greater community participation in reproductive health-care services by decentralizing the management of public health programmes and by forming partnerships in cooperation with local non-governmental organizations and private health-care providers. All types of non-governmental organizations, including local women's groups, trade unions, cooperatives, youth programmes and religious groups, should be encouraged to become involved in the promotion of better reproductive health.

7.10 Without jeopardizing international support for programmes in developing countries, the international community should, upon request, give consideration to the training, technical assistance, short-term contraceptive supply needs and the needs of the countries in transition from centrally managed to market economies, where reproductive health is poor and in some cases deteriorating. These countries, at the same time, must themselves give higher priority to reproductive health services, including a comprehensive range of contraceptive means, and must address their current reliance on abortion for fertility regulation by meeting the need of women in those countries for better information and more choices on an urgent basis.

7.11 Migrants and displaced persons in many parts of the world have limited access to reproductive health care and may face specific serious threats to their reproductive health and rights. Services must be particularly sensitive to the needs of individual women and adolescents and responsive to their often powerless situation, with particular attention to those who are victims of sexual violence.

B. FAMILY PLANNING

Basis for action

7.12 The aim of family-planning programmes must be to enable couples and individuals to decide freely and responsibly the number and spacing of their children and to have the information and means to do so and to ensure informed choices and make available a full range of safe and effective methods. The success of population education and family-planning programmes in a variety of settings demonstrates that informed individuals everywhere can and will act responsibly in the light of their own needs and those of their families and communities. The principle of informed free choice is essential to the long-term success of family-planning programmes. Any form of coercion has no part to play. In every society there are many social and economic incentives and disincentives that affect individual decisions about child-bearing and family size. Over the past century, many Governments have experimented with such schemes, including specific incentives and disincentives, in order to lower or raise fertility. Most such schemes have had only marginal impact on fertility and in some cases have been counterproductive. Governmental goals for family planning should be defined in terms of unmet needs for information and services. Demographic goals, while legitimately the subject of government development strategies, should not be imposed on family-planning providers in the form of targets or quotas for the recruitment of clients.

7.13 Over the past three decades, the increasing availability of safer methods of modern contraception, although still in some respects inadequate, has permitted greater opportunities for individual choice and responsible decision-making in matters of reproduction throughout much of the world. Currently, about 55 per cent of couples in developing regions use some method of family planning. This figure represents nearly a fivefold increase since the 1960s. Family-planning programmes have contributed considerably to the decline in average fertility rates for developing countries, from about six to seven children per woman in the 1960s to about three to four children at present. However, the full range of modern family-planning methods still remains unavailable to at least 350 million couples world wide, many of whom say they want to space or prevent another pregnancy. Survey data suggest that approximately 120 million additional women world wide would be currently using a modern family-planning method if more accurate information and affordable services were easily available, and if partners, extended families and the community were more supportive. These numbers do not include the substantial and growing numbers of sexually active unmarried individuals wanting and in need of information and services. During the decade of the 1990s, the number of couples of reproductive age will grow by about 18 million per annum. To meet their needs and close the existing large gaps in services, family planning and contraceptive supplies will need to expand very rapidly over the next several years. The quality of family-planning programmes is often directly related to the level and continuity of contraceptive use and to the growth in demand for services. Family-planning programmes work best when they are part of or linked to broader reproductive health programmes that address closely related health needs and when women are fully involved in the design, provision, management and evaluation of services.

Objectives

7.14 The objectives are:

(a) To help couples and individuals meet their reproductive goals in a framework that promotes optimum health, responsibility and family well-being and respects the dignity of all persons and their right to choose the number, spacing and timing of the birth of their children;

(b) To prevent unwanted pregnancies and reduce the incidence of high-risk pregnancies and morbidity and mortality;

(c) To make quality family-planning services affordable, acceptable and accessible to all who need and want them, while maintaining confidentiality;

(d) To improve the quality of family-planning advice, information, education, communication, counselling and services;

(e) To increase the participation and sharing of responsibility of men on the actual practice of family planning;

(f) To promote breast-feeding to enhance birth spacing.

Actions

7.15 Governments and the international community should use the full means at their disposal to support the principle of voluntary choice in family planning.

7.16 All countries should, over the next several years, assess the extent of national unmet need for good-quality family-planning services and its integration in the reproductive health context, paying particular attention to the most vulnerable and underserved groups in the population. All countries should take steps to meet the family-planning needs of their populations as soon as possible and should, in all cases by the year 2015, seek to provide universal access to a full range of safe and reliable family-planning methods and to related reproductive health services which are not against the law. The aim should be to assist couples and individuals to achieve their reproductive goals and give them the full opportunity to exercise the right to have children by choice.

7.17 Governments at all levels are urged to institute systems of monitoring and evaluation of user-centred services with a view to detecting, preventing and controlling abuses by family-planning managers and providers and to ensure a continuing improvement in the quality of services. To this end, Governments should secure conformity to human rights and to ethical and professional standards in the delivery of family planning and related reproductive health services aimed at ensuring responsible, voluntary and informed consent and also regarding service provision. In-vitro fertilization techniques should be provided in accordance with appropriate ethical guidelines and medical standards.

7.18 Non-governmental organizations should play an active role in mobilizing community and family support, in increasing access and acceptability of reproductive health services including family planning, and cooperate with Governments in the process of preparation and provision of care, based on informed choice, and in helping to monitor public- and private-sector programmes, including their own.

7.19 As part of the effort to meet unmet needs, all countries should seek to identify and remove all the major remaining barriers to the utilization of family-planning services. Some of those barriers are related to the inadequacy, poor quality and cost of existing family-planning services. It should be the goal of public, private and non-governmental family-planning organizations to remove all programme-related barriers to family-planning use by the year 2005 through the redesign or expansion of information and services and other ways to increase the ability of couples and individuals to make free and informed decisions about the number, spacing and timing of births and protect themselves from sexually transmitted diseases.

7.20 Specifically, Governments should make it easier for couples and individuals to take responsibility for their own reproductive health by removing unnecessary legal, medical, clinical and regulatory barriers to information and to access to family-planning services and methods.

7.21 All political and community leaders are urged to play a strong, sustained and highly visible role in promoting and legitimizing the provision and use of family-planning and reproductive health services. Governments at all levels are urged to provide a climate that is favourable to good-quality public and private family-planning and reproductive health information and services through all possible channels. Finally, leaders and legislators at all levels must translate their public support for reproductive health, including family planning, into adequate allocations of budgetary, human and administrative resources to help meet the needs of all those who cannot pay the full cost of services.

APPENDIX B

EXCERPTS FROM THE PLATFORM FOR ACTION OF THE 1995 FOURTH WORLD CONFERENCE ON WOMEN[1]

United Nations
FOURTH WORLD CONFERENCE ON WOMEN

Beijing, China
4–15 September 1995

. . .

(Annex II)

PLATFORM FOR ACTION

. . .

CHAPTER IV: STRATEGIC OBJECTIVES AND ACTIONS

. . .

C: *Women and health*

89. Women have the right to the enjoyment of the highest attainable standard of physical and mental health. The enjoyment of this right is vital to their life and well-being and their ability to participate in all areas of public and private life. Health is a state of complete physical, mental and social well-being and not merely the absence of disease or infirmity. Women's health involves their emotional, social and physical well-being and is determined by the social, political and economic context of their lives, as well as by biology. However, health and well-being elude the majority of women. A major barrier for women to the achievement of the highest attainable standard of health is inequality, both between men and women and among women in different geographical regions, social classes and indigenous and ethnic groups. In national and international forums, women have emphasized that to attain optimal health throughout the life cycle, equality, including the sharing of family responsibilities, development and peace are necessary conditions.

---

[1] UN, Report on the Fourth World Conference on Women, Beijing, 4–15 September 1995. UN doc. A/CONF.177/20, 17 October 1995.

90. Women have different and unequal access to and use of basic health resources, including primary health services for the prevention and treatment of childhood diseases, malnutrition, anaemia, diarrhoeal diseases, communicable diseases, malaria and other tropical diseases and tuberculosis, among others. Women also have different and unequal opportunities for protection, promotion and maintenance of their health. In many developing countries, the lack of emergency obstetric services is also of particular concern. Health policies and programmes often perpetuate gender stereotypes and fail to consider socio-economic disparities and other differences among women and may not fully take account of the lack of autonomy of women regarding their health. Women's health is also affected by gender bias in the health system and by the provision of inadequate and inappropriate medical services to women.

91. In many countries, especially in developing countries, in particular the least developed countries, a decrease in public health spending and, in some cases, structural adjustment, contribute to the deterioration of public health systems. In addition, privatization of health-care systems without appropriate guarantees of universal access to affordable health care further reduces health-care availability. This situation not only directly affects the health of girls and women, but also places disproportionate responsibilities on women, whose multiple roles, including their roles within the family and the community, are often not acknowledged; hence they do not receive the necessary social, psychological and economic support.

92. Women's right to the enjoyment of the highest standard of health must be secured throughout the whole life cycle in equality with men. Women are affected by many of the same health conditions as men, but women experience them differently. The prevalence among women of poverty and economic dependence, their experience of violence, negative attitudes towards women and girls, racial and other forms of discrimination, the limited power many women have over their sexual and reproductive lives and lack of influence in decision-making are social realities which have an adverse impact on their health. Lack of food and inequitable distribution of food for girls and women in the household, inadequate access to safe water, sanitation facilities and fuel supplies, particularly in rural and poor urban areas, and deficient housing conditions, all overburden women and their families and have a negative effect on their health. Good health is essential to leading a productive and fulfilling life, and the right of all women to control all aspects of their health, in particular their own fertility, is basic to their empowerment.

93. Discrimination against girls, often resulting from son preference, in access to nutrition and health-care services endangers their current and future health and well-being. Conditions that force girls into early marriage, pregnancy and childbearing and subject them to harmful practices, such as female genital mutilation, pose grave health risks. Adolescent girls need, but too often do not have, access to necessary health and nutrition services as they mature. Counselling and access to sexual and reproductive health information and services for adolescents are still inadequate or lacking completely, and a young woman's right to privacy, confidentiality, respect and informed consent is often not considered. Adolescent girls are both biologically and psychologically more vulnerable than boys to sexual

abuse, violence and prostitution, and to the consequences of unprotected and premature sexual relations. The trend towards early sexual experience, combined with a lack of information and services, increases the risk of unwanted and too early pregnancy, HIV infection and other sexually transmitted diseases, as well as unsafe abortions. Early child-bearing continues to be an impediment to improvements in the educational, economic and social status of women in all parts of the world. Overall, for young women early marriage and early motherhood can severely curtail educational and employment opportunities and are likely to have a long-term, adverse impact on the quality of their lives and the lives of their children. Young men are often not educated to respect women's self-determination and to share responsibility with women in matters of sexuality and reproduction.

94. Reproductive health is a state of complete physical, mental and social well-being and not merely the absence of disease or infirmity, in all matters relating to the reproductive system and to its functions and processes. Reproductive health therefore implies that people are able to have a satisfying and safe sex life and that they have the capability to reproduce and the freedom to decide if, when and how often to do so. Implicit in this last condition are the right of men and women to be informed and to have access to safe, effective, affordable and acceptable methods of family planning of their choice, as well as other methods of their choice for regulation of fertility which are not against the law, and the right of access to appropriate health-care services that will enable women to go safely through pregnancy and childbirth and provide couples with the best chance of having a healthy infant. In line with the above definition of reproductive health, reproductive health care is defined as the constellation of methods, techniques and services that contribute to reproductive health and well-being by preventing and solving reproductive health problems. It also includes sexual health, the purpose of which is the enhancement of life and personal relations, and not merely counselling and care related to reproduction and sexually transmitted diseases.

95. Bearing in mind the above definition, reproductive rights embrace certain human rights that are already recognized in national laws, international human rights documents and other consensus documents. These rights rest on the recognition of the basic right of all couples and individuals to decide freely and responsibly the number, spacing and timing of their children and to have the information and means to do so, and the right to attain the highest standard of sexual and reproductive health. It also includes their right to make decisions concerning reproduction free of discrimination, coercion and violence, as expressed in human rights documents. In the exercise of this right, they should take into account the needs of their living and future children and their responsibilities towards the community. The promotion of the responsible exercise of these rights for all people should be the fundamental basis for government- and community-supported policies and programmes in the area of reproductive health, including family planning. As part of their commitment, full attention should be given to the promotion of mutually respectful and equitable gender relations and particularly to meeting the educational and service needs of adolescents to enable them to deal in a positive and responsible way with their sexuality. Reproductive health eludes many of the world's people because of such factors as: inadequate levels of

knowledge about human sexuality and inappropriate or poor-quality reproductive health information and services; the prevalence of high-risk sexual behaviour; discriminatory social practices; negative attitudes towards women and girls; and the limited power many women and girls have over their sexual and reproductive lives. Adolescents are particularly vulnerable because of their lack of information and access to relevant services in most countries. Older women and men have distinct reproductive and sexual health issues which are often inadequately addressed.

96. The human rights of women include their right to have control over and decide freely and responsibly on matters related to their sexuality, including sexual and reproductive health, free of coercion, discrimination and violence. Equal relationships between women and men in matters of sexual relations and reproduction, including full respect for the integrity of the person, require mutual respect, consent and shared responsibility for sexual behaviour and its consequences.

97. Further, women are subject to particular health risks due to inadequate responsiveness and lack of services to meet health needs related to sexuality and reproduction. Complications related to pregnancy and childbirth are among the leading causes of mortality and morbidity of women of reproductive age in many parts of the developing world. Similar problems exist to a certain degree in some counties with economies in transition. Unsafe abortions threaten the lives of a large number of women, representing a grave public health problem as it is primarily the poorest and youngest who take the highest risk. Most of these deaths, health problems and injuries are preventable through improved access to adequate health-care services, including safe and effective family planning methods and emergency obstetric care, recognizing the right of women and men to be informed and to have access to safe, effective, affordable and acceptable methods of family planning of their choice, as well as other methods of their choice for regulation of fertility which are not against the law, and the right of access to appropriate health-care services that will enable women to go safely through pregnancy and childbirth and provide couples with the best chance of having a healthy infant. These problems and means should be addressed on the basis of the report of the International Conference on Population and Development, with particular reference to relevant paragraphs of the Programme of Action of the Conference.[2] In most countries, the neglect of women's reproductive rights severely limits their opportunities in public and private life, including opportunities for education and economic and political empowerment. The ability of women to control their own fertility forms an important basis for the enjoyment of other rights. Shared responsibility between women and men in matters related to sexual and reproductive behaviour is also essential to improving women's health.

---

[2] Report of the International Conference on Population and Development, Cairo, 5–13 September 1994 (United Nations publication, Sales No. E.95.XIII.18) chap. I, resolution 1, annex.

APPENDIX C

STATES PARTIES TO INTERNATIONAL HUMAN RIGHTS TREATIES WITH RELEVANCE TO THE RIGHT TO REPRODUCTIVE CHOICE (AS AT 1 JANUARY 1996)[1]

UNIVERSAL

Convention on the Elimination of All Forms of Discrimination against Women
adopted 18 December 1979 and entered into force 3 September 1981
(151 ratifications and accessions)

Albania, Angola, Antigua and Barbuda, Argentina, Armenia, Australia, Austria, Azerbaijan, Bahamas, Bangladesh, Barbados, Belarus, Belgium, Belize, Benin, Bhutan, Bolivia, Bosnia and Herzegovina, Brazil, Bulgaria, Burkina Faso, Burundi, Cambodia, Cameroon, Canada, Cape Verde, Central African Republic, Chad, Chile, China, Colombia, Comoros, Congo, Costa Rica, Côte d'Ivoire, Croatia, Cuba, Cyprus, Czech Republic, Denmark, Dominica, Dominican Republic, Ecuador, Egypt, El Salvador, Equatorial Guinea, Eritrea, Estonia, Ethiopia, Fiji, Finland, France, Gabon, Gambia, Georgia, Germany, Ghana, Greece, Grenada, Guatemala, Guinea, Guinea-Bissau, Guyana, Haiti, Honduras, Hungary, Iceland, India, Indonesia, Iraq, Ireland, Israel, Italy, Jamaica, Japan, Jordan, Kenya, Republic of Korea, Kuwait, Lao Peoples Democratic Republic, Latvia, Lesotho, Liberia, Libyan Arab Jamahiriyah, Liechtenstein, Lithuania, Luxembourg, Macedonia, Madagascar, Malawi, Malaysia, Maldives, Mali, Malta, Mauritius, Mexico, Moldova, Mongolia, Morocco, Namibia, Nepal, Netherlands, New Zealand, Nicaragua, Nigeria, Norway, Panama, Papua New Guinea, Paraguay, Peru, Philippines, Poland, Portugal, Romania, Russian Federation, Rwanda, Saint Kitts and Nevis, Saint Lucia, Saint Vincent and the Grenadines, Samoa, Senegal, Seychelles, Sierra Leone, Singapore, Slovakia, Slovenia, South Africa, Spain, Sri Lanka, Suriname, Sweden, Tajikistan, Tanzania, Thailand, Togo, Trinidad and Tobago, Tunisia, Turkey, Uganda, Ukraine, United Kingdom and Northern Ireland, Uruguay, Uzbekistan, Vanuatu, Venezuela, Viet Nam, Yemen, Yugoslavia, Zaire, Zambia, Zimbabwe.

---

[1] All ratifications current to 1 January 1996, as listed in Marie, 'International Instruments relating to Human Rights: Classification and Status of Ratifications as of 1 January 1996', 17 *Human Rights Law Journal* (1996), No. 1–2, except for the Signatories to the Charter of the Organization of American States, as listed in: Buergenthal et al., *Protecting Human Rights in the Americas: Selected Problems* (1990), p. 556, as updated to 1 January 1996.

International Covenant on Economic, Social and Cultural Rights
adopted 16 December 1966 and entered into force 3 January 1976
(134 ratifications)

Afghanistan, Albania, Algeria, Angola, Argentina, Armenia, Australia, Austria, Azerbaijan, Barbados, Belarus, Belgium, Benin, Bolivia, Bosnia and Herzegovina, Brazil, Bulgaria, Burundi, Cambodia, Cameroon, Canada, Cape Verde, Central African Republic, Chad, Chile, Colombia, Congo, Costa Rica, Croatia, Cyprus, Czech Republic, Denmark, Dominica, Dominican Republic, Ecuador, Egypt, El Salvador, Equatorial Guinea, Estonia, Ethiopia, Finland, France, Gabon, Gambia, Georgia, Germany, Greece, Grenada, Guatemala, Guinea, Guinea-Bissau, Guyana, Honduras, Hungary, Iceland, India, Iran, Iraq, Ireland, Israel, Italy, Ivory Coast, Jamaica, Japan, Jordan, Kenya, Republic of Korea, Democratic People's Republic of Korea, Kyrgyzstan, Latvia, Lebanon, Lesotho, Libyan Arab Jamahiriyah, Lithuania, Luxembourg, Macedonia, Madagascar, Malawi, Mali, Malta, Mauritius, Mexico, Moldova, Mongolia, Morocco, Namibia, Nepal, Netherlands, New Zealand, Nicaragua, Niger, Nigeria, Norway, Panama, Paraguay, Peru, Philippines, Poland, Portugal, Romania, Russia, Rwanda, Saint Vincent and Grenadines, San Marino, Sao Tomé and Principe, Senegal, Seychelles, Slovakia, Slovenia, Solomon Islands, Somalia, Spain, Sri Lanka, Sudan, Suriname, Sweden, Switzerland, Syrian Arab Republic, Tanzania, Togo, Trinidad and Tobago, Tunisia, Uganda, Ukraine, United Kingdom, Uruguay, Uzbekistan, Venezuela, Viet Nam, Yemen, Yugoslavia, Zaire, Zambia, Zimbabwe.

International Covenant on Civil and Political Rights
adopted 16 December 1966 and entered into force 23 March 1976
(133 ratifications)

Afghanistan, Albania, Algeria, Angola, Argentina, Armenia, Australia, Austria, Azerbaijan, Barbados, Belarus, Belgium, Benin, Bolivia, Bosnia and Herzegovina, Brazil, Bulgaria, Burundi, Cambodia, Cameroon, Canada, Cape Verde, Central African Republic, Chad, Chile, Colombia, Congo, Costa Rica, Croatia, Cyprus, Czech Republic, Denmark, Dominica, Dominican Republic, Ecuador, Egypt, El Salvador, Equatorial Guinea, Estonia, Ethiopia, Finland, France, Gabon, Gambia, Georgia, Germany, Grenada, Guatemala, Guinea, Guyana, Haiti, Hungary, Iceland, India, Iran, Iraq, Ireland, Israel, Italy, Ivory Coast, Jamaica, Japan, Jordan, Kenya, Republic of Korea, Democratic People's Republic of Korea, Kyrgyzstan, Latvia, Lebanon, Lesotho, Libyan Arab Jamahiriyah, Lithuania, Luxembourg, Macedonia, Madagascar, Malawi, Mali, Malta, Mauritius, Mexico, Moldova, Mongolia, Morocco, Mozambique, Namibia, Nepal, Netherlands, New Zealand, Nicaragua, Niger, Nigeria, Norway, Panama, Paraguay, Peru, Philippines, Poland, Portugal, Romania, Russia, Rwanda, Saint Vincent and Grenadines, San Marino, Sao Tom´ and Principe, Senegal, Seychelles, Slovakia, Slovenia, Somalia, Spain, Sri Lanka, Sudan, Suriname, Sweden, Switzerland, Syrian Arab Republic, Tanzania, Togo, Trinidad and Tobago, Tunisia, Uganda, Ukraine, United Kingdom, United States of America, Uruguay, Uzbekistan, Venezuela, Viet Nam, Yemen, Yugoslavia, Zaire, Zambia, Zimbabwe.

Optional Protocol to the International Covenant on Civil and Political Rights
adopted 16 December 1966 and entered into force 23 March 1976
(87 ratifications)

Algeria, Angola, Argentina, Armenia, Australia, Austria, Barbados, Belarus, Belgium, Benin, Bolivia, Bosnia and Herzegovina, Bulgaria, Cameroon, Canada, Central African Republic, Chad, Chile, Colombia, Congo, Costa Rica, Croatia, Cyprus, Czech Republic, Denmark, Dominican Republic, Ecuador, El Salvador, Equatorial Guinea, Estonia, Finland, France, Gambia, Georgia, Germany, Guinea, Guyana, Hungary, Iceland, Ireland, Italy, Jamaica, Republic of Korea, Kyrgyzstan, Latvia, Libyan Arab Jamahiriyah, Lithuania, Luxembourg, Madagascar, Malta, Mauritius, Mongolia, Namibia, Nepal, Netherlands, New Zealand, Nicaragua, Niger, Norway, Panama, Paraguay, Peru, Philippines, Poland, Portugal, Romania, Russia, Saint Vincent and Grenadines, San Marino, Sao Tomé and Principe, Senegal, Seychelles, Slovakia, Slovenia, Somalia, Spain, Suriname, Sweden, Togo, Trinidad and Tobago, Uganda, Ukraine, Uruguay, Uzbekistan, Venezuela, Zaire, Zambia.

Convention on the Rights of the Child
adopted 20 November 1989 and entered into force 2 September 1990
(185 ratifications)

Afghanistan, Albania, Algeria, Angola, Antigua and Barbuda, Argentina, Armenia, Austria, Australia, Azerbaijan, Bahamas, Bahrain, Bangladesh, Barbados, Belarus, Belgium, Belize, Benin, Bhutan, Bolivia, Bosnia and Herzegovina, Botswana, Brazil, Brunei, Bulgaria, Burkina Faso, Burundi, Cambodia, Cameroon, Canada, Cape Verde, Central African Republic, Chad, Chile, China, Colombia, Comoros, Congo, Costa Rica, Croatia, Cuba, Cyprus, Czech Republic, Denmark, Djibouti, Dominica, Dominican Republic, Ecuador, Egypt, El Salvador, Equatorial Guinea, Eritrea, Estonia, Ethiopia, Fiji, Finland, France, Gabon, Gambia, Georgia, Germany, Ghana, Greece, Grenada, Guatemala, Guinea, Guinea-Bissau, Guyana, Haiti, Holy See, Honduras, Hungary, Iceland, India, Indonesia, Iran, Iraq, Ireland, Israel, Italy, Ivory Coast, Jamaica, Japan, Jordan, Kazakhstan, Kenya, Kiribati, Kyrgyzstan, Republic of Korea, Democratic Republic of Korea, Kuwait, Democratic Republic of Lao, Latvia, Lebanon, Lesotho, Liberia, Libyan Arab Jamahiriyah, Liechtenstein, Lithuania, Luxembourg, Macedonia, Madagascar, Malawi, Malaysia, Maldives, Mali, Malta, Marshall Islands, Mauritania, Mauritius, Mexico, Micronesia, Moldova, Monaco, Mongolia, Morocco, Mozambique, Myanmar, Namibia, Nauru, Nepal, Netherlands, New Zealand, Nicaragua, Niger, Nigeria, Nive, Norway, Pakistan, Palau, Panama, Papua New Guinea, Paraguay, Peru, Philippines, Poland, Portugal, Qatar, Romania, Russia, Rwanda, Saint Kitts and Nevis, Saint Lucia, Saint Vincent and Grenadines, Samoa, San Marino, Sao Tomé and Principe, Senegal, Seychelles, Sierra Leone, Singapore, Slovakia, Slovenia, Solomon Islands, South Africa, Spain, Sri Lanka, Sudan, Suriname, Swaziland, Sweden, Syrian Arab Republic, Tajikistan, Tanzania, Thailand, Togo, Tonga, Trinidad and Tobago, Tunisia, Turkey, Turkmenistan, Tuvalu, Uganda, Ukraine, United Kingdom, Uruguay, Uzbekistan, Vanuatu, Venezuela, Viet Nam, Yemen, Yugoslavia, Zaire, Zimbabwe.

African Charter on Human and Peoples' Rights
adopted 26 June 1981 and entered into force 21 October 1986
(50 ratifications)

Algeria, Angola, Benin, Botswana, Burkina Faso, Burundi, Cameroon, Cape Verde, Central African Republic, Chad, Comoros, Congo, Djibouti, Egypt, Equatorial Guinea, Gabon, Gambia, Ghana, Guinea, Guinea-Bissau, Ivory Coast, Kenya, Lesotho, Liberia, Libyan Arab Jamahiriyah, Madagascar, Malawi, Mali, Mauritania, Mauritius, Mozambique, Namibia, Niger, Nigeria, Rwanda, Saharawi Arab Democratic Republic, Sao Tomé and Principe, Senegal, Seychelles, Sierra Leone, Somalia, Sudan, Swaziland, Tanzania, Togo, Tunisia, Uganda, Zaire, Zambia, Zimbabwe.

American Convention on Human Rights,
adopted 22 November 1969 and entered into force 18 July 1978
(25 ratifications)

Argentina, Barbados, Bolivia, Brazil, Chile, Colombia, Costa Rica, Dominica, Dominican Republic, Ecuador, El Salvador, Grenada, Guatemala, Haiti, Honduras, Jamaica, Mexico, Nicaragua, Panama, Paraguay, Peru, Suriname, Trinidad and Tobago, Uruguay, Venezuela.

Additional Protocol to the American Convention on Human Rights
in the area of economic, social and cultural rights
adopted 17 November 1988; not in force
(5 ratifications)

Ecuador, El Salvador, Panama, Peru, Suriname.

Charter of the Organization of American States
first adopted in Bogotá in 1948, notably amended by the Protocol of Cartagena de Indias, signed 5 December 1985 and entered into force 16 November 1988
[For purposes of the 1948 American Declaration of the Rights and Duties of Man]
(35 ratifications)

Antigua and Barbuda, Argentina, Bahamas, Barbados, Belize, Bolivia, Brazil, Canada, Chile, Colombia, Costa Rica, Cuba, Dominica, Dominican Republic, Ecuador, El Salvador, Grenada, Guatemala, Guyana, Haiti, Honduras, Jamaica, Mexico, Nicaragua, Panama, Paraguay, Peru, Saint Kitts and Nevis, Saint Lucia, Saint Vincent and the Grenadines, Suriname, Trinidad and Tobago, United States, Uruguay, Venezuela.

Convention for the Protection of Human Rights and Fundamental Freedoms
[European Convention on Human Rights]
adopted 4 November 1950 and entered into force 3 September 1953
(31 ratifications)

Austria, Belgium, Bulgaria, Cyprus, Czech Republic, Denmark, Finland, France, Germany, Greece, Hungary, Iceland, Ireland, Italy, Liechtenstein, Lithuania, Luxembourg, Malta, Netherlands, Norway, Poland, Portugal, Romania, San Marino, Slovakia, Slovenia, Spain, Sweden, Switzerland, Turkey, United Kingdom.

European Code of Social Security (Revised)
adopted 6 November 1990; not in force
(0 ratifications)

European Social Charter
adopted 18 October 1961 and entered into force 26 February 1965
(20 ratifications)

Austria, Belgium, Cyprus, Denmark, Finland, France, Germany, Greece, Iceland, Ireland, Italy, Luxembourg, Malta, Netherlands, Norway, Portugal, Spain, Sweden, Turkey, United Kingdom.

APPENDIX D

GENERAL COMMENT NO. 19 ADOPTED BY THE HUMAN RIGHTS COMMITTEE, REGARDING ARTICLE 23 (ON THE RIGHT TO MARRY AND FOUND A FAMILY)[1]

1. Article 23 of the International Covenant on Civil and Political Rights recognizes that the family is the natural and fundamental group unit of society and is entitled to protection by society and the State. Protection of the family and its members is also guaranteed, directly or indirectly, by other provisions of the Covenant. Thus, article 17 establishes a prohibition on arbitrary or unlawful interference with the family. In addition, article 24 of the Covenant specifically addresses the protection of the rights of the child, as such or as a member of a family. In their reports, States parties often fail to give enough information on how the State and society are discharging their obligation to provide protection to the family and the persons composing it.

2. The Committee notes that the concept of the family may differ in some respects from State to State, and even from region to region within a State, and that it is therefore not possible to give the concept a standard definition. However, the Committee emphasizes that, when a group of persons is regarded as a family under the legislation and practice of a State, it must be given the protection referred to in article 23. Consequently, States parties should report on how the concept and scope of the family is construed or defined in their own society and legal system. Where diverse concepts of the family, 'nuclear' and 'extended', exist within a State, this should be indicated with an explanation of the degree of protection afforded to each. In view of the existence of various forms of family, such as unmarried couples and their children or single parents and their children, States parties should also indicate whether and to what extent such types of family and their members are recognized and protected by domestic law and practice.

3. Ensuring the protection provided for under article 23 of the Covenant requires that States parties should adopt legislative, administrative or other measures. States parties should provide detailed information concerning the nature of such measures and the means whereby their effective implementation is assured. In fact, since the Covenant also recognizes the right of the family to protection by society, States parties' reports should indicate how the necessary protection is granted to the

---

[1] General Comment No. 19 (39). UN, Report of the Human Rights Committee, Volume I, General Assembly, Official Records, Forty-fifth Session, Supplement No. 40 (A/45/40), pp. 175–177.

family by the State and other social institutions, whether and to what extent the State gives financial or other support to the activities of such institutions, and how it ensures that these activities are compatible with the Covenant.

4. Article 23, paragraph 2, of the Covenant reaffirms the right of men and women of marriageable age to marry and to found a family. Paragraph 3 of the same article provides that no marriage shall be entered into without the free and full consent of the intending spouses. States parties' reports should indicate whether there are restrictions or impediments to the exercise of the right to marry based on special factors such as degree of kinship or mental incapacity. The Covenant does not establish a specific marriageable age either for men or for women, but that age should be such as to enable each of the intending spouses to give his or her free and full personal consent in a form and under conditions prescribed by law. In this connection, the Committee wishes to note that such legal provisions must be compatible with the full exercise of the other rights guaranteed by the Covenant; thus, for instance, the right to freedom of thought, conscience and religion implies that the legislation of each State should provide for the possibility of both religious and civil marriages. In the Committee's view, however, for a State to require that a marriage, which is celebrated in accordance with religious rites, be conducted, affirmed or registered also under civil law is not incompatible with the Covenant. States are also requested to include information on this subject in their reports.

5. The right to found a family implies, in principle, the possibility to procreate and live together. When States parties adopt family planning policies, they should be compatible with the provisions of the Covenant and should, in particular, not be discriminatory or compulsory. Similarly, the possibility to live together implies the adoption of appropriate measures, both at the internal level and as the case may be, in co-operation with other States, to ensure the unity or reunification of families, particularly when their members are separated for political, economic or similar reasons.

6. Article 23, paragraph 4, of the Covenant provides that States parties shall take appropriate steps to ensure equality of rights and responsibilities of spouses as to marriage, during marriage and at its dissolution.

7. With regard to equality as to marriage, the Committee wishes to note in particular that no sex-based discrimination should occur in respect of the acquisition or loss of nationality by reason of marriage. Likewise, the right of each spouse to retain the use of his or her original family name or to participate on an equal basis in the choice of a new family name should be safeguarded.

8. During the marriage, the spouses should have equal rights and responsibilities in the family. This equality extends to all matters arising from their relationship, such as choice of residence, running of the household, education of the children and administration of assets. Such equality continues to be applicable to arrangements regarding legal separation or dissolution of the marriage.

9. Thus, any discriminatory treatment in regard to the grounds and procedures for

separation or divorce, child custody, maintenance or alimony, visiting rights or the loss or recovery of parental authority must be prohibited, bearing in mind the paramount interest of the children in this connection. States parties should, in particular, include information in their reports concerning the provision made for the necessary protection of any children at the dissolution of a marriage or on the separation of the spouses.

APPENDIX E

GENERAL RECOMMENDATION NO. 21 ADOPTED BY THE COMMITTEE ON THE ELIMINATION OF DISCRIMINATION AGAINST WOMEN REGARDING EQUALITY IN MARRIAGE AND FAMILY RELATIONS[1]

. . .

ARTICLE 16

. . .

Comment

Public and private life

11. Historically, human activity in public and private life has been viewed differently and regulated accordingly. In all societies women who have traditionally performed their roles in the private or domestic sphere have long had those activities treated as inferior.

12. As such activities are invaluable for the survival of society, there can be no justification for applying different and discriminatory laws or customs to them. Reports of State parties disclose that there are still countries where *de jure* equality does not exist. Women are thereby prevented from having equal access to resources and from enjoying equality of status in the family and society. Even where *de jure* equality exists, all societies assign different roles, which are regarded as inferior, to women. In this way, principles of justice and equality contained in particular in article 16 and also in articles 2, 5 and 24 of the Convention are being violated.

. . .

Article 16(1)(e)

21. The responsibilities that women have to bear and raise children affect their right of access to education, employment and other activities related to their personal

---

[1] CEDAW, General Recommendation No. 21, UN, Report of the Committee on the Elimination of Discrimination against Women, Thirteenth Session, General Assembly, Official Records, Forty-ninth Session, Supplement No. 38 (A/49/38), pp. 1–10.

development. They also impose inequitable burdens of work on women. The number and spacing of their children have a similar impact on women's lives and also affect their physical and mental health, as well as that of their children. For these reasons, women are entitled to decide on the number and spacing of their children.

22. Some reports disclose coercive practices which have serious consequences for women, such as forced pregnancies, abortion or sterilization. Decisions to have children or not, while preferably made in consultation with spouse or partner, must not nevertheless be limited by spouse, parent, partner or Government. In order to make an informed decision about safe and reliable contraceptive measures, women must have information about contraceptive measures and their use, and guaranteed access to sex education and family planning services, as provided in article 10 (h) of the Convention.

23. There is general agreement that where there are freely available appropriate measures for the voluntary regulation of fertility, the health, development and well-being of all members of the family improves. Moreover, such services improve the general quality of life and health of the population, and the voluntary regulation of population growth helps preserve the environment and achieve sustainable economic and social development.

. . .

Reservations

41. The Committee has noted with alarm the number of States parties which have entered reservations to the whole or part of article 16, especially when a reservation has also been entered to article 2, claiming that compliance may conflict with a commonly held vision of the family based, *inter alia*, on cultural or religious beliefs or on the country's economic or political status.

42. Many of these countries hold a belief in the patriarchal structure of a family which places a father, husband or son in a favourable position. In some countries where fundamentalist or other extremist views or economic hardships have encouraged a return to old values and traditions, women's place in the family has deteriorated sharply. In others, where it has been recognized that a modern society depends for its economic advance and for the general good of the community on involving all adults equally, regardless of gender, these taboos and reactionary or extremist ideas have progressively been discouraged.

43. Consistent with articles 2, 3 and 24 in particular, the Committee requires that all States parties gradually progress to a stage where, by its resolute discouragement of notions of the inequality of women in the home, each country will withdraw its reservation, in particular to articles 9, 15 and 16 of the Convention.

44. States parties should resolutely discourage any notions of inequality of women and men which are affirmed by laws, or by religious or private law or by custom,

and progress to the stage where reservations, particularly to article 16, will be withdrawn.

45. The Committee noted, on the basis of its examination of initial and subsequent periodic reports, that in some States parties to the Convention that had ratified or acceded without reservation, certain laws, especially those dealing with family, do not actually conform to the provisions of the Convention.

46. Their laws still contain many measures which discriminate against women based on norms, customs and socio-cultural prejudices. These States, because of their specific situation regarding these articles, make it difficult for the Committee to evaluate and understand the status of women.

47. The Committee, in particular on the basis of articles 1 and 2 of the Convention, requests that those States parties make the necessary efforts to examine the de facto situation relating to the issues and to introduce the required measures in their national legislation still containing provisions discriminatory to women.

Reports

48. Assisted by the comments in the present general recommendation, in their reports States parties should:

(a) Indicate the stage that has been reached in the country's progress to removal of all reservations to the Convention, in particular reservations to article 16;

(b) Set out whether their laws comply with the principles of articles 9, 15 and 16 and where, by reason of religious or private law or custom, compliance with the law or with the Convention is impeded.

Legislation

49. States parties should, where necessary to comply with the Convention, in particular in order to comply with articles 9, 15 and 16, enact and enforce legislation.

Encouraging compliance with the Convention

50. Assisted by the comments in the present general recommendation, and as required by articles 2, 3 and 24, States parties should introduce measures directed at encouraging full compliance with the principles of the Convention, particularly where religious or private law or custom conflict with those principles.

APPENDIX F

EXCERPTS FROM GENERAL COMMENT NO. 24 ADOPTED BY THE HUMAN RIGHTS COMMITTEE, REGARDING ARTICLE 52 (RELATING TO RESERVATIONS)[1]

1. . . . Some . . . reservations exclude the duty to provide and guarantee particular rights in the Covenant. Others are couched in more general terms, often directed to ensuring the continued paramountcy of certain domestic legal provisions. Still others are directed at the competence of the Committee. The number of reservations, their content and their scope may undermine the effective implementation of the Covenant and tend to weaken respect for the obligations of States parties. It is important for States parties to know exactly what obligations they, and other States parties, have in fact undertaken . . .

. . .

4. The possibility of entering reservations may encourage States which consider that they have difficulties in guaranteeing all the rights in the Covenant nonetheless to accept the generality of obligations in that instrument. Reservations may serve a useful function to enable States to adapt specific elements in their laws to the inherent rights of each person as articulated in the Covenant. However, it is desirable in principle that States accept the full range of obligations, because the human rights norms are the legal expression of the essential rights that every person is entitled to as a human being.

. . .

8. Reservations that offend peremptory norms would not be compatible with the object and purpose of the Covenant. Although treaties that are mere exchanges of obligations between States allow them to reserve *inter se* application of rules of general international law, it is otherwise in human rights treaties, which are for the benefit of persons within their jurisdiction. Accordingly, provisions in the Covenant that represent customary international law (and *a fortiori* when they have the character of peremptory norms) may not be the subject of reservations. Accordingly, a State may not reserve the right to engage in slavery, to torture, to subject persons

---

[1] UN, Human Rights Committee, General Comment No. 24 on issues relating to reservations made upon ratification or accession to the Covenant or the Optional Protocols thereto, or in relation to declarations under article 41 of the Covenant, Fifty-second Session, UN doc. CCPR/C/21/Rev.1/Add.6, 2 November 1994.

to cruel, inhuman or degrading treatment or punishment, to arbitrarily deprive persons of their lives, to arbitrarily arrest and detain persons, to deny freedom of thought, conscience and religion, to presume a person guilty unless he proves his innocence, to execute pregnant women or children, to permit the advocacy of national, racial or religious hatred, to deny to persons of marriageable age the right to marry, or to deny to minorities the right to enjoy their own culture, profess their own religion, or use their own language. And while reservations to particular clauses of article 14 may be acceptable, a general reservation to the right to a fair trial would not be.

. . .

10. The Committee has further examined whether categories of reservations may offend the 'object and purpose' test. In particular, it falls for consideration as to whether reservations to the non-derogable provisions of the Covenant are compatible with its object and purpose. While there is no hierarchy of importance of rights under the Covenant, the operation of certain rights may not be suspended, even in times of national emergency . . . One reason for certain rights being made non-derogable is because their suspension is irrelevant to the legitimate control of the state of national emergency (for example, no imprisonment for debt, in article 11). Another reason is that derogation may indeed be impossible (as, for example, freedom of conscience). At the same time, some provisions are non-derogable exactly because without them there would be no rule of law . . . While there is no automatic correlation between reservations to non-derogable provisions, and reservations which offend against the object and purpose of the Covenant, a State has a heavy onus to justify such a reservation.

11. The Covenant consists not just of the specified rights, but of important supportive guarantees. These guarantees provide the necessary framework for securing the rights in the Covenant and are thus essential to its object and purpose. Some operate at the national level and some at the international level. Reservations designed to remove these guarantees are thus not acceptable . . . Reservations that purport to evade that essential element in the design of the Covenant, which is also directed to securing the enjoyment of the rights, are also incompatible with its object and purpose . . .

12. . . . Reservations often reveal a tendency of States not to want to change a particular law. And sometimes that tendency is elevated to a general policy. Of particular concern are widely formulated reservations which essentially render ineffective all Covenant rights which would require any change in national law to ensure compliance with Covenant obligations. No real international rights or obligations have thus been accepted . . .

. . .

16. The Committee finds it important to address which body has the legal authority to make determinations as to whether specific reservations are compatible with the object and purpose of the Covenant. As for international treaties in general, the

International Court of Justice has indicated in the *Reservations to the Genocide Convention Case* (1951) that a State which objected to a reservation on the grounds of incompatibility with the object and purpose of a treaty could, though objecting, regard the treaty as not in effect as between itself and the reserving State. Article 20, paragraph 4, of the Vienna Convention on the Law of Treaties 1969 contains provisions most relevant to the present case on acceptance of and objection to reservations. This provides for the possibility of a State to object to a reservation made by another State. Article 21 deals with the legal effects of objections by States to reservations made by other States. Essentially, a reservation precludes the operation, as between the reserving and other States, of the provision reserved; and an objection thereto leads to the reservation being in operation as between the reserving and objecting State only to the extent that it has not been objected to.

17. . . . And because the operation of the classic rules on reservations is so inadequate for the Covenant, States have often not seen any legal interest in or need to object to reservations. The absence of protest by States cannot imply that a reservation is either compatible or incompatible with the object and purpose of the Covenant . . .

18. It necessarily falls to the Committee to determine whether a specific reservation is compatible with the object and purpose of the Covenant. This is in part because, as indicated above, it is an inappropriate task for States parties in relation to human rights treaties, and in part because it is a task that the Committee cannot avoid in the performance of its functions . . . The normal consequence of an unacceptable reservation is not that the Covenant will not be in effect at all for a reserving party. Rather, such a reservation will generally be severable, in the sense that the Covenant will be operative for the reserving party without benefit of the reservation.

19. Reservations must be specific and transparent, so that the Committee, those under the jurisdiction of the reserving State and other States parties may be clear as to what obligations of human rights compliance have or have not been undertaken. Reservations may thus not be general, but must refer to a particular provision of the Covenant and indicate in precise terms its scope in relation thereto. When considering the compatibility of possible reservations with the object and purpose of the Covenant, States should also take into consideration the overall effect of a group of reservations, as well as the effect of each reservation on the integrity of the Covenant, which remains an essential consideration . . .

20. . . . States should also ensure that the necessity for maintaining reservations is periodically reviewed, taking into account any observations and recommendations made by the Committee during examination of their reports. Reservations should be withdrawn at the earliest possible moment. Reports to the Committee should contain information on what action has been taken to review, reconsider or withdraw reservations.

BIBLIOGRAPHY

BOOKS

Andreassen, Bård-Anders and Teresa Swinehart (eds.), *Human Rights in Developing Countries: 1990 Yearbook* (Kehl: N.P. Engel, Publisher, 1991).

Bartels, Dianne M., Reinhard Priester, Dorothy E. Vawter and Arthur L. Caplan (eds.), *Beyond Baby M: Ethical Issues in New Reproductive Technologies* (Clifton, New Jersey: Humana Press, 1989).

Baruch, Elaine Hoffman, Amadeo F. D'Adamo and Joni Seager (eds.), *Embryos, Ethics and Women's Rights* (London: The Haworth Press, Inc., 1987).

Benedek, Wolfgang and Wolfgang Heinz (eds.), *Regional Systems of Human Rights Protection in Africa, America and Europe: Contributions to the Programme* (Brussels: Friedrich Naumann Foundation, 1992).

Black, Maggie, *Better Health for Women and Children Through Family Planning: Report on an International Conference held in Nairobi, Kenya, October 1987* (New York: The Population Council, 1988).

Blank, Robert H., *Fertility Control: New Technologies, New Policy Issues* (London: Greenwood Press, 1991).

Bloed, Arie (ed.), *The Conference on Security and Co-operation in Europe: Analysis and Basic Documents, 1972–1993* (Dordrecht: Kluwer Academic Publishers, 1993).

Boland, Reed (ed.), *Annual Review of Population Law, 1989* (Harvard: Harvard University Press, 1989).

Bossuyt, Marc J., *Guide to the Travaux Préparatoires of the International Covenant on Civil and Political Rights* (Dordrecht: Martinus Nijhoff Publishers, 1987).

Brownlie, Ian, *Principles of Public International Law*, Fourth Edition (Oxford: Clarendon Press, 1990).

____, *Basic Documents on Human Rights*, Third Edition (Oxford: Clarendon Press, 1992).

Bryson, Valerie, *Feminist Political Theory* (London: The MacMillan Press Ltd., 1992).

Buergenthal, Thomas, Robert Norris and Dinah Shelton, *Protecting Human Rights in the Americas: Selected Problems*, Third Revised Edition (Kehl: N.P. Engel, Publisher, 1990).

Carillo, Roxane, *Battered Dreams: Violence against Women as an Obstacle for Development* (New York: UNIFEM, 1992).

Cook, Rebecca J., *Women's Health and Human Rights* (Geneva: WHO, 1994).

____ and Bernard Dickens, *Abortion Laws in Commonwealth Countries* (Geneva: WHO, 1979).

Council of Europe, *Human Rights in International Law: Basic Texts* (Strasbourg: Council of Europe Press, 1992).

____, Ad Hoc Committee of Experts on Progress in the Biomedical Sciences, *Human Artificial Procreation* (Strasbourg: Council of Europe, Legal Affairs, 1989).

Detrick, Sharon (ed.), *The United Nations Convention on the Rights of the Child: A Guide to the 'Travaux Préparatoires'* (Dordrecht: Martinus Nijhoff Publishers, 1992).

Detter, Ingrid, *The International Legal Order* (Aldershot: Dartmouth Publishing Co., 1994).

van Dijk, P. and G. J. H. van Hoof, *Theory and Practice of the European Convention on Human Rights*, Second Edition (Deventer: Kluwer Law and Taxation Publishers, 1990).

Dixon-Mueller, Ruth, *Population Policy and Women's Rights: Transforming Reproductive Choice* (London: Praeger, 1993).

Eide, Asbjørn, Catarina Krause and Allan Rosas (eds.), *Economic, Social and Cultural Rights: A Textbook* (Dordrecht: Martinus Nijhoff Publishers, 1995).

Harris, D. J., *Cases and Materials on International Law*, Fourth Edition (London: Sweet and Maxwell, 1991).

Harrison, Paul, *The Third Revolution: Environment, Population and a Sustainable World* (London: I.B. Taurus, 1992).

Hartman, Betsy, *Reproductive Rights and Wrongs: The Global Politics of Population Control and Contraceptive Choice* (New York: Harper and Row, 1987).

Higgins, Rosalyn, *Problems and Process: International Law and How We Use It* (Oxford: Clarendon Press, 1994).

Human Rights Watch, *Human Rights Watch World Report 1995: Events of 1994* (New York: Human Rights Watch, 1994)

International Bank for Reconstruction and Development (IBRD), *Effective Family Planning Programs* (Washington: World Bank, 1993).

International Labour Organisation (ILO), *Population and Family Welfare Education in the Worksetting* (Geneva: ILO, 1990).

____, *International Labour Standards and ILO Population Programmes* (Geneva: ILO, 1992).

____, *Workers with Family Responsibilities* (Geneva: ILO, 1993).

International Planned Parenthood Federation (IPPF), *The Human Right to Family Planning* (London: IPPF, 1984).

Jensen, Marianne and Karin Poulsen, *Human Rights and Cultural Change: Women in Africa* (Copenhagen: The Danish Centre for Human Rights, 1993).

Johnson, Stanley P., *World Population and the United Nations* (Cambridge: Cambridge University Press, 1987).

Kane, Penny, *The Second Billion: Population and Family Planning in China* (Sydney: Penguin Books Australia Ltd., 1987).

Lijnzaad, Elisabeth, *Reservations to UN-Human Rights Treaties: Ratify and Ruin?* (Dordrecht: Martinus Nijhoff Publishers, 1995).

Mason, John Kenyon, *Medico-Legal Aspects of Reproduction and Parenthood* (Aldershot, England: Dartmouth Publishing Co., 1990).

Meredith, Philip and Lyn Thomas, *Planned Parenthood in Europe: A Human Rights Perspective* (London: Croom Helm, 1986).

Norrie, Kenneth M., *Family Planning and the Law* (Aldershot, England: Dartmouth Publishing Co., 1991).

Nowak, Manfred, *U.N. Covenant on Civil and Political Rights: CCPR Commentary* (Kehl: N.P. Engel, Publisher, 1993).

Omran, Abdel Rahim, *Family Planning in the Legacy of Islam* (London: Routledge, 1992).

Ouguergouz, Fatsah, *La Charte Africaine des Droits de l'homme et des Peuples: une Approche Juridique des Droits de l'homme Entre Tradition et Modernité* (Paris: Presses Universitaires de France, 1993).

Patel, Vibhuti, *In Search of Our Bodies: A Feminist Look at Women, Health and Reproduction in India* (Bombay: Shakti, 1987).

Paxman, John M., *Law and Planned Parenthood* (London: IPPF, 1980).

Petchesky, Rosalind P. and Jennifer A. Weiner, *Global Feminist Perspectives on Reproductive Rights and Reproductive Health: Report on the Special Sessions Held at the Fourth International Interdisciplinary Congress on Women, held at Hunter College, New York City, June 3–7 1990* (Hunter College, City University New York: Women's Studies Program, 1990).

Plata, María Isabel and María Yanuzova, *Los Derechos Humanos y la Convención Sobre la Eliminación de Todas las Formas de Disciminación Contra la Mujer, 1979* (Bogotá: Profamilia, 1993).

The Population Council, *Safe Motherhood Partners: Emphasizing Action* (New York: Family Care International, 1992).

Raymond, Janice G., *Women as Wombs: Reproductive Technologies and the Battle over Women's Freedom* (San Francisco: HarperCollins Publishers, 1993).

Regional Institute for Population Studies (RIPS), *Ghana Population Policy* (Accra, Ghana: RIPS, 1969).

Rehof, Lars Adam, *Guide to the Travaux Préparatoires of the United Nations Convention on the Elimination of All Forms of Discrimination against Women* (Dordrecht: Martinus Nijhoff Publishers, 1993).

Renteln, Alison Dundes, *International Human Rights: Universalism versus Relativism* (London: Sage Publications, 1990).

Reuter, Paul, *La convention de Vienne sur le Droit des traités* (Paris: Librairie Armand Colin, 1970).

____, *Droit international public*, Sixième édition (Paris: Presses Universitaires de France, 1983).

Rousseau, Charles, *Droit international public*, Onzième édition (Paris: Dalloz, 1987).

Sadik, Nafis, *Population Policies and Programmes* (New York: UNFPA, 1991).

____, *The State of the World Population 1992* (New York: UNFPA, 1992).

____, *The State of the World Population 1993* (New York: UNFPA, 1993).

____, *The State of the World Population 1995* (New York: UNFPA, 1995).

Schachter, Oscar, *International Law in Theory and Practice* (Dordrecht: Martinus Nijhoff Publishers, 1991).

Shaw, Malcolm N., *International Law*, Third Edition (Cambridge: Grotius Publications Ltd., 1991).

Simma, Bruno (ed.), *The Charter of the United Nations: A Commentary* (Oxford: Oxford University Press, 1994).

Stephenson, Patricia and Marsden G. Wagner (eds.), *Tough Choices: In Vitro Fertilization and the Reproductive Technologies* (Philadelphia: Temple University Press, 1993).

Tomaševski, Katarina, *Women and Human Rights* (London: Zed Books Ltd., 1993).

United Nations, *Women: Challenges to the Year 2000* (New York: United Nations, 1991).

____, *Human Rights: A Compilation of International Instruments, Volume I (First and Second Parts)*, (New York and Geneva: United Nations, 1994).

____, Centre for Social Development and Humanitarian Affairs, *The Work of CEDAW: Reports of the Committee on the Elimination of Discrimination against Women (CEDAW), Volume I* (New York: United Nations, 1989).

____, Centre for Social Development and Humanitarian Affairs, *The Work of CEDAW: Reports of the Committee on the Elimination of Discrimination against Women (CEDAW), Volume II* (New York: United Nations, 1990).

United Nations High Commissioner for Refugees (UNHCR), *Proceedings of the Inter-Agency Symposium on Reproductive Health in Refugee Situations: Palais de Nations, Geneva, 28-30, June, 1995* (Geneva: UNHCR, 1995).

____, *Sexual Violence against Refugees: Guidelines on Prevention and Response* (Geneva: UNHCR, 1995).

United Nations Population Fund (UNFPA), *Meeting the Population Challenge* (New York: UNFPA, 1992).

____, *Population Issues (Briefing Kit 1992)* (New York: UNFPA, 1992).

____, *Index of Demographic, Social and Economic Indicators* (New York: UNFPA, 1995).

Warwick, Donald, *Bitter Pills* (Cambridge: Cambridge University Press, 1982).

Whitfield, Susan (ed.), *June Fourth Briefing Papers on China* (London: June 4th China Support, 1993).

World Bank, *Poverty Reduction Handbook* (Washington: World Bank, 1992).

World Commission on Environment and Development, *Our Common Future* (Oxford: Oxford University Press, 1987).

World Health Organization (WHO), *Female Genital Mutilation (Information Kit)* (Geneva: WHO, 1994)

_____, *The World Health Report 1995: Bridging the Gaps* (Geneva: WHO, 1995).

ARTICLES

Adjetey, Fitnat Naa-Adjeley, 'Reclaiming the African Woman's Individuality: The Struggle between Women's Reproductive Autonomy and African Society and Culture', *American University Law Review*, Vol. 44, No. 4 (1995), pp. 1351–1381.

An-Na'im, Abdullahi Ahmed, 'State Responsibility Under International Human Rights Law to Change Religious and Customary Laws', in: Rebecca J. Cook (ed.), *Human Rights of Women: National and International Perspectives* (Philadelphia: University of Pennsylvania Press, 1994), pp. 167–188.

Bayefsky, Anne F., 'Making the Human Rights Treaties Work', in: Louis Henkin and John Lawrence Hargrove (eds.), *Human Rights: An Agenda for the Next Century* (Washington: The American Society of International Law—Studies in Transnational Legal Policy, No. 26, 1994), pp. 229–296.

Beyani, Chaloka, 'Toward a More Effective Guarantee of Women's Rights in the African Human Rights System', in: Rebecca J. Cook (ed.), *Human Rights of Women: National and International Perspectives* (Philadelphia: University of Pennsylvania Press, 1994), pp. 285–306.

Bielefeldt, Heiner, 'Muslim Voices in the Human Rights Debate', *Human Rights Quarterly*, Vol. 17, No. 4 (1995), pp. 587–617.

Bok, Sissela, 'Population and Ethics: Expanding the Moral Space', in: Gita Sen, Adrienne Germain and Lincoln C. Chen (eds.), *Population Policies Reconsidered: Health, Empowerment and Rights* (Harvard Center for Population and Development Studies: Harvard University Press, 1994), pp. 15–26.

Boland, Reed, Sudhakar Rao and George Zeidenstein, 'Honoring Human Rights in Population Policies: From Declaration to Action', in: Gita Sen, Adrienne Germain and Lincoln C. Chen (eds.), *Population Policies Reconsidered: Health, Empowerment and Rights* (Harvard Center for Population and Development Studies: Harvard University Press, 1994), pp. 89–105.

Boye, Abd-el Kader, Kathleen Hill, Stephen Isaacs and Deborah Gordis, 'Marriage Law and Practice in the Sahel', *Studies in Family Planning*, Vol. 22, No. 6 (1991), pp. 343–349.

Brennan, Katherine, 'The Influence of Cultural Relativism on International Human Rights Law: Female Circumsicion as a Case Study', *Law and Equality*, Vol. 7 (1989), pp. 367–389.

Van Bueren, Geraldine, 'The International Protection of Family Members' Rights as the 21st Century Approaches', *Human Rights Quarterly*, Vol. 17, No. 4 (1995), pp. 732–765.

Buergenthal, Thomas, 'To Respect and to Ensure State Obligations and Permissible Derogations', in: Louis Henkin (ed.), *The International Bill of Rights: The Covenant on Civil and Political Rights* (New York: Columbia University Press, 1981), pp. 72–91.

Bunch, Charlotte, 'Women's Rights as Human Rights: Toward a Re-Vision of Human Rights', in: Charlotte Bunch and Roxanna Carrillo (eds.), *Gender Violence: A Development and Human Rights Issue* (New Jersey: Plowshares Press, 1991), pp. 3-18.

____, 'The Global Campaign for Women's Human Rights', *The Review of the International Commission of Jurists*, No. 50 (1993), pp. 105–108.

____, 'Strengthening Human Rights of Women', in: Manfred Nowak (ed.), *World Conference on Human Rights: The Contribution of NGOs* (Vienna: Manz, 1994), pp. 32–41.

Butegwa, Florence, 'Women's Human Rights: A Challenge to the International Human Rights Community', *The Review of the International Commission of Jurists*, No. 50 (1993), pp. 71–80.

Byrnes, Andrew, 'Toward More Effective Enforcement of Women's Human Rights Through the Use of International Human Rights Law and Procedures', in: Rebecca J. Cook (ed.), *Human Rights of Women: National and International Perspectives* (Philadelphia: University of Pennsylvania Press, 1994), pp. 189–227.

Carrillo, Roxanna, 'Violence against Women: An Obstacle to Development', in: Charlotte Bunch and Roxanna Carrillo (eds.), *Gender Violence: A Development and Human Rights Issue* (New Jersey: Plowshares Press, 1991), pp. 19–41.

Charlesworth, Hilary, 'What are "Women's International Human Rights"', in: Rebecca J. Cook (ed.), *Human Rights of Women: National and International Perspectives* (Philadelphia: University of Pennsylvania Press, 1994), pp. 58–84.

China Population Information and Research Centre, 'The Population of China: Problems and Strategies', *China Population Today*, Vol. 9, No. 4 (1992), pp. 1–16.

Clark, Belinda, 'The Vienna Convention Reservations Regime and the Convention on the Elimination of Discrimination Against Women', *American Journal of International Law*, Vol. 85, No. 2 (1991), pp. 281–321.

Coliver, Sandra, 'The Right to Information Necessary for Reproductive Health and Choice under International Law', *The American University Law Review*, Vol. 44, No. 4 (1995), pp. 1279–1303.

———, 'The Right to Information Necessary for Reproductive Health and Choice under International Law', in: S. Coliver (ed.), *The Right to Know: Human Rights and Access to Reproductive Health Information* (London: ARTICLE 19, 1995), pp. 38–82.

Cook, Rebecca J., 'The Legal Promotion of the Human Right to Family Planning', in: International Planned Parenthood Federation (IPPF), *The Human Right to Family Planning* (London: IPPF, 1983), pp. 37–49.

———, 'Reservations to the Convention on the Elimination of Discrimination Against Women', *Virginia Journal of International Law*, Vol. 30 (1990), pp. 643–716.

———, 'International Human Rights and Women's Reproductive Health', *Studies in Family Planning*, Vol. 24, No. 2 (1993), pp. 73–86.

———, 'Putting the "Universal" into Human Rights', *Populi (The UNFPA Magazine)*, Vol. 20, No. 1 (1993), pp. 12–13.

———, 'Women's International Human Rights Law: The Way Forward', in: Rebecca J. Cook (ed.), *Human Rights of Women: National and International Perspectives* (Philadelphia: University of Pennsylvania Press, 1994), pp. 3–36.

——— and Bernard Dickens, 'Ethics and Values in Family Planning: Legal and Legislative Aspects', in: Z. Bankowski, J. Barzelatto and A. M. Capron (eds.), *Ethics and Human Values in Family Planning: XXII CIOMS Conference Highlights* (Geneva: Council of International Organizations of Medical Sciences, 1989), pp. 117–140.

Correa, Sonia and Rosalind P. Petchesky, 'Reproductive and Sexual Rights: A Feminist Perspective', in: Gita Sen, Adrienne Germain and Lincoln C. Chen (eds.), *Population Policies Reconsidered: Health, Empowerment and Rights* (Harvard Center for Population and Development Studies: Harvard University Press, 1994), pp. 107–123.

Demeny, Paul, 'Human Rights in a Changing Political and Socio-Economic Environment', in: UN, *Population and Human Rights: Proceedings of the Expert Group Meeting on Population and Human Rights, Geneva, 3–6 April, 1989* (New York: United Nations, 1990), pp. 75–86.

Dixon-Mueller, Ruth, 'Innovations in Reproductive Health Care: Menstrual Regulation Policies and Programs in Bangladesh', *Studies in Family Planning*, Vol. 19, No. 3 (1988), pp. 129–140.

Dubler, Nancy Neveloff, 'The Right to Fornication: The Right to Reproduce', in: Stuart S. Spicker, William B. Bonderson and H. Tristan Engelhardt Jr. (eds.), *The Contraceptive Ethos* (Dordrecht: Reidel Publishing Company, 1987), pp. 165–181.

Eide, Asbjørn, 'Economic, Social and Cultural Rights as Human Rights', in: Asbjørn Eide, Catarina Krause and Allan Rosas (eds.), *Economic, Social and Cultural Rights: A Textbook* (Dordrecht: Martinus Nijhoff Publishers, 1995), pp. 21–40.

_____ and Allan Rosas, 'Economic, Social and Cultural Rights: A Universal Challenge', in: Asbjørn Eide, Catarina Krause and Allan Rosas (eds.), *Economic, Social and Cultural Rights: A Textbook* (Dordrecht: Martinus Nijhoff Publishers, 1995), pp. 15–19.

Ezeh, Alex Chika, 'The Influence of Spouses Over Each Other's Contraceptive Attitudes in Ghana', *Studies in Family Planning*, Vol. 24, No. 3 (1993), pp. 163–174.

Fincancioglu, Nuray, 'Contraception, Family Planning and Human Rights', in: UN, *Population and Human Rights: Proceedings of the Expert Group Meeting on Population and Human Rights, Geneva, 3–6 April, 1989* (New York: United Nations, 1990), pp. 87–103.

Fitzpatrick, Joan, 'International Norms and Violence against Women', in: Rebecca J. Cook (ed.), *Human Rights of Women: National and International Perspectives* (Philadelphia: University of Pennsylvania Press, 1994), pp. 532–571.

Freedman, Lynn P. and Stephen L. Isaacs, 'Human Rights and Reproductive Choice', *Studies in Family Planning*, Vol. 24, No. 1 (1993), pp. 18–30.

Goldstein, Anne Tierney, 'Remarks on the Panel Discussion on Civil and Political Rights and the Right to Nondiscrimination', *The American University Law Review*, Vol. 44, No. 4 (1995), pp. 1315–1318.

Gruskin, Sofia, 'Negotiating the Relationship of HIV/AIDS to Reproductive Health and Reproductive Rights', *The American University Law Review*, Vol. 44, No. 4 (1995), pp. 1191–1206.

Jacobson, Roberta, 'The Committee on the Elimination of Discrimination against Women', in: Philip Alston (ed.), *The United Nations and Human Rights* (Oxford, Clarendon Press, 1992), pp. 444–472.

Jasudowicz, Tadeusz, 'The Legal Character of Social Rights from a Perspective of International Law as a Whole', in: Krzysztof Drzewicki, Catarina Krause and Allan Rosas (eds.), *Social Rights as Human Rights: A European Challenge* (Turku/Åbo: Institute for Human Rights, 1994), pp. 23–42.

Johns Hopkins University, 'Fertility and Family Planning: An Update', *Population Reports*, Population Information Program, Series M, No. 8 (1985).

_____, 'The Environment and Population Growth: Decade for Action', *Population Reports*, Population Information Program, Series M, No. 10 (1992).

Khushalini, Yougindra, 'Human Rights in Asia and Africa', in: F. E. Snyder and S. Sathirathai (eds.), *Third World Attitudes Toward International Law* (Dordrecht: Martinus Nijhoff Publishers, 1987), pp. 321–339.

Kumado, Kofi, 'Conditionality: An Analysis of the Policy of Linking Development

Aid to the Implementation of Human Rights Standards', *The Review of the International Commission of Jurists*, No. 50 (1993), pp. 23–30.

Leary, Virginia A., 'The Right to Reproductive Health in International Human Rights Law', *Health and Human Rights*, Vol. 1, No. 1 (1994), pp. 25–56.

Lieberson, Jonathan, 'The Population Explosion and Contraceptive Ethos', in: Stuart S. Spicker, William B. Bonderson and H. Tristan Engelhardt Jr. (eds.), *The Contraceptive Ethos* (Dordrecht: Reidel Publishing Company, 1987), pp. 59–87.

Macklin, Audrey, 'Refugee Women and the Imperative of Categories', *Human Rights Quarterly*, Vol. 17, No. 2 (1995), pp. 213–277.

Mamdani, Mahmood, 'A Glimpse at African Studies, Made in the USA', *Codesria Bulletin*, Vol. 2 (1990), pp. 7–11.

Marie, Jean-Bernard, 'International Instruments relating to Human Rights: Classification and Status of Ratifications as of 1 January 1996', *Human Rights Law Journal*, Vol. 17, No. 1–2 (1996).

McLean, Sheila, 'Women, Rights and Reproduction', in: Sheila McLean (ed.), *Legal Issues in Human Reproduction* (Brookfield: Darmouth Publishers, 1990), pp. 213–232.

Medina, Cecilia, 'Toward a More Effective Guarantee of the Enjoyment of Human Rights by Women in the Inter-American System', in: Rebecca J. Cook (ed.), *Human Rights of Women: National and International Perspectives* (Philadelphia: University of Pennsylvania Press, 1994), pp. 257–284.

Meron, Theodor, 'Enhancing the Effectiveness of the Prohibition of Discrimination against Women', *American Journal of International Law*, Vol. 84, No. 1 (1990), pp. 213–217.

Morsink, Johannes, 'Women's Rights in the Universal Declaration', *Human Rights Quarterly*, Vol. 13, No. 2 (1991), pp. 229–244.

Mueller, Herta, 'Rumania: Pregnancy Police', *Connexions (Special Issue: Reproductive Rights—The Global Right)*, No. 31 (1989), pp. 22–23.

Nielsen, Linda, 'The Right to a Child Versus the Rights of a Child', in: J. Eekelaar and P. Sarcevic (eds.), *Parenthood in Modern Society: Legal and Social Issues for the Twenty-First Century* (1993), pp. 213–221.

Norrie, Kenneth, 'United Kingdom: Legal Regulation of Human Reproduction', in: Sheila A. M. McLean (ed.), *Law Reform and Human Reproduction* (Aldershot, England: Dartmouth Publishing Co., 1992), pp. 201–219.

Obermeyer, Carla Makhlouf, 'Reproductive Choice in Islam: Gender and State in Iran and Tunisia', *Studies in Family Planning*, Vol. 25, No. 1 (1994), pp. 41–51.

Oloka-Onyango, Joe and Sylvia Tamale, '"The Personal is Political" or Why Women's Rights are Indeed Human Rights: An African Perspective on International Feminism', *Human Rights Quarterly*, Vol. 17, No. 4 (1995), pp. 691–731.

Plata, María Isabel, 'Reproductive Rights as Human Rights: The Colombian Case', in: Rebecca J. Cook (ed.), *Human Rights of Women: National and International Perspectives* (Philadelphia: University of Pennsylvania Press, 1994), pp. 515–531.

Robson, Angela, 'Torture, not Culture', *Amnesty International (British Section) Journal*, No. 63 (1993), pp. 8–9.

Romany, Celina, 'State Responsibility Goes Private: A Feminist Critique of the Public/Private Distinction in International Human Rights Law', in: Rebecca J. Cook (ed.), *Human Rights of Women: National and International Perspectives* (Philadelphia: University of Pennsylvania Press, 1994), pp. 85–115.

Salaff, Janet W., 'The Right To Reproduce: The People's Republic of China', in: Stuart S. Spicker, William B. Bonderson and H. Tristan Engelhardt Jr. (eds.), *The Contraceptive Ethos* (Dordrecht: Reidel Publishing Company, 1987), pp. 89–134.

Sass, Hans Martin, 'Responsibilities in Human Reproduction and Population Policy', in: Stuart S. Spicker, William B. Bonderson and H. Tristan Engelhardt Jr. (eds.), *The Contraceptive Ethos* (Dordrecht: Reidel Publishing Company, 1987), pp. 135–157.

Sen, Gita, Adrienne Germain and Lincoln Chen, 'Reconsidering Population Policies: Ethics, Development, and Strategies for Change', in: Gita Sen, Adrienne Germain and Lincoln C. Chen (eds.), *Population Policies Reconsidered: Health, Empowerment, and Rights* (Harvard Center for Population and Development Studies, Harvard University Press, 1994), pp. 3–13.

Shaheed, Farida, 'The Cultural Articulation of Patriarchy: Legal Systems, Islam and Women', *South Asia Bulletin*, Vol. 6, No. 1 (1986), pp. 38–44.

Shiers, E. Tobin, 'Coercive Population Control Policies: An Illustration of the Need for a Conscientious Objector Provision for Asylum Seekers', *Virginia Journal of International Law*, Vol. 20, No. 4 (1990), pp. 1007–1037.

Slack, Alison, 'Female Circumcision: A Critical Approach', *Human Rights Quarterly*, Vol. 10, No. 4 (1988), pp. 437–486.

Spahn, Elizabeth K., 'Waiting for Credentials: Feminist Theories of Enforcement of International Human Rights', *The American University Law Review*, Vol. 44, No. 4 (1995), pp. 1053–1083.

Sullivan, Donna J., 'Women's Human Rights and the 1993 World Conference on Human Rights', *American Journal of International Law*, Vol. 88, No. 1 (1994), pp. 152–167.

Tomaševski, Katarina, 'European Approaches to Enhancing Reproductive Freedom', *The American University Law Review*, Vol. 44, No. 4 (1995), pp. 1037–1051.

____, 'Health Rights', in: Asbjørn Eide, Catarina Krause and Allan Rosas (eds.), *Economic, Social and Cultural Rights: A Textbook* (Dordrecht: Martinus Nijhoff Publishers, 1995) pp. 125–142.

____, 'Women', in: Asbjørn Eide, Catarina Krause and Allan Rosas (eds.), *Economic, Social and Cultural Rights: A Textbook* (Dordrecht: Martinus Nijhoff Publishers, 1995) pp. 273–288.

United Nations, 'General Assembly Looks at Means of Implementing Programme of Action', in: *Newsletter of the International Conference on Population and Development, Cairo, Egypt, 5–13 September 1994*, No. 21 (New York: ICPD Secretariat, November 1994).

____, United Nations Secretariat, 'Relationship Between Human Rights and Population Issues: Standard-Setting Activities of the United Nations, 1980–1988', in: UN, *Population and Human Rights: Proceedings of the Expert Group Meeting on Population and Human Rights, Geneva, 3–6 April, 1989* (New York: United Nations, 1990), pp. 54–74.

Welch, Claude E. Jr., 'Human Rights and African Women: A Comparison of Protection Under Two Major Treaties', *Human Rights Quarterly*, Vol. 15, No. 3 (1993), pp. 549–574.

Zulficar, Mona, 'From Human Rights to Program Reality: Vienna, Cairo, and Beijing in Perspective', *The American University Law Review*, Vol. 44, No. 4 (1995), pp. 1017–1036.

OFFICIAL DOCUMENTS

Conference on Security and Co-operation in Europe, Concluding Document of the Vienna Meeting on the Follow-up to the Conference Adopted on 15 January 1989 (CSCE: Vienna, 1989). Reproduced in A. Bloed (ed.), *The Conference on Security and Co-operation in Europe; Analysis and Basic Documents, 1972-1993* (Dordrecht: Kluwer Academic Publishers, 1993), pp. 327–423.

Council of Europe, Declaration on the Freedom of Expression and Information, adopted by the Committee of Ministers on 29 April 1982 at its 70th Session (Strasbourg: Council of Europe, 1982).

____, Directorate of Human Rights, European Parliament Resolution of 9 June 1983 reprinted in *Human Rights Information Sheet No. 13*, Doc. H/INF (83), April-October 1983.

____, Progress of Medicine, Biology and Respect for Private and Family Life

(Strasbourg: Council of Europe Press), Doc. DH–DEV (91) 1 of 1 March 1991.

Immigration and Refugee Board, Canada, Guidelines Issued by the Chairperson Pursuant to Section 65(3) of the Immigration Act: Women Refugee Claimants Fearing Gender-Related Persecution (Ottawa: Immigration and Refugee Board, 9 March 1993.

Interpreter Release (No. 70), '*Matter of Chang*' Interim Dec. 3107 (BIA 1989), 22 November 1993, pp. 1558–1561.

KELA (Social Insurance Institution), *A Guide to Benefits* (Helsinki: Government of Finland, 1994).

LC Working Group on Human Resources, *Women, Human Rights and Reproduction*, NGO–EC Liaison Committee (Brussels: European Commission, 1990).

United Nations, Amsterdam Declaration on A Better Life for Future Generations, adopted by the International Forum on Population in the Twenty-first Century, Amsterdam, 6–9 November 1989, UN doc. A/C.2/44/6.

____, Committee on Economic, Social and Cultural Rights, Report on the Fifth Session, Economic and Social Council, Official Records, 1991, Supplement No. 3 (E/1991/23) (New York: United Nations, 1991).

____, Committee on Economic, Social and Cultural Rights, Report on the Tenth and Eleventh Sessions, Economic and Social Council, Official Records, 1995, Supplement No. 3 (E/1995/22) (New York: United Nations, 1995).

____, Committee on the Rights of the Child, Concluding observations of the Committee on the Rights of the Child: United Kingdom of Great Britain and Northern Ireland, UN doc. CRC/C/15/Add.34, 15 February 1995.

____, Committee on the Rights of the Child, Provisional Agenda and Annotations, UN doc. CRC/C/47, 4 December 1995.

____, Committee on the Rights of the Child, Reservations, Declarations and Objections Relating to the Convention of the Rights of the Child, UN doc. CRC/C/2/Rev.3, 11 July 1994.

____, Contribution from the United Nations Population Fund to the World Conference on Human Rights, Preparatory Committee, Geneva, 19–30 April 1993, UN doc. A/CONF.157/PC/61/Add.9.

____, Economic Commission for Europe, Regional Platform for Action—Women in a Changing World—Call for Action from an ECE Perspective, UN doc. E/ECE/RW/HLM/8, 20 December 1994.

____, Final Act of the International Conference on Human Rights, Teheran, 22 April to 13 May 1968, UN doc. A/CONF.32/41.

____, Human Rights and Scientific and Technological Developments: Human Rights and Bioethics: Report of the Secretary-General, UN doc. E/CN.4/1995/74, 15 November 1994.

____, Human Rights Committee, General Comment No. 24 of 2 November 1994 on issues relating to the reservations made upon ratification or accession to the Covenant or the Optional Protocols thereto, or in relation to declarations under article 41 of the Covenant, Fifty-second Session, UN doc. CCPR/C/21/Rev.1/Add.6, 2 November 1994.

____, Joint Declaration of the Special Rapporteurs/Representatives/Experts and Chairmen of Working Groups of the Special Procedures of the Commission on Human Rights, UN doc. A/CONF.157/9.

____, Preliminary report submitted by the Special Rapporteur on violence against women, its causes and consequences, Ms. Radhika Coomaraswamy, in accordance with Commission on Human Rights resolution 1994/45, UN doc. E/CN.4/1995/42, 22 November 1994.

____, Provisional Summary Record of the 11th Meeting of ECOSOC (Concerning the Convention on the Elimination of All Forms of Discrimination against Women), UN doc. E/1987/SR.11.

____, Rape and abuse of women in the territory of the former Yugoslavia: Report of the Secretary-General, UN doc. E/CN.4/1994/5, 30 June 1993.

____, Report of the Committee on the Elimination of Discrimination against Women, Sixth Session, General Assembly, Official Records, Forty-second Session, Supplement No. 38 (A/42/38) (New York: United Nations, 1987).

____, Report of the Committee on the Elimination of Discrimination against Women, Eleventh Session, General Assembly, Official Records, Forty-seventh Session, Supplement No. 38 (A/47/38) (New York: United Nations, 1993).

____, Report of the Committee on the Elimination of Discrimination against Women, Thirteenth Session, General Assembly, Official Records, Forty-ninth Session, Supplement No. 38 (A/49/38) (New York: United Nations, 1994).

____, Report of the Committee on the Elimination of Discrimination against Women, Fourteenth Session, UN doc. A/50/38, 31 May 1995.

____, Report of the Fourth World Conference on Women, Beijing, 4–15 September 1995, UN doc. A/CONF.177/20, 17 October 1995.

____, Report of the Human Rights Committee, General Assembly, Official Records, Thirty-seventh Session, Supplement No. 40 (A/37/40) (New York: United Nations,

1982).

____, Report of the Human Rights Committee, General Assembly, Official Records, Forty-third Session, Supplement No. 40 (A/43/40) (New York: United Nations, 1988).

____, Report of the Human Rights Committee, Volume I, General Assembly, Official Records, Forty-fifth Session, Supplement No. 40 (A/45/40) (New York: United Nations, 1990).

____, Report of the International Conference on Population, Mexico City, 6–14 August 1984, UN doc. E/CONF.76/19.

____, Report of the International Conference on Population and Development, Cairo, 5–13 September 1994, UN doc. A/CONF.171/3, 18 October 1994.

____, Report of the Meeting of the Special Rapporteurs/Representatives/Experts and Chairmen of Working Groups of the Special Procedures of the Commission on Human Rights, UN doc. E/CN.4/1995/5.

____, Report of the Meeting of the Special Rapporteurs/Representatives/Experts and Chairmen of Working Groups of the Special Procedures of the Commission on Human Rights, UN doc. E/CN.4/1996/50, 23 October 1995.

____, Report of the situation of human rights in the territory of the former Yugoslavia submitted by Mr. Tadeusz Mazowiecki, Special Rapporteur of the Commission on Human Rights, pursuant to Commission resolution 1992/S–1/1 of 14 August 1992, UN doc. E/CN.4/1993/50, 10 February 1993.

____, Report of the United Nations World Population Conference, Bucharest, 19–30 August 1974, UN doc. E/CONF.60/19.

____, Report of the World Conference to Review and Appraise the Achievements of the United Nations Decade for Women: Equality, Development and Peace, Nairobi, Kenya, 15-26 July 1985, UN doc. A/CONF.116/28/Rev.1.

____, Question of Integrating the Rights of Women into the Human Rights Mechanisms of the United Nations and the Elimination of Violence against Women; Commission on Human Rights resolution 1994/45 of 4 March 1994. UN doc. E/CN.4/1994/132, pp. 140–145.

____, Security Council Final Report of the Commission of Experts Established Pursuant to Security Council Resolution 935 (1994), UN doc. S/1994/1405, 9 December 1994.

____, Security Council Final Report of the Commission of Experts Established Pursuant to Security Council Resolution 780 (1992), UN doc. S/1994/674, 27 May 1994.

____, Status of the Convention on the Elimination of All Forms of Discrimination against Women; Report of the Secretary-General of 12 September 1985, UN doc. A/40/623.

____, Third Session of the Preparatory Committee for the International Conference on Population and Development, 4–22 April 1994, UN doc. A/CONF.171/PC/1; and in: UN Press Release POP/94/3 of 25 April 1994.

____, Vienna Declaration and Programme of Action, World Conference on Human Rights, Vienna, 14–25 June 1993, UN doc. A/CONF.157/23, 12 July 1993.

United Nations High Commissioner for Refugees, Executive Committee, Note on Refugee Women and International Protection, EC/SCP/59, 28 August 1990.

PAPERS PRESENTED

An-Na'im, Abdullahi, remarks made following a panel discussion on religious and cultural rights at the Conference on the International Protection of Reproductive Rights held at the American University, Washington D.C., 10–11 November 1994.

Bongaarts, Jon, 'Policy Options in Population and Development Strategies'. Paper presented at the ILO/UNFPA Technical Workshops on Population Policy and Development Planning Strategies, Geneva, 25 October to 1 November 1994.

Oppong, Christine, 'ILO Standard Setting, Policy Studies and Technical Cooperation Relating to Population Issues and Women'. Briefing note presented at the ILO/UNFPA Technical Workshops on Population Policy and Development Planning Strategies, Geneva, 25 October to 1 November 1994.

PAMPHLETS AND BULLETINS

International Women's Rights Watch, *The Women's Watch*, No. 5, Issue 2 (1991).

NGO Bulletin, Information Service, United Nations Office, Geneva, INF/NGO/95/2, 27 January 1995.

United Nations, *Population Newsletter*, Population Division of the Department of Economic and Social Affairs, UN, New York (No. 4), 10 December 1967.

PRESS ARTICLES

'Cardinals Dive into the Population Fray', *International Herald Tribune*, 15 June 1994, pp. 1 and 6.

'China Brings in Tough Law to Stamp out Birth Defects', *The Guardian*, 6 June 1995,

p. 5.

'China Moves to Ban Babies with Defects', *The Sunday Times*, 5 February 1995.

'Family, Population, AIDS and Abortion', *Impact International*, Vol. 24, No. 5 (1994), pp. 14–16.

'Family Planning for All', *International Herald Tribune*, 2 December 1993, p. 4.

'Forge a Population Plan', *International Herald Tribune*, 8 June 1993, p. 6.

'Go-Ahead on Pill for Abortions', *International Herald Tribune*, 17 May 1994, p. 2.

Higgins, Andrew, 'Mystery of the "Missing" Orphans', *The Guardian*, 10 January 1996, p. 3.

'Nafis Sadik mobilise les énergies pour la 3e Conférence mondial sur la population', *Le Nouveau Quotidien: Journal Suisse et Européen (Supplément spécial)*, 31 May 1994, special insert.

'Population: Women Will be Taking More Control', *International Herald Tribune*, 27 July 1994, p. 5.

'Perish the Baby Girl', *Newsweek*, 28 August 1995, pp. 22–26.

'Pope Battles UN on Population', *International Herald Tribune*, 19 April 1994, p. 4.

'US Trials for French Abortion Pill Agreed', *The Times*, 17 May 1994, p. 12.

Walsh, James, 'Ordering up "Better" Babies', *Time Magazine*, 2 May 1994, pp. 48–49.

'Wirth Urges ICPD to Adopt Universal Family Planning', *Daily Bulletin* (of the Mission of the United States of America to the United Nations Office at Geneva), 6 April 1994, p. 4.

'The Women Get Their Say', *International Herald Tribune*, 29 April 1994, p. 6.

TABLE OF TREATIES

1945 United Nations Charter. Concluded: 26 June 1945, entered into force: 10 January 1945. 1 UNTS xvi.

1948 Convention on the Prevention and Punishment of the Crime of Genocide (Genocide Convention). Concluded: 9 December 1948, entered into force: 12 January 1951. 78 UNTS 277.

1950 Convention for the Protection of Human Rights and Fundamental Freedoms (European Convention on Human Rights; ECHR). Concluded: 4 November 1950, entered into force: 3 September 1953. ETS No. 5

1951 Convention relating to the Status of Refugees. Concluded: 28 July 1951, entered into force: 22 April 1954. 189 UNTS 150.

1952 ILO Convention (No. 103) concerning Maternity Protection (Revised). Concluded: 28 June 1952, entered into force: 7 September 1955. *International Labour Conventions and Recommendations 1919–1991, Volume I* (Geneva: International Labour Office, 1992), pp. 570–574.

1961 European Social Charter. Concluded: 18 October 1961, entered into force: 26 February 1965. ETS No. 35. Additional Protocol to the European Social Charter Providing for a System of Collective Complaints of 9 November 1995 and Explanatory Report (Provisional Version), Council of Europe, Directorate of Human Rights, Social Charter Section, H95_ 8E, 5 July 1995.

1966 International Covenant on Civil and Political Rights (CCPR), including Optional Protocol. Concluded: 16 December 1966, entered into force: 23 March 1976. 999 UNTS 171.

1966 International Covenant on Economic, Social, and Cultural Rights (CESCR). Concluded: 16 December 1966, entered into force: 3 January 1976. 999 UNTS 3

1969 Convention on the Law of Treaties. Concluded: 23 May 1969, entered into force: 27 January 1980. 8 I.L.M. 679.

1969 American Convention on Human Rights (Pact of San José, Costa Rica). Concluded: 22 November 1969, entered into force: 18 July 1978. 1144 UNTS 331. Additional Protocol to the American Convention on Human Rights in the area of Economic, Social and Cultural Rights (Protocol of San Salvador). Concluded: 17 November 1988, not yet in force. OAS Treaty Series No. 69.

1975 ILO Convention (No. 142) concerning Vocational Guidance and Vocational Training in the Development of Human Resources. Concluded: 23 June 1975, entered into force: 19 July 1977. *International Labour Conventions and Recommendations 1919–1991, Volume II* (Geneva: International Labour Office, 1992), pp. 1066–1090.

1979 Convention on the Elimination of All Forms of Discrimination against Women (Women's Convention). Concluded: 18 December 1979, entered into force: 3 September 1981. 1249 UNTS 13.

1981 ILO Convention (No. 156) concerning Equal Opportunities and Equal Treatment for Men and Women Workers: Workers with Family Responsibilities. Concluded: 23 June 1981, entered into force: 11 August 1983. *International Labour Conventions and Recommendations 1919–1991, Volume II* (Geneva: International Labour Office, 1992), pp. 1244–1247.

1981 African Charter on Human and Peoples' Rights. Concluded: 26 June 1981, entered into force: 21 October 1986. 21 I.L.M. 59.

1989 Convention on the Rights of the Child (Children's Convention). Concluded: 20 November 1989, entered into force: 2 September 1990. 28 I.L.M. 1456.

1990 European Code of Social Security (Revised). Concluded: 6 November 1990, not yet in force. ETS No. 139.

TABLE OF CASES

CANADA

Chan v. Canada (Minister of Employment and Immigration) 20 Imm.LR 2d 181, 1993.
Cheung v. Canada, (Minister of Employment and Immigration), 2 FC 314 (FCA), 1 April 1993.
Cases Nos. C89–00036 and C89–00037, 1989, Convention Refugee Determination Decisions No. 30, Immigration and Refugee Board, Canada.

COLOMBIA

Aracelly Valencia Salazar v. Hospital General de Medellín, No. 7795, Sala de lo Contencioso Administrativo, Santafé de Bogotá (1992).

COUNCIL OF EUROPE

Application No. 6482/74, *X v. Belgium and the Netherlands*. European Commission of Human Rights, Decisions and Reports 7 (1977).

Application No. 8416/79, *X. v the United Kingdom*, European Commission on Human Rights, Decisions and Reports 19 (1980).

Application No. 15666/89, *Kerkhoven, Hinke & Hinke v. The Netherlands*, European Commission of Human Rights, decision of 19 May 1992.

Case relating to Certain Aspects of the Laws on the Use of Languages in Education in Belgium (Belgian Linguistic Case), judgment of 23 July 1968. Publications of the European Court of Human Rights, Series A, No. 6.

Case of Kjeldsen, Busk Madsen and Pedersen, judgment of 7 December 1976. Publications of the European Court of Human Rights, Series A, No. 23.

Rees, judgment of 17 October 1986. Publications of the European Court of Human Rights, Series A, No. 106.

Open Door Counselling and Dublin Well Woman Centre Ltd. v. Ireland, judgment of 29 October 1992. Publications of the European Court of Human Rights, Series A, No. 246.

Case of S.W. v. The United Kingdom (47/1994/494/576). To be reproduced as Publications of the European Court of Human Rights, Series A, No. 335–B.

Case of C.R. v. The United Kingdom (48/1994/495/577). To be reproduced as Publications of the European Court of Human Rights, Series A, No. 335–C.

EUROPEAN UNION

Case C–159/90, *Society for the Protection of Unborn Children Ireland Ltd. v. Stephen Grogan and Others*, [1991] ECR I–4685

ORGANIZATION OF AMERICAN STATES

Inter-American Court of Human Rights. *Interpretation of the American Declaration of the Rights and Duties of Man within the Framework of Article 64 of the American Convention on Human Rights*, Advisory Opinion OC–10/89, of 14 July 1989. Series A, No. 10.

UNITED NATIONS

Communication No. R.14/61 *Leo Hertzberg, Ulf Mansson, Astrid Nikula and Marko and Tuovi Putkonen*. UN, Report of the Human Rights Committee, General Assembly, Official Records, Thirty-seventh Session, Supplement No. 40 (A/37/40), pp. 161–165.

UNITED STATES OF AMERICA

Carey v. Pop. Services, 431 U.S. 678 (1977).
Eisenstadt v. Baird, 405 U.S. 438 (1972).

INDEX OF TERMS

A
abortion
  forced, 51, 52, 61, 100–101, 154–155
  general, 5, 16, 44, 48, 119, 125, 144, 147, 150–151, 153
  illegal/unsafe, 3, 68, 100, 158
  of abnormal foetus, 51
  right to, 67–68, 70–75
  sex-selective (gender-based), 63–65, 144
  pill. *See* RU-486.
adolescents
  family planning needs, 76–77
  parental rights/role, 82–88
  right to reproductive choice, 82–88
aid. *See* donors.
amniocentesis, 63. *See also* technology.

B
Bangladesh, 4, 72, 83, 106, 123, 128, 131, 132, 136
beneficiary (right-holder), 76–90. *See also*: couple, disabled persons.
Brazil, 4, 116, 125, 137

C
Cambodia, 64
Canada, 89, 113, 153–155
CEDAW. *See* Commissions and Committees.
Charters/Codes:
  African Charter on Human and Peoples' Rights (1981), 24, 28, 29, 32, 35, 63, 69
  Charter of the OAS, 27
  Charter of the United Nations (1945), 20–21
  European Code of Social Security (Revised) (1990), 29, 32, 35, 62
  European Social Charter (1961), 29, 31–32, 34–35, 62, 69, 142
China:
  forced abortion/sterilization, 51, 59, 90, 154
  population policy, 10–11, 59, 101–102, 118, 154–156
  sex ratio at birth, 64
Christianity (and Catholic views), 122, 134–135, 147
coercion/coercive policies, 5, 10–11, 57, 59, 81, 95–96, 98–101, 103–105, 109, 143, 149, 153, 156, 159, 160
Colombia, 4, 95
Commissions and Committees:
  Commission on Human Rights, 78–79, 116, 143
  Committee on Economic, Social and Cultural Rights, 49, 61, 110, 117, 140, 159
  Committee on the Elimination of Discrimination Against Women (CEDAW), 60, 74, 82, 100, 116–122, 127–128, 130, 131, 133, 138–139, 146, 148, 149, 159
  Committee on the Rights of the Child, 85, 87, 116–117, 140
  European Commission of Human Rights, 62, 65, 68, 72, 79–80, 142
  Human Rights Committee (HRC), 28, 44, 47, 55, 65–66, 79, 117, 128–129, 130, 140
  Inter-American Commission on Human Rights, 38, 53, 72, 145
communications/complaints procedure:
  in the Council of Europe, 142
  to CEDAW, 119, 139
  to HRC, 119, 141
conditionality (of aid). *See* donors.
Conferences:
  International Conference on Population, Mexico (1984), 12–13, 20, 57

International Conference on Human Rights, Teheran (1968), 11, 48,
International Conference on Population and Development (ICPD), Cairo (1994), 2, 5, 7, 18, 20, 32–33, 76, 93, 98, 112, 114, 119–120, 146, 156, 158
World Conference on Human Rights, Vienna (1993), 108, 138–139
World Conference on Women, Beijing (1995), 2, 5, 18, 76, 80, 93, 156
World Population Conference, Bucharest (1974), 12
World Summit on Social Development, Copenhagen (1994), 5
contraception
access to 71, 78, 82–83,
use of 3, 4, 5, 13, 71, 100–101, 106, 112–113, 134, 157. See also: family planning methods; human right to family planning information/to access to family planning services.
Conventions and Covenants:
(Americas)
American Convention on Human Rights (ACHR) (1969), 26, 32, 54, 63, 65, 68–69, 145
Additional Protocol to the American Convention on Human Rights in the area of Economic, Social and Cultural Rights (1988), 26, 29, 32, 35, 54, 63, 69
American Declaration of the Rights and Duties of Man (American Declaration) (1948), 27, 35, 54, 63, 69, 72
(Council of Europe)
Convention for the Protection of Human Rights and Fundamental Freedoms (European Convention on Human Rights, ECHR) (1950), 25, 28, 30, 31, 52, 62, 64–65, 67–68, 72, 79, 142, 152
(United Nations/Universal)
Convention on the Elimination of All Forms of Discrimination aAgainst Women (Women's Convention) (1979), 16, 17, 27, 29, 30, 32, 33, 47, 56–57, 59, 60, 64–67, 69–70, 73–75, 78, 82, 84, 90, 92–94, 104, 106, 109, 110, 115–122, 127–128, 129–133, 136–139, 140, 148, 149, 153, 159, 160
Convention on the Prevention and Punishment of the Crime of Genocide (Genocide Convention) (1948), 24–25
Convention on the Rights of the Child (Children's Convention) (1989), 28, 29, 33, 62, 65–66, 67, 78, 83, 85–87, 89, 116, 122, 126–127, 140
International Covenant on Civil and Political Rights (CCPR) (1966), 24–26, 28, 29, 32, 43–44, 47, 51, 55, 62–66, 78, 79, 84, 91–92, 119, 127, 128–129, 137, 140–141
First Optional Protocol to the CCPR (1966), 119, 141
International Covenant on Economic, Social and Cultural Rights (CESCR) (1966), 26, 28, 29, 33, 49–50, 61, 62–63, 67, 74, 78, 91, 92, 110, 127, 140, 145
Vienna Convention on the Law of Treaties (Vienna Convention) (1969), 42–43, 115, 120–121, 128–129
cost (of family planning), real costs, 110–114. See also principle of relativity.
Council of Europe, 23, 25, 29, 31, 53, 142
couple:
married versus unmarried, 76, 78, 79
same-sex, 79, 80
versus individual reproductive choice, 79, 80–81, 152–153
Courts:
Court of Justice of the European Communities (ECJ), 67–68
European Court of Human Rights, 30–31, 62, 67–68, 79, 87–88, 142, 152
Inter-American Court of Human Rights, 27, 53
International Court of Justice, 19, 137
cultural relativism, 108, 134, 160
customs:
cultural/traditional norms/practices, 58, 81–82, 104–109, 136, 138, 160
admissibility of, 81–82

D

Declarations and programmes of action:
  Amsterdam Declaration (on population) (1989), 7, 20
  Beijing Declaration and Platform of Action (1995), 2, 18, 20, 32, 161
  Cairo Programme of Action (1994), 2, 18, 20, 32, 33, 58, 74, 114, 120, 161
  Declaration on the Elimination of All Forms of Intolerance and of Discrimination Based on Religion or Belief (1981), 135–136
  Declaration on the Freedom of Expression and Information (Council of Europe) (1982) 31
  Declaration of Social Progress and Development (1969), 11
  Nairobi Forward-Looking Strategies for the Advancement of Women (1985), 13, 20–21, 56
  Proclamation of Teheran (1968), 2, 11, 56
  Universal Declaration of Human Rights (1948), 10, 12, 22, 26, 47, 84
  Vienna Declaration and Programme of Action (1993), 108, 138
  World Population Plan of Action (1974), 12
Denmark, 8, 53, 87, 113, 125
derogable rights/(non-derogable), 129–130
disabled persons
  rights of mentally 50, 88–90
  rights of physically 50, 88–90
discrimination. *See* human right on non-discrimination.
disincentives (to bear children). *See* incentives.
donors:
  conditioning of aid, 112, 145–147, 160
  role of, 66, 112–114, 145–146
duties (of the State). *See* obligations.

E

education (link to fertility), 8–9
Egypt, 4, 123, 124, 125, 131–133, 136
equal/identical rights, 8–9, 80–82, 106–108, 120–122, 124, 125, 130–131, 133, 134, 145

F

family planning
  methods/forms of 6, 13, 70–71, 74, 77–78, 85, 87–88, 92–95, 100, 105–107, 111, 119
  programmes 6, 12, 58, 74, 99–101, 108, 112, 119
  unmet need for 3–4, 70–71, 82–83, 114
  See also: human right; cost; incentives.
female genital mutilation (FGM), 135, 143
feminist legal theory/approach, 77
France, 72, 78, 125

G

Germany, 88, 99, 113, 123, 124, 125, 136
Ghana, 4, 81, 99
Great Britain, 68, 72. *See also* United Kingdom.

H

health
  infant 5–6
  maternal 5–6, 28, 113, 144, 152
  See also human right to health.
HIV/AIDS, 5, 51, 83, 84, 88, 90
horizontal effects (*horizontalwirkung*), 94–95, 111, 152
hortatory instruments. *See* Declarations and programmes of action.
human right:
(individual)
  on non-discrimination, 14, 130
  to access to family planning services, 3, 7, 18, 32–35, 69–75, 85, 105, 108, 136, 140, 157–158
  to benefit from advances in scientific technology, 15, 45–48, 74
  to found a family, 10–12, 15, 17, 24–27, 43–54, 79, 90, 92–93, 140, 141
  to health, 15, 28, 30, 32–35, 45–46, 66–67, 69, 70, 85, 108, 120, 140

to information, family planning information, 3, 15, 17, 18, 29–32, 65–69, 83, 85–88, 92, 99, 111, 140–142
to liberty and security, 15, 94, 149, 152–153, 160
to life, 64–65, 75, 94
to marry, 15, 25, 79, 130
to privacy/private family life, 15, 55, 62–63, 84, 89, 140
to procreate, 44–48, 53–54
to reproduce. See reproductive rights.
to reproductive choice:
to decide the number and spacing of children, 6, 11–12, 14–18, 27–29, 55–65, 92, 95–96, 99, 107, 119, 120
to reproductive health. See to health.

I
ICPD. See Conferences.
incentives (for use of family planning), 94, 99–104, 118, 145, 160
India, 100, 102, 113, 125
individual petition. See communications procedure.
Indonesia, 4, 100–101, 108–109, 125
infanticide:
general 3
female 64
infertility, 44–48, 54, 143
information. See human right to information.
International Bank for Reconstruction and Development (IBRD), 74, 145
International Labour Organisation (ILO), 156–158
in vitro fertilization, 44, 46, 48, 50
Iraq, 123, 124, 125, 132–133, 136
Ireland, 67–68
Islamic law. See Sharia.

K
Korea (Republic of), 108, 128

L
Laos, 64, 116
Libyan Arab Republic (Libya), 125, 131–132, 138–139

M
Malta, 73, 125
marriage:
general 8, 53, 79, 90, 105, 122, 124, 125, 130, 137
authorization of husband for use of contraception, 82
contraceptive services 5
unmarried couple rights. See couple.
menstrual regulation, 72, 147
mentally disabled. See disabled persons.
Mexico, 4, 119, 123, 124, 125, 136, 157
mortality:
infant 5–6, 8, 34
maternal 5–6, 8, 71

N
Nairobi Forward-Looking Strategies. See Declarations and programmes of action.
Netherlands, 79, 80, 91, 113, 123, 124, 125, 136
Norway, 51, 86, 113, 125, 126

O
obligations (of the State):
general, 18, 82, 87, 91–96, 98–99, 103, 109–111, 115, 129–130, 141, 143, 145, 157, 159–161
negative (duty of forbearance), 46, 49, 52, 92–93, 111
positive (duty of performance), 60, 61, 69–70, 93–94, 111. See also principle of relativity.
Organizations:
Organization of American States, 23, 27, 54, 72
Organization of African Unity, 23
Organization for Security and Cooperation in Europe, 31

P
Pakistan, 4, 63–64
Philippines, 4, 107–108
population:
policies/planning, 2–3, 10–11, 20,

211

55–56, 57, 60, 80, 92–93, 98–104, 112, 118, 119, 146–148, 153, 155–156, 158, 160
projections, 6–7
pregnancy (forced), 60–61, 100, 144–145, 149, 152–153
principle of relativity (reasonable obligations of the State), 110–111
private sphere (State duties), 94. *See also* horizontal effects.
Proclamation of Teheran. *See* Declarations and programmes of action.
procreation. *See*: human right to procreate; technology.
Programme of Action. *See* Declarations and programmes of action.

Q
Quran, 123, 132–135

R
rape:
  as a crime against humanity, 144–145, 150–151
  impact on reproductive choice, 149–153
refugees. *See* UNHCR.
religion (religious norms influencing reproduction), 107–109, 132–136, 146, 160. *See also* reservations based on *Sharia*.
reproductive choice: decision-making, 55–63. *See also*: human right to reproductive choice; disabled persons.
reproductive health, 5–6, 32, 83–84, 88, 99, 112–113, 145, 158
reproductive rights, 2, 3, 18, 22, 53, 77, 79–80, 88, 134, 144
reproductive technologies. *See* technology.
reservations:
  based on *Sharia*, 131–135
  general admissibility, 127–132
  HRC General Comment on reservations, 128–129
  on dispute settlement, 137–138
  on ground of custom, 136
  to the CCPR, 128–129
  to the Children's Convention, 122, 126–127
  to the Women's Convention, 121–125, 127–137, 160
  See also Vienna Convention on the Law of Treaties.
resources. *See*: cost; donors; principle of relativity.
Romania, 71, 125
RU–486, 72
Rwanda, 4, 150

S
sex-determination. *See* sex-selective abortion; amniocentesis; technology.
sex ratio (at birth), 63–64
Sharia (law):
  ground of reservations, 123–125, 131–136
  interpretations of, 132–135
social:
  rights, 93, 110–111
  roles. *See*: customs; stereotyping.
sonography, 63
sources (of international law), 18–22
Special Rapporteur:
  Inter-American System, 145
  on the situation of human rights in Yugoslavia, 149, 151
  on violence against women, 64, 143–145
stereotyping (of roles), 8–9, 104–105
sterilization:
  general, 16, 44
  forced/non-consensual, 5, 25, 50, 52–53, 59, 88, 90, 95, 100, 143, 154
  persons with hereditary illnesses, 51
  mentally disabled, 51, 88–90
Sunna, 123, 132–133, 135
Sweden, 72, 78, 113, 123, 124, 125, 136

T
technology;
  assisting procreation/reproduction, 44–48, 52–54, 111–112, 144
  for sex determination, 63–65, 144

traditions. *See* customs.

travaux préparatoires:
  as sources of interpretation, 47
  CCPR, 47, 64, 78–79, 84
  Women's Convention, 47, 56–57, 70, 73, 78

treaty-bodies. *See* Commissions and Committees.

U

Uganda, 4, 8

UN bodies/organizations:
  United Nations Children's Fund (UNICEF), 156
  United Nations High Commissioner for Refugees (UNHCR), 153, 156, 158
  United Nations Population Fund (UNFPA), 7, 99, 113, 114, 156–158

United States of America, 72, 87, 89, 113, 114, 155–156

United Kingdom, 53, 86, 87, 91, 113, 142, 152. *See also* Great Britain.

V

violence (against women), 108, 143–145, 149, 158. *See also* Special Rapporteur on.

W

war crimes. *See* rape.

women (individual right to reproductive choice), 76–78, 80–82. *See also*: couple; marriage.

World Health Organization (WHO), 71, 89, 156

Y

Yugoslavia (former), 149–151